THE FEAST OF CHRISTMAS

Paul Levy was born in Kentucky in 1941 and educated at the universities of Chicago, London, Harvard and Oxford. A lapsed academic, he has for many years been both Lytton Strachey's co-literary executor and, until 1992, the Food and Wine Editor of the *Observer*. He writes frequently for the *Wall Street Journal* on general cultural matters and lives in a 17th-century Oxfordshire farmhouse with his wife, two daughters and an awful lot of cats.

Paul Levy is also the author or editor of: Lytton Strachey: The Really Interesting Question and Other Papers (Ed.); Moore: G. E. Moore and the Cambridge Apostles; The Shorter Strachey (Ed. with Michael Holroyd); The Official Foodie Handbook (with Ann Barr); Out to Lunch; and Finger Lickin' Good: A Kentucky Childhood

The Feast of Christmas

Paul Levy

with photographs by Robin Broadbent

Kyle Cathie Limited

Acknowledgements

For their practical help with this book the author wishes to thank the following: Edward Behr, Frances and Tom Bissell, Maggie Black, Raymond and Koti Cottrell, Kyle Cathie, Alan and Jane Davidson, Georgina Denison, Fiona Fairbairn, the late M. F. K. Fisher, Chris Goddard, Steve Hatt, Julia Hodgkin, Ken Hom, Hazel Horrobin, Philip and Mary Hyman, Joy Larkcom, Jenny Lo, Patricia Lousada, Penelope Marcus, John Munson, John Noble, Richard Olney, Camellia Panjabi, Namita Panjabi, Claudia Roden, Dennis Severs, Hilary Spurling, Anne Willan and Marc Cherniavsky, Hilary Bird for the index and Mark Walford.

Credits

Food for photography prepared by Mary Cadogan, styling by Penny Markham. Chicken from Bennett's Farm, Dorking, Surrey (0306 711598), cheese from Neal's Yard Dairy, ham from Dukeshill Ham Company, Bridgnorth, Shropshire (0704 635519), fish from Steve Hatt, Essex Road, London N1 (071 226 3963). The following supplied food for the cover shot: W. Bainborough Ltd and Jeroboams of Elizabeth Street, London SW1.

Picture acknowledgements

The Author and Publishers wish to thank the following for permission to use illustrations:

Bridgeman Art Library pages 15, 23, 25, 42, 58, 85, 89, 90, 144; Windsor Castle, Royal Library, © 1992 Her Majesty the Queen page 19; Jacqui Hurst pages 35, 39, 114, 116; Sonia Halliday and Laura Lustington page 24; Illustrated London News pages 24, 83; Mary Evans Picture Library pages 78, 111, 177; Harrods Ltd Company Archives page 95; the Stilton Cheese Makers' Association and Osborne Publicity Services Ltd pages 143, 144, 145; and Appleby's of Hawkstone page 148.

The television series, **The Feast of Christmas**, is a Malone Gill Production for Channel 4, produced by Georgina Dennison and directed by Chris Goddard.

Contents

Acknowledgements

For their practical help with this book the author wishes to thank the following: Edward Behr, Frances and Tom Bissell, Maggie Black, Raymond and Koti Cottrell, Kyle Cathie, Alan and Jane Davidson, Georgina Denison, Fiona Fairbairn, the late M. F. K. Fisher, Chris Goddard, Steve Hatt, Julia Hodgkin, Ken Hom, Hazel Horrobin, Philip and Mary Hyman, Joy Larkcom, Jenny Lo, Patricia Lousada, Penelope Marcus, John Munson, John Noble, Richard Olney, Camellia Panjabi, Namita Panjabi, Claudia Roden, Dennis Severs, Hilary Spurling, Anne Willan and Marc Cherniavsky, Hilary Bird for the index and Mark Walford.

Credits

Food for photography prepared by Mary Cadogan, styling by Penny Markham. Chicken from Bennett's Farm, Dorking, Surrey (0306 711598), cheese from Neal's Yard Dairy, ham from Dukeshill Ham Company, Bridgnorth, Shropshire (0704 635519), fish from Steve Hatt, Essex Road, London N1 (071 226 3963). The following supplied food for the cover shot: W. Bainborough Ltd and Jeroboams of Elizabeth Street, London SW1.

Picture acknowledgements

The Author and Publishers wish to thank the following for permission to use illustrations:

Bridgeman Art Library pages 15, 23, 25, 42, 58, 85, 89, 90, 144; Windsor Castle, Royal Library, © 1992 Her Majesty the Queen page 19; Jacqui Hurst pages 35, 39, 114, 116; Sonia Halliday and Laura Lustington page 24; Illustrated London News pages 24, 83; Mary Evans Picture Library pages 78, 111, 177; Harrods Ltd Company Archives page 95; the Stilton Cheese Makers' Association and Osborne Publicity Services Ltd pages 143, 144, 145; and Appleby's of Hawkstone page 148.

The television series, **The Feast of Christmas**, is a Malone Gill Production for Channel 4, produced by Georgina Dennison and directed by Chris Goddard.

The Feast of Christmas

Paul Levy

with photographs by Robin Broadbent

Kyle Cathie Limited

For Tatyana and Georgia

First published in Great Britain by
Kyle Cathie Limited
3 Vincent Square London SW1P 2LX

Copyright © 1992 by Paul Levy
Copyright © 1992 in the food
    photographs by Robin Broadbent

ISBN hardcover 1 85626 070 4
    paperback 1 85626 071 2

A CIP catalogue record for this book is
available from the British Library

Photoset by Rowland Phototypesetting
Ltd, Bury St Edmunds, Suffolk
Printed in Great Britain by
Butler and Tanner Ltd,
Frome and London

Introduction

Once a year our dismal diet disappears, and the gloom of national culinary mediocrity lifts. (Americans have the bonus of a twice-a-year food high, thanks to Thanksgiving.) For the rest of the year, we may merely eat, snack, graze or nosh; but at Christmas we feast.

Poor old Anglo-Saxons. We have to get ourselves in a special frame of mind to eat better than we usually do. We have to decorate our houses and buy presents for our children, just to get us in the mood. How unlike the run of mankind we are in this respect. I have known students in Shanghai who were actually *hungry* (a condition little known in the junk-food overfed West) and who, when invited to a dinner at a restaurant they could never afford, and offered food of a quantity and quality they may seldom or never have seen, showed a critical appreciation of what was set before them. They did not wolf down the delicate steamed fish with its slivers of ginger and garlic, though that was probably the method usually employed to get through their twice-daily ration of half a pound of gritty boiled rice with a couple of tablespoons of vegetables and a scrap of fatty pork. These students, who had latched on to our party to practise their English, and not in the hope of getting a square meal, showed by their demeanour, their table

manners and the fashion in which they savoured every bite, slowly and reflectively, that though they may have been almost starving, they knew how to feast.

The same respectful, reflective attitude towards food exists, still, in most European countries: the meanest peasant, who may subsist, involuntarily, on a diet of grains and vegetables, still knows how to feast. This grace before meals, this attitude that allows food to be savoured (or despised if it is not up to standard) is a gift given by the culture; a gift transmitted by parents and grandparents, which is the direct result of the closeness of their association with the soil. Of course this gift is no blessing if the soil has let them down, if the crops have been poor and nature has been mean. But when there is food on the table (and, usually, wine in the glass), the person with the talent for feasting is capable of having an experience of enjoyment, of the enhancing of life, that is all but denied to us who get our food shrink-wrapped from a stripbulb-lighted supermarket.

Still, once a year we are given a glimpse of what food can mean to man. Instinctively we know the importance of feasting. Indeed, we feel at Christmas that it is everyone's *right* to feast. It is not only in hospitals, factory canteens and army messes that a special effort is made at Christmas; even those who are nourished only by soup kitchens, and prisoners in their jails, are given better food at this time of year.

What is it that distinguishes the attitude of the feaster from that of the ordinary eater? In what frame of mind do we approach the feast? First, of course, there is the anticipation of sensory pleasure – we expect to enjoy ourselves more than usual (and some to enjoy themselves more than enough; it is idle to deny that for some people the pleasure of the feast includes licensed gluttony). Secondly, there is the prospect of social pleasure, of at least a short time of comradeship and good fellowship, even if it is limited to a few hours around a table.

But thirdly, and this may be startling if you have never thought about it before, there is an intellectual reward. The ancients knew this: after all, there was a bite to eat served with the wine at Plato's Symposium. The pleasures of the table are enhanced by reflecting on them (despite the horrid upper-class English ban on discussing the food at table, which lasted well into the 1960s). Curiosity about what we put in our mouths is a very good thing, and a pleasurable cast of mind. Why is this turkey so moist, when another cook's version of this bird is a dry and sorry thing? Where did the turkey originate? How did it get its name? Why do we eat it at Christmas?

At the feast, everyone is a critic.

If we have enough food, we take it for granted. It is only when there is too little, or more than enough, that we reflect about what we chew and swallow. Food is surrounded by myths, some of which are nonsense (such as that 'toadstools' are poisonous, but mushrooms are delicious; that you can tell one from the other by peeling them, or cutting them with a silver knife). Each item of food has its own history (what was Italian food like before Columbus discovered the Americas and tomatoes, or Indian food before Portuguese travellers brought them chillies?). Food has glamour (why do we prize caviar, when the sailor, tasting it for the first time, said 'Hello, this jam tastes like fish'?). We are obsessed by food (there are chocoholics who can't get enough of it, and anorexics for whom any amount is too much). There are dangers in some foods (I once contracted salmonella from an egg, and the Japanese devotees of *fugu*, poisonous blow-fish, risk death with each bite). Food is surrounded by taboos (Muslims and Jews won't eat pork, many Americans shun animal fat).

Even the most ordinary pedestrian, everyday meal reveals, when reflected upon, curious facts of history, science and human relations. One of the most fascinating books of recent years was written by a Canadian classicist who, peeling and chopping onions for a familiar Elizabeth David recipe, suddenly stopped and asked herself why onions stung her eyes, why some were hard to peel and others easy, why some were red and some yellow or white. Where did they come from? Was it true that onions were the main food of the Egyptian workmen who built the pyramids? How do onions figure in folk medicine? Margaret Visser visited the library the next day, and began the research that culminated in *Much Depends on Dinner*, in whose 300-odd pages she analyses every aspect of a representative North American meal. History – and not just the history of food – will never be the same. She has breathed intellectual life, and new and exciting savours, into an activity most of us do three times a day.

I hope to do something like that for our annual midwinter binge, to inspect the feast course by course, and follow my nose, taste buds and curiosity wherever they take me. The investigation will take me to some peculiar places because my own family's Christmas menu is eclectic, and in what follows I examine the Christmas feast that my family and friends have held for several years. Though we basically eat the sort of meal that is customary in English-speaking countries, our family celebrations were formerly held in France, and as a result we have acquired some Frenchified ways.

Moreover, I am Jewish by birth. Though not observant, I have a strong Jewish cultural strain – in my being and in what anthropologists uncharmingly call 'foodways'. Though born in America – another important strand in explaining the food I put on our table – I live with my family in Britain; and Britain now has a culture, especially as regards food, made up of several ethnic and national traditions. We – all of us – are now as likely to go out for an Indian or Chinese meal as for fish and chips. This is as true for those living in small towns as for those living in cities. Our own Christmas turkey, as you will see from the following pages, is just as likely to be cooked with soy sauce and star anise, or to be studded with black truffles, as to be plainly roasted and stuffed with sage, onion and breadcrumbs.

This book proceeds, as does the television series it accompanies, course by course.

Paul Levy
OXFORD
JUNE 1992

CHAPTER ONE

The case for Christmas

Every family has its own, personal Christmas traditions. Ours involve elaborate planning and – to tell the truth – prolonging and emphasising as much as possible the pleasurable anticipation of the feast. We are seldom fewer than 18 at table for the Christmas meal, which has evolved into a stately chorus line, choreographed by my wife and me with the help of the principal dancers, who include some well-known professional cookery writers, and supported by the teamwork of the rest of the guests. At noon we gather in front of the fire in the drawing room and drink champagne while the children open their presents. Guests wander in through the front door of our 17th-century Oxfordshire farmhouse from noon until we sit down to eat at four.

Anyone who comes before four is either co-opted for kitchen duty, or follows my wife, Penny, on a long and strenuous walk down into the Combe Valley. The younger men are enlisted to move the furniture: the kitchen deal tables are put end to end, and the lower raised on four bricks that are stored in the pantry. The white damask tablecloths have been ironed with sugar. The fruit, flowers and foliage are arranged on the table. The menu cards, made by my younger daughter Georgia, are put out as the table is laid with all the cutlery and glasses we can muster.

The kitchen, a converted milking parlour and dairy, is about forty feet long. The table is set up at one end, while the cooks gather around the Aga at the other end. On the table side, the oyster-openers are at work, while other guest-workers are in the garden picking the sprouts, salad and herbs. Frances Bissell, *The Times* cook, is supervising the turkey, while Claudia Roden, the leading authority on Middle Eastern food, leads her team down to the cellar to collect the apples to go with the truffled *boudin blanc*. Somehow, every year, as if by magic, we are ready to crowd around the table precisely at four. Penny has done the seating plan, which is tricky, as the chief cooks have to be able to get to the Aga.

Though we introduce some (usually subtle) variations each time, the menu is basically fixed. Champagne with Middle Eastern nibbles prepared by Claudia. Then, at table, oysters (raw, plus cooked for the squeamish) with an alternative of smoked salmon. *Boudin blanc* with apples. Sometimes a large whole fish, or a terrine of scallops and turkey. The bird, formerly goose or pheasant, but now turkey (since the discovery of turkey-farmer John Munson's old-fashioned birds), is treated a little differently each year. One year it was quickly roasted, unstuffed, and carved so rapidly you could scarcely follow his movement by the celebrated chef Raymond Blanc, who then proceeded to reconstruct it, and brought it to the table still hot. Another year the entire meal was cooked single-handedly by Ken Hom, the Chinese-American cookery teacher and writer, who was too tired to carve the turkey so he lifted the breasts and sliced them into thick, succulent steaks. One year someone gave me a truffle. We shaved it thinly and placed the slices under the skin, thus producing the famous dish of turkey *en demi-deuil* – in half-mourning, because of the black of the truffles.

Frances hates Brussels sprouts, so Anton Mosimann taught me a trick to win her around to them: we shred them finely, and stir-fry them in the wok with garlic and ginger. Next we always have a green salad; we cultivate the garden with an eye to having salad all year round. The cheese is always Colston Bassett stilton (not the same since the farmers who make up the Colston Bassett cooperative took fright in the listeria scare of 1988 and went over to pasteurisation, but still the best stilton there is), a medium-sized truckle of Mr Keen's cheddar, aged 18–24 months, and a small truckle of Mrs Appleby's cheshire. Christmas pudding comes from Anton Mosimann and is served flaming with the lights out (it is always dark outside by this stage of the meal), followed by a huge Moroccan filo pastry 'snake', filled with almond paste scented with rosewater and orange-blossom water, made in advance by Claudia.

At this point we pull the crackers, put on our funny hats and read the bad jokes to each other. Chocolates, dried fruits and cobnuts from the garden are on the table with the port. And anyone with the energy to do it makes the coffee.

We try each year to drink some of the same wines as the year before, and pretend that we are assessing the vintage. In fact, we think carefully about the wines for the meal, and plan as far in advance as possible. There's always plenty of champagne, and we usually have an interesting still white wine, a claret and either a burgundy or a wine from the south of France.

We are positively burdened with Christmas traditions; we have collective nostalgia. Though the guest list changes a little every year, the hard core is unchanging. All of us are interested in food and wine, and there's always a mother-in-law and an honorary aunt or two, plus some of our children's godparents; the rest of us are the gastronomic waifs and strays, some without children, some whose children have grown up and left home – though a surprising number of this last category end up around this same table every year.

THE LEVY FAMILY CHRISTMAS REALLY BEGINS WHEN we go out to the orchard and dig up the Christmas tree from its parking space, where we put it each January 6, and lug it into the house; then we cut the holly from one of our old trees. Though the Romans used to decorate trees at this time of year, and even bring them into the house, the Christmas tree itself was introduced, both to England and America, by German immigrants in the 1830s and 1840s. As the British royal family were of German background, Christmas trees were introduced in the reigns of both George III and William IV, though of course they really caught on when Victoria and Albert erected their tree at Windsor in 1840. (The famous scene of Victoria and Albert and the royal family by their

Christmas tree appeared in the *Illustrated London News* in 1848.)

Our ritual continues with the search in the glory hole for the wicker hamper with the family decorations, and we go through the usual process of cursing on finding that the fairylights are fused because one tiny bulb isn't working. We painstakingly search for the culprit light, and we resist the usual demands of the children to make the tree as gaudy as possible. We remark on what a pity it is that all this work must be undone in 12 days' time, and explain to the children the superstitions connected with leaving the greenery up beyond Twelfth Night.

Oddly enough, though, the traditions of decorating the house with evergreens and lights and exchanging gifts did not come from the northern European Yule tradition, but from the southern European midwinter festivals of the later Roman Empire, particularly Saturnalia, which started on December 17. Saturnalia was a feast presided over by a Master of the Revels, sometimes the Lord of Misrule. Everything was turned upside down: masters waited on their servants (as still happens in the messes of the British Army on Christmas Day); gambling and drunkenness, forbidden during the rest of the year, were encouraged; children cheeked their parents; and there was licence even in matters of dress. Men wore animal skins or dressed as women, and women dressed as men.

If that puts you in mind of the Christmas pantomime, that's precisely where its cross-dressing traditions have come from. Our local pantomime, in the town of Chipping Norton, takes place every season in a tiny theatre converted from a chapel. Many of the same people attend every year, and there is a cosy feeling because many of the audience are acquainted with the actors as well as each other. The children are extremely well rehearsed, and know when to hiss and boo, and at what point the sweets will be thrown from the stage. Perhaps the pantomime itself will involve making a particularly butch male member of the audience come on to the stage and put on a frock, as it did the year before last.

Back at home as we wrap the presents we think about gift-giving and the other winter festivals. The Jewish Hanukkah is 'the feast of lights', commemorating the Maccabees' successful recovery of the temple, when one day's supply of oil miraculously lasted for eight days. Children get presents, sometimes on each of the eight days, a candle is lit each night; and there are special foods – latkes, particularly (see page 118 for recipe). Hindu Dewali is also a festival of light, and for the two weeks before it people exchange gifts of sweetmeats – the sweet shops are absolutely full of goods during the period.

Our own customs come from gift-giving at Kalends, the Roman New Year, a tradition still maintained by the French and, until this very generation, by the Scots, who have only recently begun to celebrate Christmas as well as Hogmanay, for Scotsman John Knox's condemnation of Christmas had much more effect than the dislike of it expressed by Cromwell and the English Puritans.

The real key to Christmas, though, is nostalgia. Even the children worry that the coming Christmas will not be as good as past ones, and are very conservative about, for example, having the red lacquer apples on the tree in the same places as last year, and having turkey rather than ham or beef for the main Christmas meal. Psychologists will tell us that family traditions continue because all parents consciously seek to preserve bits of their own past, of their own childhood.

My own family's Christmas traditions were fairly thin on the ground. The Levys of Lexington, Kentucky, the small town in the southern states of America where I was born, were the children of Russian Jewish immigrants, and at first they tolerated Christmas rather than celebrated it. But by the time I was 12 they had given in to the customs of the majority of the neighbours, at least in the matter of Christmas presents. I owe my present indifference to chocolates to the Christmas when a Roman Catholic step-aunt gave my brother and me each a two-pound box of chocolates. I had eaten most of them by the time the grown-ups woke up on Christmas Day, and have never wanted to repeat the experience. So, like the Victorians, I entertain a nostalgia for a Christmas that never really was. The difference is that the Victorians (mis)placed their ideal Christmas in the 18th century, probably the one era in modern British history when Christmas was least celebrated.

To see why that was so, we must just look very briefly at the history of Christmas. Saturnalia, the direct ancestor of Christmas, was celebrated, following Julius Caesar's reform of the calendar, on December 17. Augustus decreed that the 17th should be sacred to Saturn and the 18th to Ops, Saturn's wife. From then on these two days were celebrated as Saturnalia, though the holidays were later extended by several days. The Romans identified Saturn with the Greek Cronus (or Kronos), the agricultural god of harvests. Though not much is known about his cults (he may well have been the divinity of a pre-Hellenic people), his reign was regarded as a Golden Age. In the Roman version, Saturn fled to Italy after the fall of the Titans and settled on the Capitoline Hill. He civilised the people and taught them the skills of farming. In celebration of his mission to Rome gifts were exchanged, schools and courts were closed, war was forbidden and slaves and masters ate at the same table. This celebration, called the Saturnalia, was the origin of the topsy-turvy tradition. The traditions lingered on into the 19th century. In 1856, Frederick Law Olmstead, the remarkable historian of American slavery, said he had noticed in his travels in the Confederacy that 'from Christmas to New Year's Day, most of the slaves, except house servants, enjoy a freedom from labour; and Christmas is especially holiday, or Saturnalia, with them'. It is curious to reflect that the upside-down aspects of Christmas celebrations from the Middle Ages to our own day all derive from this noble Roman seasonal respite from slavery. At the winter solstice we laugh, we gamble, we even drink a little too much, perhaps because we share this folk memory of a Golden Age.

The early church did not celebrate the birth of Jesus – indeed, not much notice was taken of anybody's birthday, as its celebration was largely a pagan practice. In any case, there wasn't much point in marking the Incarnation as early Christians expected the Second Coming to happen in their own time. Thus it wasn't until the 4th century that the Bishop of Rome, Julius I, declared Christmas a feast. Naturally enough, when it came to setting the date the Church, as eager to keep its own members from lapsing as to

The Last Night of Hanukkah by Charles Spencelayh (1865–1958)

make new converts, took advantage of the fact that there were already some winter feasts celebrated more or less universally. Chief among these by the 2nd century AD was the Mithraic feast day, Dies Solis Invicti Nati, the day of the birth of the unconquered sun – December 25. On this day the sun reaches its highest point in the ecliptic and appears to stand still before going back on its apparent course through the zodiac. Up to this point the nights have been getting longer, the days shorter; now the days lengthen, and one can see that spring will definitely come again. To

a pastoral people, this was an annual reassurance that the world would not come to an end – yet – and that there would be at least one more growing season.

No wonder this was the feast day of the cult of Mithras, for Mithras, though he was a minor god in India and Persia until the 6th century BC, had become, only a century later, the principal god of the Persians, the god of wisdom and light, and associated with the sun. With the growth of the Persian empire his cult expanded all over the old world. By the 2nd century AD, Mithraism was the main rival to Christianity, and especially favoured by the Roman legions, who admired Mithras as the divine comrade and fighter. The Roman soldiers were an immensely important target in the programme of the conversion of the Gentiles, and the religion of the entire later Roman Empire could easily have been Mithraism rather than Christianity.

In Mithraism there is a struggle between the forces of good and evil. Mithras, whose followers believed they could achieve immortality, was the hero of the powers of light and the enemy of the powers of darkness. Mithras was captured, a sacred bull was sacrificed, from whose blood and body sprang all the good things of the earth, and the commemoration of this sacrifice was the central mystery of the cult. Mithraism was an ethical religion, and its observances included fasting and abstinence. The celebrations of its mysteries were confined to men and were secret; but they included sacraments such as baptism and a sacred banquet. To a Roman legionnaire its similarities to the new Christian religion must have appeared greater than its differences, and the early church viewed its decline in the 3rd century AD with a good deal of relief. Thus it made good sense to co-opt the main feast of Mithraism on December 25, and integrate it into a Christian celebration – a case of joining those you'd rather not fight.

So much for the Gentiles. What about the Jews? The church also had plans for them; after all, the apostles and the first disciples were all Jews, and they observed all the traditional Jewish ceremonies. The re-birth of the unconquered sun was a solar event, the solstice, but there was also a lunar celebration that influenced the choice of a date for Christmas. Hanukkah had been celebrated since it was instituted by Judas Maccabaeus in 165 BC; and though its date is determined by the lunar calendar, the date of the Dedication of the Temple was always 25 Kislev, which falls near enough to 20 or 21 December to make clear that it, too, is a winter solstice festival.

Jesus and the apostles definitely celebrated this Feast of Lights several centuries before the church established the nativity of Jesus Himself as a Festival of Light, and the early church probably took this into account when fixing the day for Christmas. Judas Maccabaeus was the third son of Matthias the Hasmonean, whose family was devoted to the Jewish struggle (that lasted from about 170 to 160 BC) against the Seleucidae dynasty, in particular the Syrian king Antiochus Epiphanes (175–164). In 162 BC Antiochus IV had profaned the temple by trying to force the Jews to sacrifice to heathen gods. The date of the first Hanukkah was that of the reconsecration of the temple, after an insurrection of about three years, which incidentally resulted in a dynasty of Maccabee priest-kings that lasted until Herod took over in 37 BC.

The events are recorded in two of the Apocryphal books of Maccabee, both of which were current in Jesus's lifetime. The tradition had grown up that the rededication of the temple was attended by a miracle. When they came to relight the eternal light that stands over the altar as it also does in every Christian church, the Jews found only a single unprofaned cruse of specially consecrated olive oil, enough for just one day. It burned, though, for eight days, long enough to procure new supplies. The kinship of the symbolism of this to the winter solstice is evident; and to this day observant Jews celebrate Hanukkah for eight days, by lighting an additional candle every night in an eight-branched candelabrum called a menorah.

To complete the parallels with the folk customs of the Roman and Christian feasts of light, gifts are now exchanged, or at least given to children at Hanukkah. In the past, however, it was traditional only to give coins, Hanukkah *gelt*, which the children were expected to gamble in a game involving spinning tops called *dreidls*. The tops had a Hebrew letter incised in each of the four sides, an acronym for a Hebrew expression meaning 'a great miracle happened there'. (At least, this was true in the diaspora; in Palestine and later Israel, one of the letters differs, for there the acronym stands for 'a great miracle happened *here*'.) Each child stakes one coin. One letter means that you take out a coin from the pot; another that you put in a coin; if the top lands on the third letter, nothing at all happens; but if you get the fourth letter you take the entire pot. In Rome, remember, gambling was generally forbidden; but it was licensed and even encouraged at Saturnalia; and from the Middle Ages until the Reformation, gambling, even by children, was allowed by the church uniquely at Christmas. Moreover, drinking, though not specifically enjoined on the pious at Hanukkah, as it is for the feast of Purim, when it is a Jew's religious duty to get a little tipsy, is always smiled upon at festivals, and many Jewish families break out a bottle at Hanukkah.

There are also some special foods eaten at Hanukkah. Interestingly, these all have a symbolic connection with the event. Jews of European descent, the Ashkenazim, eat potato latkes (see page 118), grated with an onion and bound with egg and matzo meal; Sephardic Jews (and now many Ashkenazim as well) eat doughnut-like pastries (see page 121). What these foods have in common is that they are deep-fried in oil, to commemorate the Hanukkah miracle. In America Hanukkah has almost been assimilated to Christmas. Presents are given to children, sometimes one a day for each of the eight days; cards are bought and sent; and the house is decorated – sometimes with a 'Hanukkah bush'. This sends shivers down religious Jewish spines, for the proper observance of Hanukkah requires only lighting the menorah, preferably in a window where it can be seen from the street, as testimony to the commemoration of the miracle. But there is little reason for Jewish parents to worry about the Christmas-isation of Hanukkah; it is the older festival, and has common roots with Christmas in the winter solstice celebrations and in Saturnalia.

The more vulgar aspects of the winter solstice festivities have not been lost; they continue to flourish in unlikely places. Christmas celebrations have got a little out of hand in Japan, for example, where, although less than one per cent of the population is Christian, the commercial side of the season has great appeal. Everyone has heard the tale, although I can't establish its truth, of the Tokyo department store that decorated its eight-storey atrium with a gigantic Father Christmas. The details were a little wrong: the designer represented Santa crucified on the cross. Similarly, I think the rabbinical authorities might be slightly distressed to read, in the *New Yorker*'s 'Edge of Night Life' column for 6 January 1992, about the Jackie 60 club at 14th and Washington Streets: 'The club's Country Christmas featured a Hanukkah Hoedown, with breast-baring cowgirls making cowboys beg for presents, a presentation of fashions to keep Santa from going back up the chimney, a video by Len Whitney featuring the carolling Mitch Miller singers, two drag queens so tall they had to stoop to get through the catacombs downstairs, and Pedro Almodovar hogging the pool table. "He must feel right at home here," said our friend. Ahhh.'

UNTIL 1752 LADY DAY, MARCH 25, WAS THE BEGINNING of the legal and financial year. In the church calendar, Lady Day marked the Annunciation, and had been called 'St Mary's Day in Lent' to set it apart from other days in honour of the Virgin. I have heard some churchmen espouse the theory that the date of Christmas was selected merely because it was nine months after Lady Day, and therefore simply allowed for the gestation period.

But this explanation won't do at all, even from the point of view of the English church. For one thing, December 25 marked the first day of the Anglo-Saxon year and the existing Yule celebrations in England. When St Augustine undertook his mission to England, Pope Gregory the Great encouraged him to assimilate the Anglo-Saxon pagan rites into his own pro-gramme. As almost to the present day, Yule was the killing time, when the livestock that couldn't be fed over the winter was slaughtered. Even today in rural Europe, peasants kill the pig, have an orgy of fresh meat and offal, and cure and preserve the rest for the winter and spring. Pagan sacrifices accompanied this time of year in Anglo-Saxon England, and Pope Gregory nudged St Augustine to chivvy his flock to change the recipient of the sacrifices from the pagan 'Devil' to the Judaeo-Christian God.

Even so, right up to the time of the Norman Con-quest (when the word 'Christmas' first gained cur-rency in England), the pagan elements of the feast were more numerous and important than the specifi-cally Christian ones. The church was troubled by the sensuous pastimes of eating and drinking, the burning of Yule logs, bringing evergreens into the house, the wassailing of the apple, plum and medlar trees by pouring libations of ale upon them, and especially the mummers' plays. With their themes of death and subsequent resurrection, and their characters of Green Men, fools and hobbies, and their attendant ritual games that have come down to us as pin-the-tail-on-the-donkey, blind-man's buff and leapfrog, they were uncomfortably close to their origins as fer-tility rites.

The post-Conquest kings started the pattern of conspicuous consumption at Christmas. In 1252 Henry III gave a Christmas banquet to a thousand peers and knights at York; it cost so much that he received a contribution of 600 oxen and £2,700 to help with the expenses from the Archbishop of York. As we know from Anglo-Saxon poems, English feudal lords had always been expected to feed their depend-ents. But by the time of Richard II (d. 1399) the Nor-man king was providing 10,000 meals daily.

Of course there were political reasons for these great Christmas feasts; they, like the institution of present-giving itself, were the cement of feudalism, binding men to their masters. They were also a matter of economic necessity to the poorest peasants and feudal retainers, who might not have survived the winter without help from their lord and master.

Despite the Conquest, though, the English Christ-mas remained obdurately less Christian than on the continent. Pagan practices were simply accepted and re-labelled. Thus the holly (from the 'holy bush') came to be interpreted, by the church, if not by the people, as a symbol of the crown of thorns. But the English Christmas remained non-Christocentric. For example, there was no English celebration or even marking of the nativity; and both nativity plays and carols were imported.

Even in the Tudor and Stuart reigns, the 12 days of Christmas were a time for indulgence – feasting, gambling, drinking too much and holding sporting events. The religious element was not absent, but not madly important, either. The Puritan backlash against Christmas was inevitable. As no reference to the feast exists anywhere in scripture, it had to go. So Martin Luther, who had a soft spot for Christmas, spoke out against its excesses; Calvin and Cromwell condemned it; and John Knox banned it.

In any case, Christmas was falling into desuetude in urban England. As the poor harvests and economic decline of the 16th and early 17th centuries forced people to drift to the towns, the observance of

The Queen's Christmas Tree: Windsor Castle, 1850

Christmas declined too. In the country it remained a time when land-owners still gave feudal support to their retainers, but gifts of blankets, coal and food were a necessity, rather than a celebration of a church feast. Indeed both Elizabeth I, and James I had to force the upper classes to return from court to their estates at Christmas and remember their obligations to their tenants and dependents.

By 1644 keeping Christmas as a feast was *mal vu*. An ordinance promulgated that year ordained that Christmas Day should actually be kept as a fast. For the next decade, Parliament sat on Christmas Day, and soldiers were dispatched to see that the shops stayed open and the churches shut.

Though the laws against Christmas were abolished with the Restoration of 1660, by the 18th century little remained of the festivities except at the country seats of those Tory squires who still observed their almost feudal duties to their staff and neighbours. This was the reality of the 'Merrie England' that the Victorians harkened back to when they reinvented Christmas. The earlier features of the feast, both religious and secular, were kept alive only in parts of America, such as the Episcopalian-tending colony of Virginia. Puritan New England took the same dim view of Christmas as did their English and Scottish co-religionists. In Massachusetts the General Court enacted a law fining anyone who observed Christmas 'by abstinence from labour, feasting or any other way' the sum of five shillings. It was not repealed until 1681.

To recapture the spirit of Christmas, the Victorians had to look back to an imaginary 18th-century England, and over the seas to the American colonists, where the feast was kept more vigorously by the merchant class in the towns than it was by rural farmers. In 1791 the Constitution established the principle of separation of church and state; but by that time in America, Christmas was no longer an occasion for theological dispute, but a secular, folk festival, to which many of the now-disparate churches were happy to attach themselves.

The best place to see this Victorian idealisation of an 18th-century Christmas is in Dickens's saccharine description of Christmas at Dingley Dell in *Pickwick Papers* (1836), with its good-natured squire, huge, roaring fires, jolly coachman and grateful and happy friends and relations, as illustrated by Phiz. The contrast with Bob Cratchit's family celebrations in *A Christmas Carol* (1843) shows how rapidly the Vic-

torian invention of the modern Christmas developed. In those few years the idea of Christmas was altered to reflect the value the Victorians placed upon the family unit, with Christmas seen chiefly as a celebration of the virtues – some economic – of family life; and the emphasis also altered to accommodate the Victorian view of social progress. From now on, writers of fiction as well as the press were as interested in Christmas in the workhouse as they were in Christmas in the manor house. Christmas became a time to worry about the underprivileged. The narrative poem, 'In the Workhouse: Christmas Day', was written by George R. Sims who was born in 1847, practically the contemporary of the fictional characters Tiny Tim, Bob Cratchit and Ebenezer Scrooge, but who lived on until 1922, just 20 years short of being able to hear Bing Crosby sing 'White Christmas' in *Holiday Inn*. It begins: 'It is Christmas Day in the Workhouse,/And the cold bare walls are bright/With garlands of green and holly,/And the place is a pleasant sight:/For with clean-washed hands and faces,/In a long and hungry line/The paupers sit at the tables,/For this is the hour they dine.' (See pages 28–29.)

The theme of poverty at Christmas, or rather, the contrast between the comfortable Christmas of the Victorian bourgeoisie and the plight of the poor at winter, was the theme of the first Christmas card. George Buday, the most serious writer on the history of the Christmas card, has proved conclusively (in 1954) that the first such article appeared in 1843. (This was no mean feat of detection, as its designer, John Calcott Horsley, by then a Royal Academician, mistook the date himself in a letter to the Editor of *The Times* he wrote in the 1880s, by which time he was an old man.) It is only fair to let Mr Buday describe the lithographed, hand-coloured first Christmas card in his own words: 'The main panel shows a homely family party in progress, including three generations, in true Victorian fashion. We can count eleven people, including four children. They are toasting the health of the absent friend, the addressee, with red wine, and only the three smallest children are not holding wine-glasses, but are busily engaged in tasting the plum pudding.'

The central panel includes the motto 'A Merry Christmas and A Happy New Year to You' on a cloth draped over the central trellis that divides the card into a triptych. Here, however, is the really stunning aspect of the world's first Christmas card. One side panel depicts poor people being clothed, the other shows a pauper and a child being fed. Are these instances of the spirit of charity? Are they intended to remind the recipient of his own good fortune in not being dependent on charity at Christmas? Or are they a smug Victorian gesture, enhancing the addressee's sense of his own well-being by contrasting it with the misfortunes of others? Victorian attitudes to poverty differed greatly, but most well-off people distinguished between the deserving poor and those whose plight was their own fault. I am made just a little uncomfortable by the scene depicted on the first Christmas card. I find myself a little happier with the frankly commercial Father Christmas cards of the 1870s or even the sentimental robin of the 1850s and '60s with its maudlin religious motto.

Of course the Christmas card, being a late developer, did not spring from nowhere; it had its antecedents in the tokens the Romans exchanged at Kalends, the New Year. At first these were bits of greenery, bay or olive branches gathered from groves sacred to the Sabine goddess of health, Strenia (new year gifts were called *strenae*); then they became edible, in the form of dried fruits or honey; then under the Caesars coins bearing the head of Janus; and finally decorated bowls, oil lamps and the like. As the Saturnalia celebrations were taken over by the church, so were the *strenae*. With the invention of printing, the tokens evolved into cards, and by the 15th century birds and flowers had been added to the religious motifs on the hand-coloured cards. The habit of exchanging cards at the New Year rather than Christmas persists to this day in France and the rest of Europe. There were New Year's cards in England (and of course Scotland) as well, but the true ancestor of the English Christmas card was the Valentine card, the manufacture of which had been big business for fifty years or more before the 1843 Christmas card.

The most persistently popular subject for the British Christmas card is the robin. (It is marginally less popular in America, possibly because the bird Americans call a 'robin' is not a cuddly, plump little chap with a red breast, but an elongated member of the thrush family.) Common sense suggests that the robin is a symbol of winter simply because robins do not migrate, and the male, the most territorial of all garden birds, defends his territory so visibly and noisily – especially at Christmas, when robins mate, and the hen is allowed to encroach on the cock's territory. In folklore, though, there is a persistent confusion, or perhaps one should say amalgamation, of the robin with that other very small bird, the wren.

Wrens (which also featured on Victorian Christmas cards) and robins were, until recent times, considered sacred birds, and protected very vigorously indeed by countryfolk (along with the migratory martin and swallow). In a Warwickshire verse, 'the robin and the wren,/are God Almighty's cock and hen', and in one from Essex 'robins and wrens are God Almighty's shirt and collar'. Also in Essex young boys were taught to leave alone the nests of the protected birds:

> The robin aye the redbreast,
> The robin and the wren,
> If you take out the nest,
> Ye'll never thrive again.
> The robin and the redbreast,
> The martin and the swallow,
> If you touch one of their eggs,
> Bad luck will surely follow.

In his chapter on robins as Christmas card motifs, Buday collected a similar rhyme from the northern counties of England: 'The robin and the wren,/Him that harries their nest,/Never shall his soul have rest', and from Cornwall, 'He who hurts the robin or the wren,/Will never prosper sea or land,'/On sea or land will ne'er do well again.' The British attitude to small birds is obviously superstitious.

Yet in the 1880s there was a vogue for Christmas cards showing small dead birds, especially robins. Not the roast goose or turkey, mind you, but one dead bird, still in its plumage, lying on its back, tiny claws in the air. The mottoes included morbid ones such as 'Sweet messenger of calm decay and Peace Divine' and all but inexplicable ones such as 'But peaceful was the night,/wherein the Prince of Light,/His reign of peace upon the earth began.'

The Victorians enjoyed a good weep, and I suppose this could be the Christmas card equivalent of Tiny Tim's crutch or the death of Little Nell, but I've not seen anything so mysterious and sinisterly surreal until I saw Glen Baxter's card of bird-masked men bound hand and foot with ropes and bearing the motto, 'It was going to be the usual dull Christmas . . .'

There is, though, always the possibility that the dead bird is a reference to Wrenning Day. Maybe there is still a folk-memory of this grisly ceremony, once widespread both in Britain and in France. Even into this century on the Isle of Man, the custom of hunting the wren was observed on St Stephen's Day, which we now generally call Boxing Day, December 26. In the 18th century it was done on Christmas Eve or Christmas morning. After prayers, when the bells rang at midnight, all the servants of the household went to hunt the wren. When they found one of these little birds they killed it and, says Frazer in *The Golden Bough*, 'fastened it to the top of a long pole with its wings extended. Thus they carried it in procession to every house chanting the following rhyme:

> We hunted the wren for Robin the Bobbin,
> We hunted the wren for Jack of the Can,
> We hunted the wren for Robin the Bobbin,
> We hunted the wren for everyone.'

Think of our horror at Europeans who *eat* songbirds. Yet Buday says that 'as a result of more recent

'Bright be your Christmas': a Victorian greetings card

confusion' it was sometimes a robin that was hunted by all the men of the village, young and old, and that the pole was decorated with evergreens and red braid; or else the dead bird was transported 'in a glass case on an improvised small hearse. Villagers who obtained a feather, a protective charm, were supposed to have good luck throughout the coming year.' Dr Brewer, in his *Dictionary of Phrase and Fable*, thought that the wren was stoned to death in commemoration of St Stephen, the first Christian martyr, who met his death in this way. The difficulty with this theory is that Brewer, writing in 1870, did not seem to be aware that the ceremony was not invariably conducted on St Stephen's Day; indeed, Christmas Eve seems to be the older date for the rite. Buday's view was that it was a late survivor of the ancient practice of killing the king, a human sacrifice to avert disaster. Frazer more modestly finds the ritual akin to others that allow the whole community to share in the benefits of sacrificing a sacred animal.

In any case, it makes one turn with relief to the Christmas cards featuring Santa Claus. Or does it? Jolly old St Nicholas, Sir Christmas, Old Christmas, Father Christmas, Kris Kringle, and the latest of these, Santa Claus – the smiling, gift-giving aspect of Christmas. Or is he? An early iconographic ancestor was Odin, the chief Norse god. But in our northern European pre-occupation with the darkness before the winter solstice and the waning of the sun, even Odin became a monster at Yule-tide. In Scandinavia in more recent times, 'Julebuk' was represented in a satanic mask and horns, though he too brought presents to children. In rural Germany even today there are those who can remember Klausauf, a demotic assistant to St Nicholas. There is always the implied threat that the same figure who brought especially nice presents to good children would devour those who were bad.

The idea of Christmas as a special time for children goes back to Saturnalia, when there was a time of Juvenilia for the children. And soon they acquired their own patron saint. St Nicholas, the patron saint of children and sailors, was the 4th-century Bishop of Myra in Asia Minor. The miracles attributed to him touch on the deepest fears of children, of being eaten, or mutilated, or otherwise mistreated by the evil demons of the dark forest; a substitute, say many modern psychologists, for the fear children have of their own parents. Certainly the theme of the child-devouring parent was as common in the myths and tales of antiquity as is the theme of the child-abusing parent in our own times.

St Nicholas assuaged these fears – or pandered to them. His chief miracle was to restore to life three little boys who had been cut up and pickled in a barrel of salt by a butcher. St Nick is also supposed to have heaved three bags of gold through the window of a house, quite anonymously, as a dowry for the three daughters of a poor man, thus saving them from prostitution. St Nicholas's three bags of gold have given us our pawn-broker's symbol.

The cult of St Nicholas was immensely popular in the Middle Ages. It was celebrated on his day, December 6, with ceremonies descended directly from the topsy-turvy world of Saturnalia, usually the election of a boy bishop, whose authority over cathedrals, college chapels and even the king's private chapels lasted at least until December 28, Holy Innocents'

Day (which commemorated the slaughter of the Innocents by King Herod). The boy bishop was elected from the ranks of the choristers. He and his entourage had the right to conduct visitations to parish churches and to local great houses, and to collect money. From his collection the boy bishop was obliged to host a great feast for all the clergy; but he was allowed to keep any change from the cost of the banquet, and quite often made a profit of a pound or two – a good deal of money for a medieval child. Each of the orders of the clergy elected its own Lord of Misrule and revelry was encouraged. Gambling was allowed, and it seems likely that even the choir boys were allowed enough beer to make them squiffy. Hereford Cathedral revived its boy-bishop ceremony some years ago, and it is now part of its regular Christmas observances.

The British Father Christmas of the 17th and 18th centuries was sometimes called Sir Christmas (looking like Shakespeare's Falstaff) or Old Christmas (in which he sometimes bore a resemblance to the Green Man) or even Captain Christmas (usually with the bearing of a good-living country squire). Post-Reformation England and Scotland had banished St Nicholas along with the rest of what the Puritans saw as the Papist-cum-Pagan paraphernalia of Christmas. Paradoxically, the image of Father Christmas that replaced St Nick was even more Saturnalian. Sometimes Father Christmas was represented as a naughty, bibulous Lord of Misrule, with a drink-related red nose, but sometimes as a wizened old man, looking rather like the figure of old Father Time, with which we associate the disappearance of the old year at New Year.

A 16th century French image of St Nicholas

A bibulous Father Christmas as Lord of Misrule

Santa Claus, whose name comes from St Nicholas via the Dutch, was imported wholesale from the United States in the 19th century. His immediate popularity was so great that Father Christmas was totally swallowed up by and assimilated to the new-comer. The extraordinary thing was that Santa Claus was cut from whole cloth in a single poem by Professor Clement Clark Moore, who lived in upper New York State. Poor Professor Moore would doubtless have preferred to be known to posterity by his scholarly work on his Hebrew lexicon, or for his translation of the Roman satirist Juvenal. Instead, we remember him only as the man who invented Santa Claus.

His dreadful poem, universally known as 'The Night Before Christmas' but actually entitled 'A Visit from St Nicholas', was published anonymously in his local paper, the *Troy Sentinel*, in 1823. Everybody remembers it, even now: ''Twas the night before Christmas, when all through the house/Not a creature was stirring, not even a mouse.' In this poetically modest verse is contained every element of the Santa story: 'a miniature sleigh, and eight tiny reindeer' ('Now Dasher! now Dancer! now, Prancer and Vixen!/On, Comet! on, Cupid! on, Donner and Blitzen!' Today's children will have to be reminded that Rudolph is not one of the original reindeer.) For the first time, Santa enters the house by the chimney, where children have hung their stockings, though they never did before; above all, Santa Claus is now definitively and forever a fat, white-bearded man dressed in a red suit trimmed 'all in fur, from his head to his foot', carrying a bag full of toys. The illustrations of the poem by Thomas Nast for *Harper's Weekly* in 1863 literally set the cap upon the image of Santa Claus, although it was at first a stiff, fur-trimmed cap that rose to a bobble-topped peak, and only later did he draw the floppy red stocking cap with white bobble.

Our present-day Christmas exactly reflects these Victorian values: we indulge ourselves and our families, but it is the one time of year when charity workers can be guaranteed of catching our attention. We may feel cynical about Christmas, a season in which fad succeeds fad, and teenage Ninja mutant turtles give way to Nintendo in the affections of children, while massed pop stars admonish us to 'Feed the World' from the privacy of our own television sets. But it was the Victorians, not us, who first commercialised Christmas. After all, what is a better reflection of the famous entrepreneurial energy of the Victorian age, than the history of the Christmas card?

Christmas in the English-speaking countries has always been closer to its pagan roots than to their Christian adaptations. Our carols celebrate wassailing, pouring libations of cider to the apple trees to ensure next year's apple crop, quite as often as they remember the nativity. The crèche, and even the nativity play, are relatively recent arrivals in Britain, for they were transplanted from Italy and France after the Reformation and never really took root in Protestant soil. The wayside crèche in England is more rare than the pub where they maintain the ancient tradition of firing their shotguns into the boughs of the trees to frighten evil spirits away, or the coven of Wiccans, dancing around a flaming cauldron (symbolising the birth of the Child of Light) to welcome the winter solstice, and searching in their puddings for runic fortune-telling charms. As for the holly and ivy, any of the tens of thousands of pagans who still practise their antique religion in Britain will tell you that the holly is the spirit of the winter as the ivy is the spirit of the summer and that the fairy on the top of the Christmas tree has been there forever – for she is the goddess. As you can imagine, these followers of the Old Religion have no difficulty about the celebration of Christmas – they're quite certain they've been about it much longer than the rest of us; the alignment of the standing stones at Stonehenge, Avebury and elsewhere quite clearly do have something to do with the two solstices, don't they?

We are bound to conclude that mankind has always had need of some sort of midwinter festival. The convergence of customs and habits across cultures and religions is astonishing, but convincing. The only possible course of action is to enjoy it thoroughly.

Wassail - The foam at the top is lamb's wool, exploded apple. When you pour the hot spiced cider into a glass mug, you must be sure to put in a silver spoon first to prevent the glass cracking from the heat of the liquid. The same is true if you serve it in a glass punchbowl: a metal ladle touching the side and bottom of the bowl will conduct the heat and avoid an expensive calamity

WASSAIL

Mull cider, scrumpy if you can get it, with sweet spices, such as cloves, cinnamon, nutmeg, ginger and cardamom, in a retrievable muslin bag. Strengthen with applejack or calvados if you like (but vodka will do at a pinch). Don't boil! Unless you've used very dry cider, you probably won't need much sugar.

Lamb's Wool, with which you decorate the wassail, is made by heating apples, which in theory explode when they come into contact with the hot cider. In practice, it is best to gently simmer the apples in a bit of cider until they go woolly, and then pick out the cores, pips and skins before spreading the pulp decoratively over the surface of the wassail.

MULLED WINE

There are only two essential things to know about mulling wine. The first is that it is a waste to use really good wine. The second is that boiling it will drive off the alcohol and, with it, most of the point of drinking it.

So, to each bottle of *drinkable*, stout red wine (delicate pinot noir, for example, is useless), add one-tenth to one-fifth its volume of grape spirits, brandy or armagnac, or port or both. Warm this gently in a large, heavy saucepan containing a lemon, orange or several kumquats stuck with a few cloves, a stick of cinnamon and a blade of mace plus any other sweet spices you like tied up in a muslin bag. The longer it infuses the better, but it's ready when it's piping hot. Check for sweetness, and add white sugar to taste.

IN THE WORKHOUSE: CHRISTMAS DAY
by George Robert Sims
(1847–1922)

It is Christmas Day in the Workhouse,
  And the cold bare walls are bright
With garlands of green and holly,
  And the place is a pleasant sight:
For with clean-washed hands and faces,
  In a long and hungry line
The paupers sit at the tables,
  For this is the hour they dine.

And the guardians and their ladies,
  Although the wind is east,
Have come in their furs and wrappers,
  To watch their charges feast;
To smile and be condescending,
  Put pudding on pauper plates,
To be hosts at the workhouse banquet
  They've paid for – with the rates.

Oh, the paupers are meek and lowly
  With their 'Thank'ee kindly, mum's';
So long as they fill their stomachs,
  What matter it whence it comes?
But one of the old men mutters,
  And pushes his plate aside:
'Great God!' he cries; 'but it chokes me!
  For this is the day *she* died.'

The guardians gazed in horror,
  The master's face went white;
'Did a pauper refuse their pudding?'
  'Could their ears believe aright?'
Then the ladies clutched their husbands,
  Thinking the man would die,
Struck by a bolt, or something,
  By the outraged One on high.

But the pauper sat for a moment,
  Then rose 'mid a silence grim,
For the others had ceased to chatter,
  And trembled in every limb.
He looked at the guardians' ladies,
  Then, eyeing their lords, he said,
'I eat not the food of villains
  Whose hands are foul and red:

'Whose victims cry for vengeance
  From their dank, unhallowed graves.'
'He's drunk!' said the workhouse master,
  'Or else he's mad, and raves.'
'Not drunk, or mad,' cried the pauper,
  'But only a hunted beast,
Who, torn by the hounds and mangled,
  Declines the vulture's feast.

'I care not a curse for the guardians,
  And I won't be dragged away.
Just let me have the fit out,
  It's only on Christmas Day
That the black past comes to goad me,
  And prey on my burning brain;
I'll tell you the rest in a whisper –
  I swear I won't shout again.

'Keep your hands off me, curse you!
  Hear me right out to the end.
You come here to see how the paupers
  The season of Christmas spend.
You come here to watch us feeding,
  As they watch the captured beast.
Hear why a penniless pauper
  Spits on your paltry feast.

'Do you think I will take your bounty,
  And let you smile and think
You're doing a noble action
  With the parish's meat and drink?
Where is my wife, you traitors –
  The poor old wife you slew?
Yes, by the God above us,
  My Nance was killed by you!

'Last winter my wife lay dying,
  Starved in a filthy den;
I had never been to the parish –
  I came to the parish then.
I swallowed my pride in coming,
  For, ere the ruin came,
I held up my head as a trader,
  And I bore a spotless name.

'I came to the parish craving
  Bread for a starving wife,
Bread for the woman who'd loved me
  Through fifty years of her life;
And what do you think they told me,
  Mocking my awful grief?
That "the house" was open to us,
  But they wouldn't give "out relief".

'I slunk to the filthy alley –
  'Twas a cold, raw Christmas eve –
And the bakers' shops were open,
  Tempting a man to thieve;
But I clutched my fists together,
  Holding my head awry,
So I came to her empty-handed,
  And mournfully told her why.

'Then I told her "the House" was open;
She had heard of the ways of *that*,
For her bloodless cheeks went crimson,
And up in her rags she sat,
Crying, "Bide the Christmas here, John,
We've never had one apart;
I think I can bear the hunger –
The other would break my heart."

'All through that eve I watched her,
Holding her hand in mine,
Praying the Lord, and weeping
Till my lips were as salt as brine.
I asked her once if she hungered,
And as she answered "No,"
The moon shone in at the window
Set in a wreath of snow.

'Then the room was bathed in glory,
And I saw in my darling's eyes
The far-away look of wonder
That comes when the spirit flies;
And her lips were parched and parted,
And her reason came and went,
For she raved of our home in Devon,
Where our happiest years were spent.

'And the accents, long forgotten,
Came back to the tongue once more,
For she talked like the country lassie
I'd wooed by the Devon shore.
Then she rose to her feet and trembled,
And fell on the rags and moaned,
And "Give me a crust – I'm famished –
For the love of God!" she groaned.

'I rushed from the room like a madman,
And flew to the workhouse gate,
Crying, "Food for a dying woman!"
And the answer came, "Too late."
They drove me away with curses;
Then I fought with a dog in the street,
And tore from the mongrel's clutches
A crust he was trying to eat.

'Back, through the filthy by-lanes!
Back, through the trampled slush!
Up to the crazy garret,
Wrapped in an awful hush.
My heart sank down at the threshold,
And I paused with a sudden thrill,
For there in the silv'ry moonlight
My Nance lay, cold and still.

'Up to the blackened ceiling
The sunken eyes were cast –
I knew on those lips all bloodless
My name had been the last;
She'd called for her absent husband –
O God! had I but known! –
Had called in vain, and in anguish
Had died in that den – *alone*.

'Yes, there, in a land of plenty,
Lay a loving woman dead,
Cruelly starved and murdered
For a loaf of the parish bread.
At yonder gate, last Christmas,
I craved for a human life.
You, who would feast us paupers,
What of my murdered wife!

'There, get ye gone to your dinners;
Don't mind me in the least;
Think of the happy paupers
Eating your Christmas feast;
And when you recount their blessings
In your smug parochial way,
Say what you did for *me*, too,
Only last Christmas Day.'

CHAPTER TWO

Let the feast begin

Is there a typical first course for Christmas lunch or dinner? In Paris, the answer would be *oui*: oysters, smoked salmon or foie gras; and many French families will lash out on one – or all three – of these luxuries for at least one of the *réveillons*. (Tradition is on their side: 'Oysters are the usual opening to a winter breakfast ... indeed they are almost indispensable', pronounced the *Almanach des Gourmands* in 1803.) The same is increasingly true in Britain. And why not? After all, Scottish smoked salmon is certainly the best in the whole world, and I would make the same claim for English native oysters, if only they were more easily available for people to test whether I'm correct or not.

Historically, though, oysters have the strongest claim on our attention. Well into the present century they were the normal first course for the Christmas feast in Britain and America, as in France. Now, as the farming of oysters brings down their price, they are once again taking their place on the English-speaking Christmas table. In a way, they never lost that place in America, though they were often cooked, especially in the southern states, and they will appear in this form in a later course in this book.

In *North Atlantic Seafood*, the most authoritative book on the subject, Alan Davidson reckons that America has more recipes for cooked oysters than do the French or British because of the relative abundance of the bivalves on that side of the Atlantic. It is true that the cheaper oysters become, the more frequently they are cooked or even used as flavouring than eaten raw. In our own day the success of *ostréiculture* in driving prices down led those chefs connected with the *nouvelle cuisine* to derive ever more exquisite ways to cook oysters. In fact, all the cooking an oyster needs is to warm it through until its edges curl just a little (and then they can be eaten with impunity, even by people like my wife who has acquired a sort of 'allergy' to oysters from having once eaten a bad one). Or you can wrap them in blanched lettuce or spinach leaves and poach them for seconds in their own liquor plus a little cream, before replacing them in their shells and napping them with a reduction of the cooking liquid.

This is a counsel of *luxe*, for times when good things get less scarce than they have formerly been. But John Munson, who farms turkeys near Colchester, told me he can remember his grandmother adding oysters to steak and kidney pie not so much for their flavour as to increase the bulk, because they were so much cheaper than beef. This was borne out by Dickens in *Pickwick Papers*, when Sam Weller says 'It's a wery remarkable circumstance, sir, that poverty and oysters always seem to go together.'

Dickens thought oysters intrinsically funny – the only writer I can think of, except Lewis Carroll, who did so. There is a wonderful passage in *Martin Chuzzlewit*, Chapter 4: '"The name of those fabulous animals (pagan, I regret to say) who used to sing in the water, has quite escaped me." Mr George Chuzzlewit suggested "Swans." "No," said Mr Pecksniff. "Not swans. Very like swans, too. Thank you." The nephew . . . propounded "Oysters." "No," said Pecksniff . . . "nor oysters. But by no means unlike oysters; a very excellent idea; thank you, my dear sir, very much. Wait. Sirens! Dear me! sirens, of course."'

As Eleanor Clark points out in *The Oysters of Locmariaquer* (1965), which is not only the best book on oysters but one of the best books I have ever read on any subject, most of the references in literature to oysters have got it wrong. They always associate oysters, not with poverty, but with pearls. Oysters don't make pearls; at least, they don't make pearls worth having. Any old bivalve will build up a coating of something resembling a pearl around an intrusive object that annoys it; but it won't be pretty or valuable. The creature that produces the best pearls is called *Meleagrina margaritifera*, and the substance with which it coats the grit in its shell is aragonite. It doesn't even look much like an oyster. I believe it is edible, though, as I was once promised (though never got), in the former pearl-fishing town of Broome, Australia, a taste of 'pearl meat'.

The association of oysters with pearls, though false, has been rich for literature. Eleanor Clark cites Shelley ('He is a pearl within an oyster shell'); Shakespeare ('Rich honesty dwells like a miser, sir, in a poor house; as your pearl in your foul oyster' from *As You Like It*, where 'foul' does not mean that the oyster is off, only that it is outwardly unprepossessing), and again ('The firm Roman to great Egypt sends this treasure of an oyster' from *Antony and Cleopatra*); and Swinburne ('Then love was the pearl of his oyster'; the remainder of this couplet from 'Dolores' is 'And Venus rose red out of wine'). She even cites Browning because he mentioned oysters repeatedly and '*never* associated them with pearls': 'Than a too-long opened oyster', 'And laying down a rival oyster bed', 'Turn round: La Roche, to right, where oysters thrive'. 'It took real intellectual stature to think of them like that, considering the set of the centuries before; it is rather grand,' said Miss Clark.

She leaves out of account, though, Saki's pronouncement in *The Quest*: 'Oysters are more beautiful than any religion . . . There's nothing in Christianity or Buddhism that quite matches the sympathetic unselfishness of an oyster.'

Though I used personally to feel like the chap in W. S. Gilbert 'who had often eaten oysters, but had never had enough', I now find it difficult to get through as many as a dozen, unless they are particularly good English natives or French *plates* (meaning simply 'flats'). I am one of the lucky people who has never had a bad one; I know from many first-hand accounts that that is a painful experience. Prudence helps. If you open your own oysters and sniff each one immediately, you will never eat a bad one. An oyster that is 'off' has an unmistakable smell; one whiff will convince you to throw it away. Yet the warning smell disappears rapidly and sometimes the oyster-opener is working so fast that he forgets to smell each one as he opens them; otherwise no one would ever suffer from oyster-poisoning. If you have had the misfortune to ingest a bad oyster, you probably cannot bear the idea of ever eating another one. But if you are brave and want to try again, start with cooked oysters, as mentioned above.

In both Europe and America you can now encounter the rock oysters of the Pacific – usually from New South Wales, Australia. These were originally from New Zealand and are two different species. The warm-water oyster comes from the northern part of North Island and is *Ostrea crassostrea*, similar to the Portuguese and American rock oysters; the deep-water oyster needing colder waters, and therefore less long-lived and less easy to store, is *Ostrea sinuata*, and comes from South Island. The fact that these have been transplanted to Australia and flourished there reveals one of the most interesting aspects of the culture of oysters: they profit (or at least *we* do, because their flavour and texture are improved) by being moved about. A pity this was not known in Lewis Carroll's time, as he would have relished the paradox of the transportation of the unmoving oyster:

> Four young Oysters hurried up,
> All eager for the treat;
> Their coats were brushed, their faces washed,
> Their shoes were clean and neat –
> And this was odd, because, you know,
> They hadn't any feet.

Lewis Carroll was slightly wrong. The infant oyster, anyway, does have a foot. In the larval 'spat' stage the oyster possesses a tiny foot that allows it to attach itself to another object – which is usually the shell of another oyster. Though classified as a pelecypod, meaning that it has a hatchet-shaped foot like a clam or scallop rather than being a stomach-footed gastropod such as a snail or limpet or head-footed like the octopus, the oyster loses its foot early in its development, and is condemned thereafter never again to move by its own agency.

Out of the 300 or so species in the world, we confine our attentions in this hemisphere to only four species of oyster. Chief of these, at least gastronomically in my opinion, is *Ostrea edulis*, the flat native oyster of Britain, though its 'gratifyingly extensive' natural range says Alan Davidson in *North Atlantic Seafood* extends from the Norwegian Sea to the Mediterranean and Morocco. The large-scale culture of this oyster began in the Morbihan in the south of Brittany, and is the specific subject of Eleanor Clark's book. But diseases such as the recent plague of bonamia as well as changes in the market have made many oyster growers change over to other species. The best *edulis*, I think, are Colchesters and Whitstables, of which I have eaten some splendid specimens in recent years. These have become rare and expensive, and I do not think I have ever even tasted a Royal Whitstable (or just plain 'Royal'), marketed exclusively by the Whitstable Oyster Company.

In the recent past, most of the seed came from France and was relaid. But this has always been the practice; as we have seen oysters benefit from a change of water. Even the famous Belons of France were generally grown at Belon, rather than bred there. Colchester Pyefleets, too, were from the celebrated fattening grounds of Pyefleet creek in the Colne estuary, where these Essex oysters have been relished since Roman times, and the Borough of Colchester has a document from Richard I defining the area from which they may come. Other well-known British natives come from Cornwall, where 'Duchy oysters' are also known as 'Helford river' oysters, Devon 'Yealm' and Essex 'Roach', though I don't ever remember being offered any of these in the thirty years during which I have been an avid consumer of British oysters. John Noble and Andrew Long are experimenting with *edulis* at their Loch Fyne oyster farm in Argyll. They believe they have found a reliable and good source of spat, oyster larvae, and hope soon to have a marketable crop of Scottish natives.

In France the district of Marennes-Oléron is responsible for 60 per cent of the country's production of *edulis*. The oysters are called by the name of the place where they have been grown, and other famous flat oyster names, says Davidson, are Arcachon, the Bay of l'Aiguillon, the Ile de Ré, the Morbihan (of which the oyster capital is Auray), the Rade de Brest and the coast of the Channel from St-Brieuc to Cancale. Belgium boasts the oysters of Ostend, The Netherlands Zeeland, and Denmark Limfjord.

Two other species are eaten in Europe. The Portuguese oyster, *Cassostrea angulata* (Lamarck), was formerly the most important after the native. Its range was from Spain and Portugal to Morocco, and its extremely frilly shell is still familiar to most oyster eaters. This oyster is more robust and faster growing than *edulis*, and came close to replacing the natives both in France and England, though recent bouts of disease have led to its being replaced almost every-

where by the giant or Pacific oyster, *Crassostrea gigas* (Thunberg). This last can grow to a huge size – Davidson says the maximum is a 'dismaying 25 cm' (10 in). In fact, smaller ones are perfectly delicious, as most of the oyster's taste and texture derive from the waters in which it is fattened.

The tale is often told of the introduction of the Portuguese oyster into France as the cargo of a ship named the *Morlasien*. In the 1860s the ship had to take shelter, against storms, in the Gironde river. An unpleasant smell caused the master to think that his cargo had spoiled, so he ordered it dumped overboard, where those oysters that remained alive found the waters of the Gironde so agreeable that they bred there, and eventually overtook the native oyster in numbers. Until fairly recently almost all *huîtres creuses* were C. *angulata*, even the *fines de Claires* raised in former salt basins, and the particularly delicious green-tinged Marennes (which get their colour from their diet of a special creature, which defies exclusive classification as either animal or vegetable, but which contains chlorophyll). Now even these, and the *huîtres spéciales* (formerly *angulata* grown with special attention in small quantities in oyster parks along with *edulis*) are almost always the giant *gigas*.

The fourth species commonly grown and eaten in the northern hemisphere is the American or Eastern oyster, *Crassostrea virginica* (Gmelin). They flourish from New Brunswick to the Gulf of Mexico; and they differ so much in appearance that it is difficult to believe that the Blue Points, Robbins Islands, Gardiners Bays and so on from Long Island, the unpronounceable Chincoteaugue Bays from Chesapeake

Native French flat oysters – a bargain at 60 francs for 12!

Bay, and the Cape Cod Wellfleets, Warehams or Chathams are all the same species. I have eaten as many as thirteen different named varieties of American oyster at a single sitting at the Grand Central Station Oyster Bar in Manhattan. They all tasted much more like each other than any of them tasted like a European oyster, let alone an *O. edulis*. But their shells were fantastic in appearance, with all the colours of the ocean floor represented on one plate, and so different in size that one might have imagined that some of them were different creatures altogether. This begs the question: are *any* of them as good to eat as those from the other side of the Atlantic? The answer, I'm sorry to say, is no.

But any oyster is better than no oyster at all, even the Sydney rock oyster that is now opened at a central depot in New South Wales and there *washed*, so that every trace of briny flavour disappears down the Aussie plughole. Some say you can understand this once you've seen the pollution levels on Bondi Beach; others point out that central distribution keeps the price of oysters down so that they are still a working man's food in Australia. Oyster poisoning is, I believe, unknown. Still, I once managed to eat a Sydney rock oyster fresh from the sea (I opened it myself, which may be against the law for all I know). It was wonderful, pure essence of the Pacific.

One of the reasons the *gigas* oyster is available the year round (as was the Portuguese) is that, on the whole, it does not breed in British or northern French waters, so it is never out of season. I'm not altogether convinced that the breeding season is the only reason *O. edulis* is not eaten in months that lack the letter 'R' – they are, after all, the warmer months when it was dangerous to transport shellfish before there was refrigeration. But it is true that *edulis* is larviparous, and lays its eggs inside its valves, keeping them inside the parent for a week following fertilisation. The late Tom Stobart wrote in *The Cook's Encyclopaedia* that this made them 'nasty to eat in the breeding season'; it only makes the oyster unpleasantly milky, as the shells are scarcely formed when the babies are expelled from the parent.

The *Crassostrea* species are oviparous, and cast their eggs on the waters to be fertilised – as Eleanor Clark puts it. The fascinating part of the oyster's sex life is that it changes sex, and the self same oyster is sometimes a father and sometimes a mother. M. F. K. Fisher in *The Art of Eating* explains the sex change, in 'Consider the Oyster': 'For about a year this oyster – *our* oyster – is a male, fertilising a few hundred thousand eggs as best he can without ever knowing whether they swim by or not. Then one day, maternal longings surge between his two halves in his cold guts and gills and all his crinkly fringes. Necessity, that well-known mother, makes him one. He is a she.'

Nobody but the oyster seems to know when it is appropriate to produce milt and when to produce ova; but every oyster produces both in the course of a lifetime. This might be expected to make *ostréiculture* an even more interesting vocation. But in fact, the oyster's sex habits do not affect the oyster farmer at all: he never needs to worry about whether he's got too many mama or too many papa oysters. The bivalves themselves see to the balance of nature; all that's necessary is that they be adults.

Millions of baby larval oysters are produced as a result of these unconventional pairings. The spat are free-swimming at first, and can even steer a bit by virtue of a cilium, that gives way to a foot at the end of about a fortnight's activity. Normally they anchor themselves to something, such as a cluster of other oysters, and keep up the attachment for life. 'This is known as their free-swimming or pelagic period,' says Eleanor Clark; 'they are carried here and there by currents, but grow a little hairlike rudder that gives them some say in the matter, and also, at the end of this vulnerable but perhaps happy time, a tiny foot with which to attach themselves to something, which they must do when the time comes or die. Once "fixed", as the process is called, the oyster loses its foot and swimming apparatus and will never move again under its own power; an awesome requirement, but then all nature fixes in some fashion, even if only in being existentially "engagé", and by and large there seems to be about the same proportion of will to

'Now if you're ready, Oysters dear, We can begin to feed.'
Tenniel's walrus and carpenter from *Through the Looking Glass* by Lewis Carroll

chance in human fixations as in those of the sessile mollusc. Freedom, as they say, is relative.'

Oysters are farmed by the agency of man collecting the spat and placing them somewhere to feed on plankton and grow, with protection from the common predators, such as crabs, starfish and whelks, and free from the competition of mussels for food and space. In the south of Brittany, as Miss Clark recounts, the larval oysters are placed in limed hollow white tiles, where the tiny creatures can literally get a foothold when the spat fall in June. They remain there for eight to ten months, and are then moved from the tiles when they weigh about a gram, and are grown on in parks or basins (of which the *claires* of Marennes are the best known). These basins need a constant supply of sea water as each oyster filters between one and six litres (two to ten pints) an hour, the equivalent, says Alan Davidson, of a human being working 'through the contents of a large public swimming-pool every day'.

It is not easy to visualise these Breton tiles if you have never seen them. But they are being replaced, in any case, by large plastic mesh bags, like those I saw in use at Loch Fyne. The size of the mesh varies according to the size of the oysters it is meant to contain. The bags are placed on metal trestles on the foreshore, so they are washed by the tides, and progressively moved into deeper water. The bags are regularly removed, and the oysters in them graded, before being put back into bags with oysters of the same size, or else marketed after a period of 'training'. This means that the oysters are handled a good deal, which smooths the rough edges off their shells and curbs any tendency to chambering, or collecting tiny pools of stagnant water in blisters in their shells. This handling is, on balance, a good thing. It is the stage of development the French call *élevage*.

At the age of three or four years, the French tend to move their oysters into the best feeding grounds for a period of a few months of what they call *affinage* (the same word is used for the final ripening of cheese before it is sold). After that comes the stage of *l'expédition*, which the Scots and English more prosaically call 'training', when the oysters spend a few weeks in shallower water, more exposed at low tide, so that they learn to protect themselves by shutting tightly when out of water. This teaches them how to survive the ten days or so they may require to make the journey from the oyster bed to the diner's plate.

At this point, provided you have an oyster knife and the know-how (cup the oyster in the left hand, flatter side up; I insert the knife two-thirds of the length up from the hinge, which should cut straight through the adductor muscle), there's nothing left but to find the lemon and the pepper mill. Mignonette sauce, Tabasco and all those other things are needed only if the oyster is weak in flavour, or to disguise the texture of oysters grown in warm water (I think all oysters get crisper and firmer in texture when the weather turns colder).

To judge by their over-representation in ancient kitchen middens or dustbins, oysters have been eaten by man for a very long time. The emperor Nero said he could identify the origin of any oyster just by tasting it. The Romans are supposed to have had the bad habit of eating oysters with *garum*, 'rotten fish' sauce, the equivalent of Thai *nam pla* and Vietnamese *nuoc nam*, made, then as now, by allowing fish, mostly anchovies, to ferment. It is further said that the special pungency of these sauces came from leaving in the intestines of whatever fish was being fermented. Maybe. I attended an academic meeting on food at Oxford once when a distinguished French professor said that this was the one universal sauce; that every culture had its own version of it; but that only one country continued to make it on an industrial scale. That country, he said, was England, and the product is called Worcestershire sauce.

Perhaps, as Eleanor Clark suggests, oysters were eaten with *garum* 'as an antidote to any slight putrefaction'. She goes on to say that 'of the several varieties of garum the most prized was from Cartagena in Spain. It was the most expensive liquid in the world, had a bitter taste and a horrible smell, and was wildly exciting to the appetite, at least of those jaded eaters. An inferior version was still being sold in fish stores in Constantinople not so long ago.' (She was writing in 1959.)

Despite the fact that we now think of it chiefly as a source of red wine, the region of Bordeaux has always provided very good oysters. Ausonius liked them as much in the 4th century as Montaigne did in the 16th, when he wrote that 'they are so agreeable, and of so high an order of taste, that is it like smelling violets to eat them; moreover they are so healthy: a valet swallowed up more than a hundred without any disturbance'.

This figure is not so amazing. Casanova, after all, dispatched fifty every night with his punch. The aphrodisiac reputation of oysters is doubtless based on their resemblance to female genitalia; but there may be better reason. (It is generally assumed that the male sex is the beneficiary of the oyster's aphrodisiac powers, but in 'Consider the Oyster' M. F. K. Fisher reported in 1941 that 'there is one man named Mussolini who lives near Biloxi, in Mississippi, who swears that he has cured seven frigid virgins by the judicious feeding of long brownish buck-oysters from near-by bayous'.) The latest theory is that they contain a lot of zinc which, taken progressively, is supposed to give a boost to male potency. Funnily enough, for all the inadequacy of his science Brillat-Savarin almost got there when he commented on the aphrodisiac effects of a fish diet: 'A still profounder analysis has discovered an . . . even more active cause of the sexual effects of a fish diet: the presence of phosphorus, which occurs already formed in the milt, and which always appears in decomposition.

'These physical truths were without doubt unknown to the ecclesiastical lawmakers who imposed a Lenten diet on various priestly orders, such as the Carthusians, the Franciscans, the Trappists, and the barefoot Carmelites as reformed by Saint Theresa; for it is impossible to believe that they could deliberately have wished to make even more difficult that vow of chastity already so antisocial in its observances.' (The translation is by M. F. K. Fisher.)

The ultimate story of oysters as a first course is an oyster-eating anecdote in Brillat-Savarin, quoted by Eleanor Clark, that puts in our places those of us whose limit is a dozen: 'In 1798 I was at Versailles, in a post as commissioner of the Directory, and was in rather frequent contact with M. Laperte, court recorder of the department. He was a lover of oysters, and complained of never having eaten his fill of them, or as he put it, never having stuffed on them. I decided

Whitstable oysters

to procure him this satisfaction, and to that effect, invited him to dine with me the next day. He came. I kept him company to the third dozen, after which I let him go on alone. So he went on to the thirty-second [dozen], that is for more than an hour, for the maid opening them was not very skilful.

'Meanwhile I had nothing to do, and as it is at table that that is really distressing, I stopped my guest just when he was going strongest. "My friend," I said, "It is not your fate to stuff on oysters today; let us dine." We dined, and he behaved with the vigour and bearing of a man only then starting to eat.'

Should you be thinking of cooking your oysters, the ultimate recipe is that descended from Richelieu's chef, and involves stuffing one thing inside another for purposes of cooking, and then discarding everything but the innermost bit. M. F. K. Fisher's version starts with the oyster. 'You put it inside a large olive. Then you put the olive inside an ortolan (a wee bird called "the garden bunting," in case you are among the under-privileged), and the ortolan inside a lark, and so on and so on. In the end you have a roasted oyster. Or perhaps a social revolution.'

What should one drink with oysters? Grimod de la Reynière, author of the *Almanach des Gourmands* and the first proper food writer of the modern era, was in no doubt. Chablis is 'the inseparable friend of the oyster and its most appropriate companion'. Mrs Fisher on the whole agrees: 'The safest wine, probably, to order with these winter pleasures is a good Chablis. It travels well, and if it is poured at the same temperature as the oysters it can be good whether it comes in a bottle from the Valmur vineyard's best vintage or in a carafe with the questionable name "Chablis Village".'

But oysters do not often grow in the same places where the vine flourishes. In France the best oysters come from Brittany, the one region in all France where no wine at all is made. I have heard that wine was made near Whitstable in the 9th century or so;

but I am certain neither you nor I should have liked to drink what must have been poor, thin stuff. I agree on the Chablis question; its characteristic flinty steeliness makes a splendid foil to the sweet salt tang of oyster flesh, and its usually good acid levels balance the fat plumpness found in all the best oysters. I've tasted many other white burgundies against oysters, but found them less satisfactory – if I may generalise just a little. The trouble is that uncooked oysters seem to react almost chemically with some very fine white wines (when tasted on their own) to produce unwelcome new, almost 'off' flavours in the mouth. I remember one tasting where a particularly delicious, nutty and buttery Meursault began to taste sulphurous when it was introduced to some very superior native oysters.

One white wine that never has any problems tolerating oysters is champagne; but then champagne has much in common with Chablis, such as the chardonnay grape and good acidity levels. Fortunately, champagne and oysters are frequent bedfellows at Christmas, that being the time when both the French and the British consume more of each than at any other season.

Red wine is impossible with uncooked oysters (though not with steak, kidney and oyster pie or pudding) as the wine acquires an extremely unpleasant metallic taste from the association; and I'm not too keen on white wine with any perceptible sweetness or too much oaky flavour. That does limit the choice a little, but there are some magnificent un-oaked New Zealand sauvignon blancs and not over-oaked California and Australia chardonnays, plus a handful of wines made from both these grape varieties from Italy, Oregon and Washington state, that will fit the bill very nicely indeed.

There is no need, though, to drink wine with oysters. Mrs Fisher points out that 'Oysters, being almost universal, can be and have been eaten with perhaps a wider variety of beverages than almost any other dish I can think of . . . and less disastrously. They lend themselves to the whims of every cool and temperate climate, so that one man can drink wine with them, another beer, and another fermented buttermilk, and no man will be wrong.' 'In England,' she continues, 'ales are the rule with the fat round oysters of the coastal beds, and any pub can recommend its own brew when the season's on. And of course sherry is safe.' Well, up to a point – the point being that sherries are sweetened for the British palate. Any sherry drunk as it is in Jerez will partner oysters beautifully, but I know you'll forgive me if I decline the Bristol Cream with my six number twos.

PEOPLE HAVE BEEN KNOWN TO REFUSE OYSTERS. I have never known anyone, man, woman or child, who disliked smoked salmon; it is the ideal, if easy, luxury first course. As nothing is required except slicing it and putting it on a plate, it is also the quickest food imaginable. If of good quality, it goes with any of the drinks mentioned above (though beware ruining good white burgundy with inferior smoked salmon), with the bonus that ardent spirits do it no harm. Vodka, plain or flavoured but ice cold, is a perfect match for the naturally oily fish; and a tot of junipery genever gin is a superb foil for the buttery delicacy.

We knew all about smoked salmon when I was a child in land-locked Kentucky; only we called it lox, bought it in tiny quantities from the Kosher butcher and ate it with bagels and cream cheese. I am not altogether certain we knew it was fish. For one thing, it came in paper parcels – and I think I remember tins. It was strictly a Jewish delicacy, and a rare one. Supplies were never certain, and I fantasised that an underground railway, such as was used by slaves escaping to the north in the Civil War, still existed, but now travelling in the opposite direction, bringing Jewish gastronomic dainties such as lox and corned (i.e. salt) beef south to the land of corn bread and grits. I confess I was astonished, on my first day in England, to discover that the wonderful smoky pink flesh was sliced from half a large fish.

Of course the best smoked salmon is Scottish. And to my taste, the best of that is smoked by the Jewish trade in London. This is a more delicate smoke than the Highland variety, and I fear it is getting increasingly rare. It's no more difficult to achieve than the stronger sort, and depends less on the cure than on the time the cured fish is left to smoke in the kiln, and on what sort of sawdust is employed to smoulder and impart its flavour to the fish. It seems that the public increasingly favours the stronger taste.

In America there is a parallel. Ordinary lox is the stronger; the milder, sometimes less salty smoked salmon is called Nova Scotia. Both usually come not from the Atlantic salmon, *Salmo salar*, but from one of the Pacific species of the genus *Onchorhynchus*, whose flesh is invariably coarser and less fine than the true Atlantic salmon, yet whose flavour can be equally interesting. Norwegian salmon is much prized in France, but the French are wrong to think it the equal of the Scottish fish. Canadian salmon of the Pacific

species used commonly to be employed for smoking salmon in Britain; but the advent of salmon farming has made this unnecessary. Irish salmon is excellent for smoking, as it is for eating fresh. The rule for smoked salmon is the same as the old rule for determining the quality of data produced by computers: garbage in, garbage out. The smoked article can be no better than the fresh fish was. Before widespread salmon farming, frozen salmon was used to ensure a constant supply; the fish, says Tom Stobart, came from all the countries mentioned, as well as from England, the colours of the flesh varied from 'the very pale Polish Delta to the rich red of Canadian' and the fat content varied from 3 per cent to 20 per cent. The quality of smoked salmon bought in Britain is now much more uniform.

But the taste still varies. In a recent blind tasting done at the *Observer*, the panel found that of samples from the five leading British supermarket chains, three were satisfactory and two excellent. The best was the mildest smoke, and a sixth sample was smoked so strongly that the panel found it unpalatable and did not include it in the report. You can try a simple test for yourself on any sample of smoked salmon: can you imagine eating it without bread and butter? I prefer smoked salmon where this is possible; but it is getting increasingly difficult to find.

The correct term for smoking salmon is 'kippering' – as in herring. *Küppen* means to spawn in Dutch and Tom Stobart thinks that the original purpose of kippering salmon was to disguise poor specimens that were out of season (they are at their worst after spawning) and could not be eaten fresh. The first references to kippered salmon are to 'kipper

Still Life of Salmon by Henry Leonidas Rolfe, exhibited 1881

times', and these are to do with the 14th-century Thames salmon fishery.

In a modern smokehouse the process of smoking salmon is a simple one. The gutted fish are beheaded and split into two filleted sides. The backbone is removed with a sharp boning knife, as are the ribs and, if the filleter is skilled, most of the pin bones. This process is carried out on a bed of coarse salt, to give the workmen better purchase; but the salt is rinsed off before the curing, which consists of nothing but an application of salt mixed with unrefined brown sugar. The resulting quality is better if the cure is applied by hand, as its desirable thickness can be

judged more accurately by an experienced craftsman than by a machine. Some people are rumoured to use whisky or even Drambuie at this stage; but I can find no one who will admit to it. Some curers still use a brine, rather than a dry cure. Brining is said to give a better appearance to the finished side of salmon; but it slows down the whole process, as the sides then have to be dried before going into the kiln.

The salt mixture is generally left on anywhere from 4 hours for a grilse or 1-year-old salmon (one that has become sexually mature early and weighs 1.5–3 kg or 3–6 lb), to 24 hours for a normally large fish. This is washed off and the sides are dried on racks – now often horizontally, whereas they were formerly hung vertically by their tails. Modern kilns are easy to control and the element of chance has disappeared from the smokehouse. The smoke is dense and is produced by smouldering sawdust. It is this that imparts the final flavour. Hardwoods of various sorts can be used, and so can peat or juniper. At Loch Fyne, for example, they use sawdust made from spent whisky barrels. Some of these once contained sherry or Bourbon whiskey, so the aromas of the smokehouse can be complex.

Sawdust is used instead of wood chips, because wood chips would catch fire rather than smoulder, and salmon is cold smoked. (Arbroath smokies, small brined haddocks, are hot-smoked, which is to say that the flesh is actually cooked.) In cold smoking the food is not cooked; which is why smoked salmon is closer in texture to cured gravadlax than to grilled or poached salmon, no matter how lightly cooked. The best temperature for cold smoking is 24–27°C (75–80°F), though any temperature from 10 to 29°C (50–85°F) would still qualify as cold rather than hot smoking (which would be a maximum of about 82°C (180°F) for fish, though much higher – up to 150°C (240°F) – for poultry, meat or game). The smoking is completed when the salmon has lost 17–18 per cent of its preprocessing weight; and salmon is now generally smoked in batches of sides of equal weight, so that the process can be timed. How long the salmon remains in the kiln varies from smokehouse to smokehouse. Indeed, it is one of the secrets of the trade, for the longer it is smoked (in proportion to is weight, of course), the stronger the flavour. But the smoking is always a matter of hours rather than days.

The 'Jewish' cure consists of salting with virtually no sugar and smoking for as little as six hours.

Smoked salmon is one of the few cold smoked foods that is eaten raw. Kippered herrings, Finnan haddock and smoked bacon are cold smoked, but cooked before eating.

Freshly smoked salmon, Butley, Orford, Suffolk

As a guide to buying smoked salmon, Tom Stobart says that 'the finished side should have a pleasant smoky aroma and feel firm when pressed with the finger-tips at the thickest part'. Don't buy it if it feels tacky or sticky, or has too powerful a smell. As most smoked salmon is now sold in vacuum packs, this advice is a little academic. Smoked salmon freezes extremely well, by the way, and you might find it more convenient to buy an unsliced side, rather than the more expensive sliced, interleaved and laid-back side, and keep it in the freezer. Frozen salmon is easier to slice thinly, and you can remove what you want and replace the side in the freezer.

Slice salmon with a long thin blade, such as a ham knife. Start about a third up from the tail end, and slice, at a very slight angle, towards the tail. Start each successive slice a tiny bit closer to the gill end, and you should end up with thin slices and no waste.

As for eating it, I'm sure you need no advice. But if you are eating Scottish salmon for the first time, try it without onion or any of the usual flavour-boosters. Thinly sliced brown bread spread with sweet, unsalted butter is essential; a squeeze of lemon and freshly milled coarse black pepper is optional. By the way, there is absolutely nothing wrong with a bagel spread with Philadelphia cream cheese, a slice of red onion and a quarter-pound of lox. Though it would make an eccentric start to Christmas dinner.

SOLOMON'S ROLLS

George Lassalle's *The Adventurous Fish Cook* (1972) gives this interesting recipe for salmon-stuffed salmon.

450 g (1 lb) fresh Scotch salmon, poached
¼ teaspoon freshly ground black pepper
1 Tbsp mayonnaise
6 spring onions, finely chopped
450 g (1 lb) smoked salmon, finely sliced
5 lemons
1 crisp lettuce

Skin and fillet the salmon and pound to a paste; add the pepper, the mayonnaise and a squeeze of lemon juice, and continue to pound all together until the mixture is creamy. Add the very finely chopped white of the spring onions.

Place a portion of this creamy mixture at one end of each slice of smoked salmon and roll into good tight cylinders. Serve, with segments of lemon, on crisp lettuce leaves. This quantity serves ten people.

GRAVLAX (OR GRAVADLAX)

This is nothing more than a pickled salmon. The name (and the recipe) stems from a time before refrigeration, when Scandinavians used literally to bury the fish in the frozen ground. The proportions given in this recipe are Jane Grigson's, and they provide a good rule of thumb. Ask the fishmonger to sell you a tail piece of salmon weighing slightly less than 1 kg – the proportions given here are perfect for a piece weighing 1½–2 lb. Get him to slice it lengthways in half and remove the backbone; be careful, when you get the two pieces of fish back home, to remove the pin bones with a pair of tweezers or long-nosed pliers. You can feel them easily by running your thumb along parallel to the backbone. If you are feeding a lot of people, or salmon is cheap, get the fishmonger to prepare a whole fish as though it were two sides of smoked salmon, and double or treble the quantities of the cure.

The cure
1 heaped Tbsp sea salt
1 rounded Tbsp brown sugar
1 tsp crushed black or white peppercorns
1 Tbsp brandy, schnapps or vodka (optional)
1 Tbsp fresh dillweed *or* ½ Tbsp dried

Combine everything except the dillweed in a bowl. Put half the fish skin-side down in a dish shallow enough to allow you to put a board carrying a weight on top of the two halves of the fish. Spread half the mixture and half the dill on one cut side and most of the other half of the mixture and the dill on the other cut side of the fish. Then sandwich the two cut sides together and sprinkle whatever cure mixture is left on the top. Weight with a board and another weight – I find a large saucepan full of water does the job. Put in a cool place to cure for at least a day, turning the fish once or twice. The longer you leave the fish – Jane Grigson says 5 days is the maximum – the stronger the taste. To serve, drain the fish and slice like smoked salmon, but not quite so thin. Thin sliced dark rye bread is good with this, and the French serve it with a sweet mustard sauce, on the lines of a mayonnaise but sometimes made with 1–2 tablespoons of mashed potato substituting for the egg yolk. A small quantity of this sauce goes a long way, to my taste, and it will do no good at all to the wine. But if you have a sweet tooth and are drinking chilled vodka, by all means double the quantity of sauce.

The sauce
2 Tbsp mustard, preferably sweet Swedish mustard, but Dijon will do
1 Tbsp granulated white sugar (omit if using Swedish mustard)
1 large egg yolk
150 ml (5 fl oz, generous ½ cup) peanut or corn oil (not olive)
2 Tbsp white wine vinegar *or* lemon juice
salt, white pepper
1 tsp fresh dillweed or ½ tsp dried

Add mustard and sugar, if used, to the egg yolk and whisk, adding oil drop by drop until the emulsion thickens. Flavour with vinegar and season with salt, pepper and dill.

FRANCES BISSELL'S POTTED OYSTERS

Makes 12 small ramekins or pots, or 12 oyster shells
12 very fresh oysters, shucked, drained and dried
    thoroughly
250 g (8 oz, 2 sticks) softened unsalted butter
5 anchovy fillets
freshly ground white pepper
freshly grated nutmeg or ground mace
lemon or lime juice to taste
clarified butter, made by heating unsalted butter and
    straining off the milky solids

Chop the oysters coarsely, then process for a moment
with the rest of the ingredients, except the butter.
Drizzle clarified butter over the top and chill until
required. You can make oval, quenelle shapes with
the mixture, using two teaspoons, and put each oyster
'sausage' into an oyster shell. Garnish with parsley
and lemon and serve with thin, hot toast.

This dish should be treated as fresh oysters, and
eaten as soon as possible after making: remember,
the oysters are not cooked.

OYSTER STEW

This recipe is taken from M. F. K. Fisher's 'Consider
the Oyster' and she took it from a *New England Cook
Book* for which she paid 15 cents in 1936.

Serves 4–8 (see note below)
900 ml (32 fl oz, 1 quart) oysters (2 dozen large-ish
    ones)
450 ml (16 fl oz, 2 cups) oyster liquor (which you
    must save when opening the oysters)
450 ml (16 fl oz, 2 cups) double or heavy cream
4 Tbsp butter
celery salt
white or cayenne pepper

You make a broth by heating half the oyster liquor
until it foams. Skim it, and add the cream, butter and
seasoning to taste. Warm the oysters through in the
remainder of the oyster liquor, just until the edges
curl; certainly no more than 5 minutes on a gentle
heat. Add the oysters to the creamy broth and serve
immediately – with oyster crackers, of course. This
would serve much too large portions to four New
Englanders, a reasonable amount to six, or a tiny
ramekin-ful to eight sensible eaters.

LADY LOUSADA'S OYSTERS ROCKEFELLER

Patricia Lousada is a first-generation American, now settled in England. Her mother was Italian, and she learned some of her best recipes from George Balanchine when she was a ballet student. She wrote this recipe for me for an *Observer* series on alternative Christmas feasts. The stuffing can be made in advance and the oysters opened in the microwave.

Serves 4–6

24 oysters
75 g (3 oz, 5 Tbsp) unsalted butter
1½ shallots, finely minced
½ stalk of celery, very finely chopped
40 g (1½ oz, 3–4 Tbsp *after chopping*) watercress leaves, chopped
40 g (1½ oz, 3–4 Tbsp) well-drained cooked, chopped spinach
2 Tbsp mixed finely minced fresh herbs – parsley, tarragon and chives
4 heaped Tbsp fresh soft breadcrumbs
1 Tbsp Pernod or other pastis (optional)
freshly ground black pepper

Sweat the shallots and celery in a third of the butter until soft. Stir in the watercress and cook until wilted. Put in a food processor or liquidiser with the spinach, herbs, breadcrumbs, Pernod and remainder of the butter. Process and then taste and season with black pepper but no salt.

Place the oysters, hinge end down, in a 5-cm (2-in) deep dish. Cover with microwave wrap and cook (in microwave) on high for 4 minutes. (Give any oysters that haven't opened 1 more minute.) Allow them to cool enough to handle and remove the oysters and pry them open with a blunt knife. Pour off a little of their juices into the sauce mixture. Free the oysters from their shells and tidy up any bits of broken shell. Place the oysters in the deeper, cupped half shell on a pan of rock salt. Stir the sauce until blended, then place a teaspoonful over each oyster. Bake in a preheated 225° (425°F, gas mark 7) oven for 5 mins, or until just heated through. Don't overcook!

GRILLED OR MICROWAVED OYSTERS

You can actually open oysters over (or under) the grill or broiler or even on a hot electric ring, as well as in the microwave on full power (though you must be careful to keep your face well away from any oyster that hasn't opened fully – see method in last recipe). Of course you have to contrive to keep the cupped side of the oyster down, and steady, so the juices don't run out. The usual way to do this is by balancing them in a hollow of coarse salt.

Whether you open your oysters over heat, or more conventionally with a knife, they are cooked when they are just warmed through. Too much heat, and they shrivel up and become tough little nuggets. The object of cooking oysters (besides making it possible for people who can't eat them raw to enjoy them) is usually to impart some extra flavour.

This should be as subtle as possible; usually a knife-tip of butter or a spoonful of thick cream with a pinch of cayenne or a drop of Tabasco (much nicer with cooked oysters, I think, than grainy black pepper) is quite enough. But a tiny quantity of chopped raw or cooked spinach, or white of leek, or minced shallot could be forgiven, provided it is put on to the oyster at a stage where it, too, can cook for a few seconds. So, having opened your oysters somehow or other, either pop the butter or cream on the already hot oyster, or prop them up properly, add the flavourings and put them under the grill just until the edges of the oyster begin to look a little frazzled.

HANG TOWN FRY

I have eaten memorable oyster omelettes in Singapore, and I think I dimly perceive in them the original of this San Francisco dish given by Mrs Fisher. The only reason I include it, besides that it has some of the status of a classic, is that Christmas is the only time of year that I can imagine anyone having the surplus of oysters that would be necessary before you'd even consider making a dish like this. Mrs Fisher doesn't say how many this recipe serves, and I think from the context that she thought one heroic man or two normal ones might demolish this omelette for their breakfast with 'two or three links of tiny browned breakfast sausages and shoestring potatoes'. It will serve three or four New Men or Women.

On kitchen paper you dry 2 dozen medium oysters, season them with salt and pepper, roll in flour, then dip in beaten egg and dredge in fine white breadcrumbs. Fry to a golden brown on one side only in butter in a hot frying pan. Then you add to the pan 4–5 lightly beaten eggs, and leave to set for one minute, before turning the whole omelette to brown on the other side: 'The resulting dish will look like an egg pancake with oysters mixed in.' This is just the thing for New Year's Day breakfast.

CHAPTER THREE

The second course

Extravagance is a necessary part of feasting. The courses must be more numerous than for an ordinary meal, but also more lavish. This is true even in institutions. Raw army recruits are given a special meal at Christmas (one regiment where I witnessed the officers serving lunch to their men allowed two pints of lager to each squaddie, and the turkey wasn't even overcooked). In prison, where policy demands that treats are rare, Christmas is marked by a meal of better quality food. Indeed, on Christmas Day in the workhouse, as Sims's poem tells us (see pages 28 29), 'the guardians and their ladies . . . put pudding on pauper plates'. As for the paupers, 'so long as they fill their stomachs,/What matter it whence it comes?'.

Whether the festive meal is eaten on Christmas Eve, or is lunch or dinner, it characteristically has at least one extra course. In the USA, where there is usually only an 'entrée' (called this, presumably, because normally it is the start to the meal, though it is always the main course) and dessert, almost every family has an appetiser course. In France and Britain, as in most of Europe where three courses are often the pattern of the meal, at least one extra course is inserted between the starter and principal dish.

For many English-speaking families, this means merely that a solid dish is consumed before or after the soup. In the case of my squaddies, this was cream of tomato; a more fussy choice would probably not have been welcomed by these hundreds of hungry 17-year-old boys. At many private tables, however, this is the time for a seafood bisque, a consommé or a hearty game soup – even if they come out of tins.

At this point in the feast, though, the dependable French eat *boudin blanc*, white pudding. At least, they do nowadays. Some sources say they used to eat plain old *boudin*, blood or black pudding. In one of her wonderfully quirky notes to her translation of Brillat-Savarin's *The Physiology of Taste*, M. F. K. Fisher reminds us that 'in Paris spicy *boudin* used to be served on Christmas Eve. It seems to me that a little earlier in the year it was brought around, sizzling and rich and *free*, in the larger cafés of Burgundy. And I remember that the prostitutes would snatch at it, daintily of course but with avidity, as if it could give them some magic strength. If the waiter liked them they could have two or three pieces, and for once there would be no joking about the bulls it had been drawn from. Each fashionably thin pale woman would eat-eat-eat, in a silence straight from *The Golden Bough*.'

Lest there be any doubt that *boudin*, the black one, was, as Robert Courtine says (in *The Hundred*

Glories of French Cooking, which sounds so much better as the original *Cent Merveilles de la Cuisine Française*), 'for a long while one of the indispensable concomitants of Christmas feasts', he gives Achille Ozanne's verse-recipe for it. It begins: '*Préparez des oignons, hachés menus, menus.*'

Extraordinarily, I have two translations of these verses by this poet-cook in front of me; but I think I can improve (the sense), though prosaically, on both:

Prepare the onions, mince them fine,
Add them to their own weight in fat over a gentle
    flame,
Stir them, until they become golden,
And their sweet aroma invades the whole
    space . . .
Mix everything with the blood, then season well
With salt, pepper, nutmeg and any other spices;
A glass of Cognac; after this: you stuff it
Into the pig's intestine, one end of which you've
Tied in advance, and when you've filled it,
Tie up the other end, and into barely simmering
    water
Plunge all your *boudins*! These labours finished,
Drain them after twenty minutes' cooking.

Courtine's version goes on with a quatrain about lazing in front of the Yule log while the black puddings simmer. And the 1960 edition of *Larousse Gastronomique* says explicitly: 'Black pudding is the traditional French dish served at supper after Christmas midnight mass. Large quantities of both black and white puddings are eaten at this meal.'

In his *The Food of France* (1958) Waverley Root

said, in his chapter on the Touraine: '*Boudin blanc* comes under the head of *charcuterie*, and you may find it listed with the hors d'oeuvre on a bill of fare, though it is more likely to be offered as one of the principal dishes. You will find this name on menus throughout the country, especially at the Christmas and New Year holiday season, when *boudin blanc* and *boudin noir* (blood pudding) are traditionally paired on *réveillon* menus (they are unfortunately disappearing under the influence of the commercialisation of these two midnight feasts, whose exaggerated prices restaurants have a habit of justifying by forsaking the hearty old dishes for what they consider more elegant and more expensive new ones).'

Larousse thinks that black pudding is of Assyrian origin, 'one of the few Assyrian dishes which have come down to us still greatly resembling those made by the pork butchers of Tyre, who, it is said, excelled in this type of preparation'. Though Courtine, who has written the 'Plaisirs du Table' column for *Le Monde* since 1949 using the nom de plume 'La Reynière', wrote the preface for that edition of *Larousse Gastronomique* (for which Patience Gray made some of the translations), he disagrees about the origins of black pudding. He queries its attribution to the Assyrians and Phoenicians, and even to the Greek cook Aphtonetes: 'Certainly there were preparations based on blood already in existence before Aphtonetes, such as the Spartans' black broth, the *myma* of Epaenetes, and the recipe given by the cook Erasistrates for a certain *hyposphagma*, which was a cooked mixture of blood, honey, cheese, salt, caraway and silphium.' (Silphium was a herb cherished by Roman cooks. An idea of its taste and smell can be given by the fact that, when it became scarce, the sulphurous, evil-smelling asafoetida was substituted for it.)

'Blood drinking, or eating,' says Reay Tannahill in *Food in History*, 'has been common in pastoral communities throughout most of recorded history. Before Islam laid a taboo on it, the Arabs were fond of a composite dish of camel hair and blood mixed together and then cooked on the fire.' I think we might draw the culinary equivalent of a veil across the rest of the history of blood-eating, until we come to the point: 'In Tyrone and Derry the blood was preserved for the lean months by being allowed to thicken in layers "strewn with salt until a little mound was formed, which was cut up into squares and laid by for use as food in the scarce time of year".' This is recognisably the ancestor of black pudding, and, says Mrs Tannahill in a note, drisheen, a kind of black pudding still eaten today in County Cork.

Courtine enquires into the etymology of *boudin*. He speculates on its relation to Old French *boudine* ('big belly, swelling') and to the Spanish word for the dish, *embutinos*. He asks: 'Which came first, "pudding" or *boudin*? The word "pudding" on its own does not imply the use of blood, you may say.' Here he is wrong. The *Oxford English Dictionary*, in a long, learned note, surveys the difficulties of connecting 'pudding' with *boudin* and concludes that, in spite of the different forms, they are very likely identical. And the very first entry for 'pudding' (a word that occupies several columns of the *OED*) gives it in the sense of black pudding. Both the French and the English words became current in the 13th century.

You can, says Courtine, with absolute correctness, make *boudin* with all sorts of stuffings: rabbit, cray-fish, meat, game, even bread; and some white *boudins* 'are no more than what the French think of as "pudding" stuffed into an intestine'. The great Ali-Bab, indeed, gives recipes for many of these in the definitive *Gastronomie Pratique* (1928).

The questions to be answered are why did (or do) the French eat black pudding at Christmas, and how did it come to be replaced (if it was) with *boudin blanc*? Courtine gets close to the answer. First he does a sort of round-up of recipes. The classic recipe uses one quart (1 litre) of blood to a pound (½ kg) of onions, a pound of fresh, finely chopped pork fat, a cup of cream (⅓ pint, 250 ml), a handful of bread-crumbs, salt, pepper, fennel and parsley. Variations abound – Larousse gives 15, both black and white, and the Gault et Millau *Guide Gourmand de la France* (the best book of its kind ever written) gives 18, but not all of them involve blood or even meat.

Waverley Root, I think, got his generalisations about the recipe for *boudin blanc* slightly wrong: '*Like boudin noir, boudin blanc* is a soft sausage, and its stuffing in most parts of the country is composed largely of bread.' His specific remarks, however, are, as always, trustworthy: 'In the Touraine, the bread is replaced by breast of chicken. The Touraine *boudin blanc* is thus the finest variety of this sausage to be found, and there is a further refinement called *boudin de volaille à la Richelieu*.' Root is amused because Richelieu, despite its gastronomic fame for several sorts of *charcuterie*, had a population in the 1950s of less than 2,000. The recipe used in this tiny village is for *boudin* 'in which truffles and mushrooms are combined with the white chicken meat, and all of them are creamed together in an elaborate sauce. By the time this has been done, one hardly dares refer to the product any longer as a sausage; it is more of a chicken croquette.'

Courtine lists Poitou, where spinach is added, Lyon where the cream and breadcrumbs are omitted but red pepper is used; and even a recipe involving a small glass of rum and a pinch of sugar. Then he gets on the real trail:

'The best *boudin* of all is in fact the simplest: that of the "*Tua*," as they call the annual pig-killing in those country districts where they also refer to the pig himself, with great respect, as "Monsieur." And the death of Monsieur is at once a ritual celebration and an act of grace toward the dispenser of all food.

'The literature of folklore is full of fine pages on this December death, the prelude to the celebration of the Nativity. In the crib, we read, He lay between the ox and the ass. But where was the pig, that encyclopaedic animal, that divine gift to man's appetite? Without a pig the crib is empty.'

This stunningly Franco-centric view of the universe overlooks that fact that where He was born pigs were not kept and eating them was forbidden. Jesus was, after all, subject to the Mosaic dietary laws.

One of the reasons for the formulation of the Jewish dietary laws might well have been connected with *boudin* and the reasons the modern French eat it at Christmas. There is a respectable theory that the dietary laws of *kashrut* were not promulgated (at any rate solely) for hygienic reasons, but to keep the Hebrews apart from their neighbours, by making them view some of the food of their neighbours as unclean. Thus the Jews acquired holiness by abstaining from these foods. Dionysus, the god of pagan revels, whom we

At the Market by Joachim Beuckelaer (c.1530–73)

know to have had Middle Eastern origins, is often pictured not only with his wine glass or flagon, but with a ring of sausages around his neck.

Sausages, of which *boudin* is the prototype, have been the food of revelry since antiquity. The medieval Christian Church took over the *boudin* with the rest of the midwinter festival; the killing time was assimilated into the calendar of the Church, and the primitive sacrifice of the pig identified with the mystery of God's sacrifice. It still goes on.

'In the countryside of the Auvergne,' Courtine writes, 'killing the pig is called *faire mongougne*, and the woman who comes in to help the farmer's wife, the farmer's daughter and his servants to make the sausages and *boudins* is called *la mongougnière*. And the children, having learned their catechisms, all know full well that the greatest feast of the year is not Christmas, or Corpus Christi or Easter but "the day we kill Monsieur."'

It is very recently in human history, Margaret Visser points out in *The Rituals of Dinner* (1991), that killing animals for food has been done every day and automatically as part of the food chain and normal economy of a country. In the past, before refrigeration, killing an animal meant a feast; such bits of the meat as could not be cured and kept had to be used up before it spoiled. This meant sharing it with other people, with members of the extended family, or sometimes with non-family members. Even as an economic fact of life, though, killing an animal had something solemn about it. A dead animal can't give milk or breed; so 'its loss had to be calculated,' Mrs Visser points out, 'and deemed worthwhile.' The surplus produced by the killing was appropriate for celebrations, as festivals 'helped force owners of animals to stop saving and enjoy', and getting rid of the surplus meat led to desirable 'social side effects'.

From the point of view of the person doing the killing, slaughtering domesticated animals for our dinners is different from hunting. With the modern, sanitised abattoir it no longer happens that the animal

is 'known' to the human being who does the killing, although that was formerly the universal case, as it still is in the sort of peasant society Courtine was writing about, above. There, Mrs Visser noted, 'in order to affect people, such a death must be witnessed by them, and not suffered out of sight, as we now arrange matters; attention is deliberately drawn, by means of ritual and ceremony, to the performance of killing. This is what is meant by "sacrifice," literally the "making sacred" of an animal consumed for dinner.' While we no longer gild the horns and place garlands of flowers around the necks of animals that are to be sacrificed, the killing of the pig is still done openly, even publicly, in parts of rural France.

Boudin is thus, symbolically, the perfect food for the feast. It cannot fail to remind the eaters of the sacrifice; it is, after all, made of the blood itself. Before modern food-storage technology, it could only be eaten when a pig had been killed. Moreover, says Mrs Visser, 'there is a tendency, also, to associate very dark food, such as coffee, chocolate, truffles, caviar and *cèpes*, as well as plum cake, with excitement and luxury. We feel obscurely that such strange dark stuff must be meaningful and ancient.' *Boudin*, remember, is one of the few foods that is almost *black* in colour.

Why, then, do the French now eat *boudin blanc* or white pudding (though at Christmas and the New Year they are often speckled black with truffles)? There are two answers to this question, I think.

First, in spite of what Margaret Visser says, luxury foods are more often white than black (brown). Just think of white rice and white bread. In fact, these did not come to be luxury foods solely on account of their cost. Though it does cost more to mill white flour, unbleached brown flour with all its bran takes longer to prove, longer to bake and therefore costs more of the baker's time and more in fuel for the oven, and so on. It was sumptuary laws that made white foods cost more than dark ones; this owed everything to fashion and little to economics.

But secondly, and the real reason, I think, is that being able to have black pudding at Christmas is dependent on the fickle European weather. No peasant ever kills a pig (or any other animal) when he can feed it for free. When the animal's fodder stops growing, unless it has been an exceptionally good year and the grain and cereal reserves have surpluses that can feed livestock as well as man, the animal's days are numbered. The killing time comes, inevitably, with the first frost.

Blood, though, is highly perishable. It 'goes off' well before muscle tissue and fat. If the frost is very late and persists from its first appearance until winter, why then the blood sausage might keep until Christmas. This, however, is a very rare combination of circumstances. Normally, therefore, being able to serve *boudin* at Christmas must have been dependent on there being sufficient stocks of feed to keep the pig alive until just before Christmas. In some years this would be out of the question. But *boudin blanc* is made from the lean meat of the pig, which stores much better than blood.

It does seem possible that black pudding used to be the preferred Christmas treat for the French peasant. It seems to me probable that white pudding was originally a *pis aller*, a make-do eaten only at the Christmas *réveillon* in years when the weather made the black version out of the question. But it was more dependable and predictable, so convenience, as it always does, weighed more heavily than tradition. Eventually, studded with truffles, flavoured with port or combined with chestnuts, *boudin blanc* took over, and itself became the traditional food of the *réveillon*.

Jane Grigson, whose *Charcuterie and French Pork Cookery* remains the authority on the subject in both English and French, points out that *boudins noirs* are the one thing you cannot fail to recognise in the French delicatessen shop; whether they're pitch black or chestnut brown, hanging in a long string or coiled on a basketwork tray, they don't look like anything else. They're cheap, even today, and delicious. Though already cooked when sold, they are usually sliced and fried, or grilled, and served with a purée of apple or potato or used to stuff a roast chicken. If you are used to English black puddings, Mrs Grigson wrote, 'you will find the French ones a lot lighter in texture.' This is because they're made to a different recipe: 'The blood is mixed with pork fat, onions and cream, rather than barley, flour and oatmeal. They are spiced, too, with considerably more finesse.' English (and Irish and Scottish) black puddings are delicious in their own right, incidentally, and can be used exactly as French ones; they have a rougher, more crumbly texture, as you'd expect from the use of cereals to bind them.

Courtine admits that there are white as well as black *boudins*, but says that to the gourmet, *boudin* means black pudding: 'Its capital is Nancy, and its kingdom stretches from Flanders to the Lyonnais, even though Paris has adopted it to such an extent that' that city 'alone now consumes more than the rest of the country put together.'

On the subject of *boudins blancs* Jane Grigson says that, by contrast with the black puddings, 'these succulent creamy-white sausages are the dearest in the *charcuterie*, and also the nicest. The whitest of pork is used, or chicken, or occasionally rabbit, and cream, eggs, onions and a few breadcrumbs or ground rice to make the mixture as bland and smooth-textured as possible.' About the texture there is no disagreement; the meat is put twice through the finest blade of the mincer, or minced as fine as possible in an industrial machine. The eggs create a spongy texture that gives considerably under the pressure of the fork or knife. But M. Bourgeois, the *charcutier* whom I watched making *boudins blancs* recently in Boulogne, used flour rather than breadcrumbs, and a higher proportion of scalded milk to the other ingredients than Jane Grigson gives in her recipe for *Boudins Blancs de Paris*.

Even more controversially, Jane Grigson uses equal quantities of pork and chicken (which may be cooked or raw). In this she agrees with Ali-Bab. *Larousse Gastronomique*, however, says unequivocally that 'the white pudding is a sausage made of white pork meat and fat'. When I questioned M. Bourgeois about the use of meat other than pork in *boudin blanc*, he told me, with a mildly scandalised air, that that was unthinkable. Yet though Avranches is not all that distant from M. Bourgeois's Boulogne, the *boudin blanc* for which the town is famous has breast of chicken, sweetbreads, fish fillets and soft roes bound with *crème fraîche*. This is no doubt the case where the exception proves the rule, for Le Mans, equally celebrated for *boudins blancs*, varies from Bourgeois orthodoxy only by the addition of onion,

which is, in any case, allowed by both Jane Grigson and Ali-Bab. Still, in *A Concise Encyclopedia of Gastronomy* (1952 edition) André Simon says that *boudin blanc* is a 'fat sausage made with white meat and seasoned with onions; the best are made with chicken and pork; the worst with veal and breadcrumbs'.

Ali-Bab's recipe, which uses five parts milk to two of meat, plus a great deal of onion, calls for truffles. But he says, 'One can simplify the formula, which is for a *boudin de luxe*, by leaving out the truffles.' And he allows the possibility ('*dans le même esprit*') of *boudins blancs* made with game, presumably the white meat of pheasant or partridge; while he says that if you replace the chicken and pork 'with the flesh of shellfish or fish, the pork fat with a bit of butter, and add some cream and egg yolks', you'll have *boudins blancs* suitable for eating on fast days. This was written, remember, in 1928. So much for the *nouvelle cuisine* chefs who think they invented *boudins de poissons* or *de fruits de mer* in the 1970s and '80s.

This discussion, by the way, is not entirely academic. Pork blood is not easy to come by in today's cleaned-up world. (Though I remember my wife once asked a French farmer's wife how her wonderful *saucisson* was made, expecting to be told that it had a great deal of garlic, or whole peppercorns and the like, and was astonished by the reply: '*Pour commencer, Madame, il faut tuer un cochon.*' 'First, kill your pig.') Black pudding is not within the compass of the average cook; but *boudin blanc* can be made by anybody who can acquire some sausage casing, and two recipes are given for it in this book (see pages 68–69).

Still Life with Apples by Gustave Courbet (1819–1877)

My own household enthusiastically embraced the *boudin blanc* tradition, probably in commemoration of the many Christmases we spent in France. Frugality and economy, though, play some part in it too, because we regard the *boudin* as a reason for using up the apples stored in the cellar. We peel and core the apples, and cut them into quarters or rough chunks. After very gently browning the *boudins* in butter in heavy enamelled cast-iron gratin dishes, we simply put the apple under the sausages so they are resting on a plumped-up bed of the fruit, and bake for 10–20 minutes. Eating apples are better than cookers, as they have exactly the right amount of

sweetness and need no extra sugar. Some eating apples keep their shape when cooked, so that the apple has a little bite, which complements perfectly the more elastic texture of the sausage.

In some years the bounty of the orchard is just too great, and we still have the wherewithal of apple tarts well into February. But even the best varieties have lost their attraction as eating apples by then, so it is a bonus if we can use up the apple crop for the Christmas meal. There are some ancient trees in our small orchard; the best yields gigantic yellow-green apples with a distinct orange blush, and crisp, slightly scented flesh. Because the house was until recently part of the Blenheim Estate, I have concluded that the apple is a Blenheim Orange. I've planted Cox's Orange Pippin, James Grieve, Egremont Russet (my favourite eating apple) and a few others to supplement the apples that were here when we arrived. But we are lucky to live at the beginning of an apple renaissance. In 1991 the British supermarket chains began selling formerly rare varieties of apple in season; and the same thing is happening in America, where the farmers' markets are introducing city dwellers to the extraordinary gastronomic rewards to be had from older types of our commonest fruit.

There is a temptation to say 'Hurrah, no more Red Delicious, no more Golden Delicious'. But I have one tree of each of these, and have discovered that they can be a treat when well grown and harvested only when ripe. The one apple I would banish from my garden is the Bramley's Seedling. Gross, bloated and sour, this common English cooker has no purpose I can see that is not better served by one of its fellows. With the very big exception of the various reinettes, French apples are boring, as are most American commercial varieties. Again, Jonathans, McIntoshes and Winesaps can be delicious, but everything depends on the conditions in which they are grown. This is why almost any variety grown in Washington state will have merit, and why even the wonderful Granny Smith tastes only of water and cotton wool when grown elsewhere in the USA.

Just think, though. We are one of the first generations since our great-grandparents to have the thrill, in the run-up to Christmas, of choosing the contents of the fruit bowl from a list of apples whose very names are poetry. Adam's Pearmain and Autumn Pearmain, Ashmead's Kernel and Beauty of Bath; Belle de Boskoop, Court Pendu Plat, Crispin and D'Archy Spice; Devonshire Quarrenden, Ellison's Orange and Gascoyne's Scarlet; George Cave, George Neal and John Standish; Herring's Pippin and Keswick Codlin; Kidd's Orange Red and Laxton's Early Crimson; Lady Henniker and Lady Sudeley, Lords Burghley, Derby, Grosvenor, Hindlip and Lamborne; Merton Beauty, Merton Charm and Merton Knave; Monarch and Mother; Owen Thomas, Tom Putt and William Crump; Stirling Castle and Tower of Glamis; Peasgood Nonsuch and Worcester Pearmain. True, some of them are no longer at their sappy best at Christmas but we also have access now to the edible poetry of the tropics: the heady perfumes of mangoes and papayas, longan, lichee and rambutan.

THERE HAVE BEEN CHRISTMASES, I CONFESS, WHEN we have been jaded and so tired of turkey that we've treated the feast as a fast. A fish course makes a welcome addition to the festival table, of course; but there have been years when a large plump salmon has taken the turkey's place at the centre of the revels. In fact, this is standard procedure in most of Europe. Those cultures whose main meal is on Christmas Eve almost all have a meat-less fasting supper, where fish is featured.

Even in the Orthodox Church, where Christmas begins at sunset on 6 January, the Christmas fast is observed. In Russia 12 meatless dishes used to be eaten in memory of the dead. Called the Apostles' supper, it followed the long Advent fast, and its resemblance to the Jewish Passover meal was striking in the requirement to invite a stranger if possible, and to lay an extra place and pour one more glass of wine than there were guests. The traditional 12 dishes included *borscht*, roast carp, the compote of dried fruit called *uzar* and a sweet rice or wheat porridge called *kutia*. This last was weighted with symbolism. The bowl in which it was eaten stood for the crib; the cereal the straw of the manger; in the centre a hollow was made with a spoon to 'receive the baby Jesus'; the fruit in the porridge represented His body, the honey that sweetened it His blood.

Carp is *the* Christmas fish in central and eastern Europe. Catholic Poland has the December 24 Christmas Eve *Wilja* or *Wigilja*. This used to be an Apostles' supper on the Russian pattern, and many of the dishes are similar. In Poland now children watch for the first star in the sky to signal the beginning of the meal, at which an even number of people must sit down at the table, lest one of the company present die during the year. As always 13 is a taboo number of guests (the prohibition against 13 at table predates Christianity), but an extra place is laid for the Blessed Virgin, as the Passover table has a place for Elijah the Prophet. The menu is similar, too, to the Russian one, with *barszcs* using *kwas* made earlier in December by fermenting beetroot, water and black rye bread, served with *uszka*, ear-shaped dumplings; a whole fish, usually carp, possibly pike, Jewish-style; *pierogi* filled with pickled cabbage and mushrooms; and *kutia*, a fruit, wheat and poppyseed porridge, or poppyseed paste with noodles, and *kompot* of dried fruit.

German-speakers, whether Lutherans or Bavarian or Austrian Catholics, have their Christmas Eve carp simmered and served with a sauce made from beer, raisins and almonds, and a bit of *Pfefferkuchen*, honeyed spice cake. Carp turns up again on New Year's Eve. This time it is certainly a mirror carp from the fish farms, with large scales, and cooked *au bleu*. Each person saves one of these scales to put in his purse, to bring prosperity in the coming year, for with it his purse will never be empty. Even when cooked in this way, as in Jane Grigson's recipe in her *Fish Cookery*, the creamy horseradish sauce is sweet with sugar and almonds. As Mrs Grigson says, 'a strange thing about carp is the unanimity with which it is treated by cooks right across the world'. The Chinese, the Poles, the French and the medieval English all agreed on the character of the accompanying sauce, as do all the Jewish recipes. 'I do not imagine a traceable connection,' wrote Jane Grigson, 'because I suspect that the carp recipes used in Europe are living fossils of the sweet-sour style of medieval cookery.'

The other fish caught in fresh water that is eaten at Christmas Eve is the *capitone* of Rome and Milan, which can be up to 1.75 metres (5 feet) in length. In *Mediterranean Seafood* Alan Davidson says these are simply adult common eels *Anguilla anguilla*, that 'grow especially big and fat, rather like capons and perhaps because they do not mature sexually in the normal way'. He says the Christmas Eve method of preparation in southern Italy (and in the South of France where there is a 'similar dish') is to rub the pieces of fat eel with garlic, and thread them on to skewers, alternating with bay leaves. You marinate them for an hour in pepper and two parts of olive oil to one of vinegar, before spit-roasting them for half an hour. Jane Grigson says you can do this sort of *capitone arrosto* in a fairly hot 190°C (375°F, mark 5) oven on a grid or rack in a roasting tin.

'The best *capitoni*,' says Anna Del Conte in her *Gastronomy of Italy*, 'are caught at the mouth of the Po. They are eaten fresh, prepared in the same ways as small eel, or preserved under oil like tuna fish. This latter is the traditional dish in Rome and Milan on Christmas Eve.' 'In Rome and Naples,' says Raymond Sokolov in *Natural History* magazine for November, 1991, 'the tradition of the Christmas vigil dictates big, fat, unprepossessing eels, *capitoni*, caught in Ortebello and stewed with herbs.' It is irrelevant to this small and attractive disagreement about the method of preparation of *capitoni* for Christmas Eve, but at other times of year in the north of Italy they are commonly eaten with *mostarda di Cremona*, the jewel-like, slightly sweet preserve of fruits in mustard.

I have had *anguille en brochette* several times in France. Indeed, as eaten at the Lion d'Or at Arcins in the Médoc, it ranks as one of my all-time, best-ever dishes. But despite having spent a quarter of the Christmases of my adult life in the south of France, I've never encountered it there, as Alan Davidson suggests I might have done, on Christmas Eve. But then, I've never been lucky enough to be invited to a proper *gros souper* in Provence, either. (The Anglo-French household in the Var whose celebrations we shared for many years was of the oyster, *boudin* and *foie gras* school.) The *gros souper* is the Provençal Christmas Eve supper, and, unlike some of the other French celebrations, it remains a meatless fasting supper. (Strictly speaking Christmas Eve supper should be the last fast of Advent, and the *réveillon*, the 'awakening' supper, should be taken after midnight mass and mark the breaking of the fast. Thus in Armagnac there used to be a stew, in Alsace sauerkraut and *foie gras d'oie*, in the Nivernais and the Touraine a freshly killed pig preceded by its black and white puddings, in Poitu game, in Roussillon a ham. In Provence, well-off and greedy families would have the *gros souper* before church and polish off a chestnut-stuffed turkey on returning from mass.)

There is a famous passage in which the poet of Provence, Frédéric Mistral, recalled a *gros souper* at St-Rémy, at about the turn of the century (quoted in Elisabeth Luard's *European Festival Food*). He tells how the usual hanging lamp is replaced for this meal by three candles. In every culture, the Christmas Eve celebration has a superstition about something that is an ill-omen for one of the guests. In Provence it was the candle wick, says Mistral: 'If the end of the wick should by chance turn towards one of the diners, that is a sign of some disaster to come.' The tablecloth had to be white, and Mistral speaks of the dishes upon the table as being 'sacramental': 'The snails which each diner winkles from the shell with a brand-new pin, the fried salt-cod, the *muge* [gurnard] stuffed with olives, chard, cardoons, *céléri à la poivrade*, followed by a host of delicious sweetmeats, such as the *gâteau à l'huile*, grapes, nougat, quinces and above all, the Christmas bread – not to be broached until one quarter has been given to the first poor man who passes by.

'At the end of the table, in a little dish, sprouts a tuft of wheat which on St Barbara's feast [December 4] was planted and watered so that it would germinate.' It was also the tradition to bring in the *tréfoir* or Yule log on Christmas Eve. The youngest child would baptise it in wine '*in nomine patris, et filii, et spiritus sancti . . .*' and it would be retrieved from the fire, to be burnt bit by bit over the 12 days of Christmas. Its ashes were used in health-giving potions, and any unburned piece of it kept under the bed would protect the whole house from lightning.

Elisabeth Luard had the good fortune to share a Christmas Eve supper relatively recently with Mademoiselle Paulette, a retired accountant in Villedieu near Vaison-la-Romaine. The menu for the supper, which started about seven o'clock, after sundown, was based on a *soupe aux lasagnes*, with fresh pasta, cabbage, leeks, turnips, chard, celery and carrots, finished with garlicky aïoli. The supporting dishes were cardoons and chard, snails and salt cod. (The 13 desserts were served after mass *chez* Mlle Paulette and these will feature in a later chapter.) Elisabeth Luard gives a recipe for salt cod, *morue en raito*, which comes from Josephine Besson of Cannes, but born in Marseille, who uses the recipe for her own family's fasting supper. Interestingly, it lacks the red wine that Richard Olney, who also lives in Provence, seems to think the essential feature of the dish. In his great book, *Simple French Food*, Olney calls for 0.75 l (1¼ pints) of red wine to 750 g (1½ lb) of salt cod. Indeed, he translates *morue en raito* as 'cod in red wine sauce', and says in his championship aside to his recipe that: '*Raito* is the name of the sauce in which any number of fish – eel, conger eel, whiting, halibut, fresh haddock – sliced, filleted, or cut into sections, may be gently stewed after having been lightly pan-fried. Salt cod, alone, is prepared in a *raito* (or sometimes in a *capilotade* – chopped onions cooked in olive oil, flour stirred in, moistened with water and vinegar to taste, bouquet garni, and a handful of capers; in parts of the Var, the vinegar is replaced by a glass of *vin cuit*, a homemade sweet wine, reserved usually for Christmas and prepared at the time of the grape harvest from the unfermented grape must reduced and skimmed – a certain amount of marc or distilled alcohol is often added to it) as one of the traditional dishes of the Provençal Christmas Eve *gros souper*.'

Quite the best description of the *gros souper* is in Olney's book. He says: 'The ritual, pre-midnight mass, Christmas Eve supper in Provence is strictly a family affair. A certain flexibility of detail exists within its nonetheless rigid form: garlic soup (*aïgo bouido*) may or may not preface the meal, followed by or replaced by either *petits-gris* (a variety similar to but smaller than the huge Burgundy snails that are tinned and exported – they are first starved for a few days, bathed in salt and vinegar, well washed, and cooked for 2 or 3 hours in a heavily fennel-flavoured white wine court bouillon) and *aïoli* or crisp celery hearts and *anchoiade* (a thick vinaigrette whose body derives from pounded garlic and anchovy fillets); salt cod and its alternative *raito* or *capilotade* sauces, although traditional, are sometimes dethroned by other fish and other sauces (an octopus *daube*, for instance, which takes the quaint appellation of *tripes de mer*, or "sea tripe"); gratins of spinach and hard-boiled eggs, creamed chard ribs or salsify are common follow-ups, but any winter vegetable preparation may supplant or supplement them. Each element seems to have been chosen for its humble and homely character . . .'

It was the old custom of the Advent fast that determined the Christmas Eve menus both in the Catholic south of Europe and in Protestant Scandinavia, and, as Raymond Sokolov says in an article about cod in the magazine *Natural History*, 'The Universal Penitential Fish': 'There seems to be no doubt that these fish meals preserve the idea of penitential food best known from Friday and Lenten "meager" meals, at which the pious, until quite recently, abstained from meat and substituted fish.' Another aspect of ritual cod-eating at Christmas that seems to have gone unnoticed is its association with red wine. Though it doesn't seem an obvious gastronomic marriage, the Scandinavians routinely drink red wine with their Christmas Eve cod or *lutefisk*; and, as we can see from Richard Olney's recipe for *raito*, the Provençaux *cook* the salt cod in red wine.

The taste for salt cod is one I share, and its popularity is easy for me to understand. Less so is *lutefisk*, which Alan Davidson in *North Atlantic Seafood* says is 'stockfish prepared in a special way'. It does not have to be cod; ling is common, and other fish of the same family can be used. 'At first sight or smell,' says Davidson, *lutefisk* 'is a puzzling phenomenon.' In Norway, Finland and Sweden alone, it is a Christmas tradition to soak stockfish first in water and then in lye, and then again in running water before cooking it. The process is laborious and takes several days. *Lutefisk* is not a practical suggestion for those looking for an additional course for their Christmas meal, and even a dish of salt cod with red wine is not to everybody's taste.

IF YOU CAN'T BUY BOUDIN BLANC, CAN'T GET sausage casings, or just don't fancy the idea of making your own, but want a savoury meat course, a home-made terrine can be simplicity itself. Of course it's easy to make any one of the liver-based terrines in advance and leave it to develop its flavours for Christmas Day – game would be an obvious choice for this time of year, and you can give yourself plenty of time to marinate the flesh of a partridge or pheasant, or even a pigeon; and farmed venison and even wild boar are available. I confess that I have, in the past, parked the livers of the turkey or goose in the freezer, with the idea of making future pâtés of them. But you wouldn't want to leave them under a layer of hoarfrost for a whole year; so they tend to get used up well before the next Christmas.

Moreover, I think it's important that the dishes of the Christmas meal have an air of elegance about them, and many of these terrines are what Richard Olney calls agrestic, or rustic. Not so rustic, but hearty and flavourful nonetheless, is the turkey and scallop terrine Frances Bissell made one year to occupy this slot in the Christmas feast (see page 76). For vegetarians, this is an obvious place to have a vegetable terrine, which can be particularly pretty when sliced, with jewel-like cross-sections of just-blanched, still crisp, tiny green beans, globe artichoke bottoms and baby carrots. Unfortunately, the very best recipes for vegetable terrines all use a mousse of chicken breast or veal to bind the vegetables.

If you have begun the meal with something fishy, or oysters, but not smoked salmon, you might find a slice of raw ham would go well at this point in the menu. It is not uncommon to encounter a thick-ish slice of *jambon de Bayonne* in France at this point, especially at the St-Sylvestre or New Year *réveillon*; and many restaurants follow the practice of bringing the whole ham to the table in a highly polished silver

63

slicing frame with spikes that make it resemble the medieval torturer's iron maiden.

All hams that can be eaten raw are cured, of course, and some of them are also smoked. The cure should be salting or brining, and not injection, which is more like embalming than curing; but the cheaper injection method is all too common nowadays. *Jambon de Bayonne*, the most famous French ham, comes mostly from Orthez, which is a little east of Bayonne itself. It is cold-smoked after curing, which makes it taste different from the similar but unsmoked hams of Spain and Italy. The ham of the Morvan in Burgundy is highly prized in France, as are those of the Auvergne, of Alsace and Lorraine, and of Toulouse. The best *prosciutto crudo* is that from Parma, which should be sliced paper thin, and is actually cured in winter and thus ready to eat just when the figs and melons, its ideal accompaniments, are ripe. The ham of San Daniele in Friuli is cured differently and is also very fine. *Jamón serrano*, the mountain ham of Spain, is at its best when made from a lean, black Iberian pig; it's wildly expensive, so most of what one sees today, even in Spain, is made from fatter white hybrid pigs. German Westphalian hams are from pampered pigs that are elaborately prepared, cured and smoked. The smoking is done over beechwood sawdust with quite a lot of juniper twigs and berries, so that the smoky flavour is more pronounced than in, say, *jambon de Bayonne*.

One reason for slicing raw ham thinly is that it can otherwise be tough. This is especially true of Spanish hams, which, as Tom Stobart says in his *Cook's Encyclopaedia*, are made from particularly 'well exercised pigs'. In any case, you'll probably be getting the delicatessen to slice your ham for you. I do not recommend buying a whole ham of this sort, anyway, unless you are certain you can finish it up fairly soon after buying it. Even when hung in a cool cellar, uncooked hams dry out and toughen. I was once caught out like this, and took a near-fossilised ham to our English butcher, who re-brined it. It did soften enough to slice, but everyone who ate as much as a mouthful of it came out in spots.

We generally have a ham of the other sort at Christmas – one that has to be cooked before it is served – but we save it for Boxing Day, and Chapter 5.

In my childhood in Kentucky we often followed the standard practice of the American south and had a dish of scalloped oysters as the second course. This was a good way of using oysters, usually Bluepoints, which didn't have too far to travel from Chesapeake Bay, that came in cans with a little transparent window near the top, made of plastic or stiffened cellophane I suppose. They were 'shucked' (removed from their shells) and packed in their own liquor. I don't remember how long they were supposed to keep in their tins, but we bought them at the A&P from a counter covered in crushed ice. The principle of the dish was a simple one – the oysters and their liquor were just warmed through in the oven, with cream or butter and some seasoning (always cayenne, but I think I remember a blade of mace being involved). Some starchy material had to be used as a base. At home, this was invariably crushed saltine crackers (like crisp cream crackers with salt). I think we knew that this was a substitute for more glamorous dishes whose preparations involved proper fresh oysters.

Whatever food you choose to come second in the order of service of the Christmas feast, it is important to remember the theatrical dimension of feasting. This means paying careful attention to the dramatic sequence of the wines you serve. This is not idle advice for the very rich, those who can afford vintage champagne and real burgundy: those on a budget need to pay even greater heed to matching the wines to the food and to arranging everything in the best order. For example, if you've got over the hurdle of which white wine to serve with a fishy first course, what do you drink next with soup? Or with *boudin blanc*? Or with a meat-based terrine or ham? Or, most difficult of all, with a vegetarian dish?

The easy way out is to drink sparkling wine as apéritif and also with the food until a red wine becomes appropriate. This is not such a silly idea. If your pockets are deep enough to accommodate champagne, it is the near-ideal match for every food mentioned so far, and certainly never worse than second-best. The new crop of fizzy wines from Australia and New Zealand and the older, more established ones from California, almost all have real character and benefit from being drunk with food. If you've taken the trouble to choose your New World bubbly with care, your guests will be impressed to see how it changes its character from being drunk on its own to being matched with food.

I don't much like soup for a celebration meal. When you're paying attention to the wine, I feel that soup makes the whole meal too liquid. Still, many people disagree with me. It is a good chance to drink an unusual fortified wine, too. Many's the Madeira that would go unopened were soup not drunk on Christmas day. And a fine consommé is a very good excuse for a glass of an Almacenista fino or amontillado sherry.

The great thing, to my mind, about a meaty second course, such as *boudin blanc*, terrine or raw ham, is that they will equally well tolerate red or white wine. Such a course gives you the chance to put your best glass forward, as any Alsace wine with character, for example, will show off gloriously with such food. A young gewürztraminer from a decent vintage will glitter, but so will a rich, sweetish *vendange tardive*. A soft red from the south of France will flatter and be flattered in turn, and both white and red burgundies will be in good company. It would not be out of the question, if you were having a well-flavoured pâté of chicken livers, for instance, to have the traditional accompaniment to *foie gras*, a glass of sauternes or of a fortified muscat such as Muscat de Rivesaltes, or even the hackneyed Beaume de Venise. The only wine I'd really counsel against in this position is a tannic red, though it might line up well against a very liver-y terrine. Otherwise, save it for the turkey.

Remember that what you're aiming for is to build up a sequence of wines of increasing power and drama, not of increasing subtlety and refinement. It's all very well to save the best wine for last. But if the best wine is an old and delicate burgundy, and requires a fresh palate for its maximum appreciation, it's no use serving it after a succession of aggressively oaked New World chardonnays and cabernet sauvignons. If you have a special bottle, either save it for the appropriate plain grilled fish or meat, or construct a very carefully planned pathway of wines so that it sits comfortably at the summit.

LADY LOUSADA'S TORTELLINI IN BRODO

Patricia Lousada's Italian mother always started her otherwise traditional American Christmas meal with this pasta dish. Lady Lousada says that wonton wrappers from oriental shops work beautifully for stuffed pasta, and 'they make the whole affair a snip to prepare'. In place of the broth, you could serve them with a little extra grated fresh parmesan and melted butter, or with a light tomato sauce.

Serves 8
32 wonton wrappers
1 shallot, finely minced
knob of butter
150 g (5 oz) fresh spinach
100 g (4 oz, ½ cup) ricotta cheese
1 Tbsp double or heavy cream or soft mild goat's cheese
20 g (¾ oz, 1½ Tbsp) finely grated parmesan cheese
a few gratings of nutmeg
salt and pepper
egg wash, made from one egg mixed with 1 tsp water
hot clear chicken or turkey broth for 8 servings

Soften the shallot in the butter, add the washed spinach leaves and turn until just wilted. Drain, squeeze out excess moisture and chop. Mix with the ricotta, cream or goat's cheese, parmesan and seasoning. Put one teaspoon of the stuffing in the top half of a wonton square. Brush with egg wash around the edge and fold in half, pressing the edges to seal. Cut into a semi-circle with a cookie or biscuit cutter. Continue until you have made 32 tortellini. Place them on a lightly floured cloth until ready to use.

Bring a large quantity of water to the boil. Don't salt the water, as the wonton wrappers contain salt. Slide the pasta parcels into the water and bring back to the boil, then simmer gently for 4–5 mins. Use a slotted spoon or large Chinese flat sieve to remove from the water and place in the individual bowls of broth. The broth should just cover the pasta, unless you prefer a more generous helping. Serve at once with a few chopped chives or parsley.

JANE GRIGSON'S BOUDINS BLANCS DE PARIS

In her *Charcuterie and French Pork Cookery* Jane Grigson gives several recipes for *boudin blanc*. As she says, it is normal in France to buy these from the *charcutier*; and you can buy them in London from Harrods and the Boucherie Lamartine, as you can from French butchers in New York, Chicago and Los Angeles. But away from the bright lights and big cities, you just have to make your own. If you can get sausage casing (make a friend of your butcher), it is not difficult; and, as Jane Grigson says, it's a good way of using up leftover chicken. The quantity produced by this recipe adaptation depends on the diameter of the sausage casing.

250 g (8 oz) roast chicken or uncooked breast
250 g (8 oz) lean pork, such as loin
500 g (1¼ lb) hard back fat mixed with flare fat from
    around the kidney
350 g (12 oz, generous 2 cups) onion, chopped
50 g (2 oz, 1 cup loosely packed) breadcrumbs,
    soaked in 4–6 Tbsp hot milk or light cream
3 eggs
1 level Tbsp salt
1 tsp white pepper
1 tsp *quatre-épices* or ground allspice

For the poaching
600ml (1pt, 2½cups) milk

The meat and fat must be very finely minced. Put them through the finest mincer blade twice, seasoning with salt, pepper and the spices and adding the onions for the second mincing. Or process with the steel blade, adding the seasonings and onions, then the soaked breadcrumbs and the eggs. If not using a food processor, beat in the breadcrumbs and eggs as thoroughly as possible. Fill the skins slackly; they will burst or explode if they're too full. Tie them with thread to make sausages of 15 cm (6 in).

For their first cooking, in a fish kettle or large saucepan simmer the milk plus 1.2 litres (2 pints, 5 cups) water. Lower the sausages gently into the liquid in the poaching tray, or use a metal basket. As the sausages rise to the surface, prick them gently with a needle to keep them from exploding; they need about 20 mins total simmering, and the liquid must never boil. Raise them gently out of the poaching liquid and leave them to drain. The next day they are ready to eat and can be grilled, brushed with melted butter or fried.

Our own method is to brown them very carefully in butter, and then place them on a bed of peeled, cored and sliced apples in a gratin dish, and bake for 10–20 mins in a preheated 190°C (375°F gas mark 5) oven.

ALI-BAB'S BOUDINS BLANCS

In this general recipe the chicken and pork can be replaced by game. Ali-Bab also says you can substitute fish or shellfish for them as well, and use 'a bit of butter' instead of the pork fat, adding some cream and egg yolks.

30 g (1 oz, 2 rounded Tbsp) rice
500 ml (1 pint, 2 cups) milk
100 g (3½ oz, 1 cup loosely packed) shredded flare (kidney) fat
2 large onions, chopped
100 g (3½ oz, generous ½ cup) raw pork, chopped
100 g (3½ oz, ½ cup) breast of roast chicken, chopped
truffles, cooked and finely diced (optional)
salt, pepper, freshly grated nutmeg
1 egg

Cook the rice in the milk until soft. Melt the fat in a large, heavy saucepan, and sweat the onions in it, without letting them colour, along with the pork. Then add the cooked rice, the chicken breast and truffles, if the budget stretches to them, and season with salt, pepper and nutmeg. Cool and process with the steel blade. Finally, add the egg and process for a second or two. Then stuff the sausages and poach them as in Jane Grigson's recipe (left).

M. F. K. FISHER'S OYSTER LOAF

Mrs Fisher recommends making this with a small loaf sufficient to feed two people. She doesn't say so, but a brioche loaf would make this the ultimate luxury. You cut off the top of the loaf – it obviously has to be a *loaf*-shaped loaf, if you see what I mean; a baguette won't work – hollow out the centre and discard the crumb. Then brush the bread case and lid with melted butter and put it into a hot oven to get all golden and toast slightly. In the meantime, egg and crumb enough oysters to fill the loaf, and fry them just until brown. Mrs Fisher says you can do this in deep or shallow fat. Fill the bread case with the oysters and pour melted butter over them before replacing the lid and eating the loaf on the spot. If you're tempted to make this, don't forget the cayenne. It is otherwise unthinkably rich. The bread case, though, is a very useful vehicle for humbler fillings, such as sautéed wild mushrooms in their season, or a mixture of chicken livers and cultivated mushrooms in a parsley-flecked *velouté*, or sweetbreads or scrambled egg with herbs.

JANE GRIGSON'S CHRISTMAS CARP
(KARPFEN POLNISCHER ART – POLISH-STYLE CARP)

In her *Fish Cookery* Jane Grigson notes that some German families eat their Christmas Eve carp with this sauce made sweet and sour with honeyed spice cake and beer; others have it poached *au bleu* with a horseradish sauce made with cream, sugar and ground almonds. If you are lucky enough to get a just-dispatched carp that can be poached in this way, don't wash it or scale it; just pour boiling vinegar over it, top up with a *court bouillon* and simmer. This recipe is adapted from hers for Polish carp.

Serves 6

2 kg (4 lb) carp containing soft roe
4 medium onions, sliced
3 stalks of celery heart, chopped
175 g (6 oz, 1½ sticks) unsalted butter
bouquet garni of thyme, bay leaf and parsley stalks, with 1 clove and 6 black peppercorns
100 g (3 oz, 1 generous cup) crumbled spice cake, such as honey cake or *pain d'épice*
about 2.5 litres (4 pints, 10 cups) beer
lemon juice
salt and freshly ground black pepper

Begin by soaking the cleaned carp in water acidulated with ¹/₁₀ to ¹/₂₀ parts vinegar. Leave its scales intact and do not wash it after the soaking, but take out the roe very carefully and be certain to remove the bitter-tasting sac at the back of the carp's head. Sweat the onion and celery in a third of the butter, in a pan large enough to take the carp. Add the bouquet garni

and crumble the cake over the bottom of the pan, laying the carp and its roe on top. Add beer to cover and simmer. Take the roe out carefully just as soon as it's done, which may be well before the fish. On a warmed fish platter surround the just-cooked fish with its roe, sliced, and keep it warm while you make the sauce. Sieve the cooking liquid into a clean saucepan and reduce it to 500–600 ml (¾–1 pint, 2–2½ cups). Season it with lemon juice and salt and pepper, and whisk in the remaining butter bit by bit until the sauce is shiny. The traditional accompaniment is boiled potatoes.

MY OWN BORSCHT

The perfect foil for Patricia Lousada's pirozhki (see page 77), and very correct for the vigil supper in central and eastern Europe, is borscht (however you spell it). I have developed a simple recipe for an elegant, thin borscht. Start with the best meat, poultry or game stock you can manage. Duck or goose is best; turkey is very good. Simmer the stock with fresh beetroot shredded in the food processor, along with almost any vegetables that come to hand. These can include soaked dried mushrooms and must include onions, leeks, shallots or garlic, but any or all of the following will do: celery, carrots, tomatoes, cabbage, celeriac, parsnip, turnips, swedes (rutabagas), potatoes, fennel, sorrel or spinach. Peel and grate all the vegetables. The trick is to divide the quantity of beetroot in two, and reserve half of it to finish the soup.

You might find it hard to do the next step, but steel yourself to it. Having simmered the shredded

vegetables in the stock, now fish them out and throw them away. All of them. The soup will be a deep red, and perfectly clear, even if you've used potato. Bring it back to the simmer and add the second lot of grated beetroot. Taste for salt and pepper, add some sugar, and a good slug of vinegar to fix the colour and give the soup a sweet-sour flavour. The best is either a sweet fruit vinegar – this is the time to use up your out-of-fashion raspberry vinegar, sherry vinegar, or 'balsamic' vinegar (you certainly should not waste the real thing on this dish). Taste it – you'll know when it's right.

The result is a limpidly clear soup, with a few shreds of beetroot but no other vegetation in each serving. Serve either hot or chilled, with a dollop of soured cream or *crème fraîche*.

GRILLED AND BAKED FISH EN PAPILLOTE

I learned this trick from Sonia Blech, chef of Mijanou restaurant in London. It works for any fish fillets, and for any small, whole fish. I can accommodate a 2-kg (4-lb) salmon on the top of my Aga cooker, and I could get an even bigger one on the Weber barbecue – but perhaps not at Christmas.

The idea is simple. You take any number of fish fillets, in a single layer or with the flavourings sandwiched between them, or a whole, cleaned and scaled fish, with or without its head, and seal it loosely in buttered or oiled cooking foil, and cook it first on a hot grill pan or barbecue, or directly on an electric ring or the hot surface of the Aga; then you finish the cooking rapidly in a hot oven. The result is moist, well-flavoured fish, with a savoury, crusty skin – if you've left the skin on.

So, for example, for a 1.5 kg (3–3½ lb) salmon: take enough foil from the packet to wrap the fish in a double layer; fold it in half and oil the side that will touch the fish. Season the fish inside and out liberally with salt and pepper and, if you want an Oriental flavour, light soy or Thai *nam pla*, plus a dusting of cayenne. Inside the fish's cavity place whatever flavouring elements you fancy. Garlic, ginger, spring onion, lemon grass, shredded Kaffir lime leaves and a crumbled dried chilli, for a Southeast Asian touch; lemon slices and fresh tarragon; basil, garlic and sun-dried tomatoes and a drizzle of good olive oil; or a knob of butter with onion or shallot and parsley or basil. The combinations are infinite and great fun to think up. Splash a little dry vermouth, white wine (or red – surprisingly good with butter and shallot), or

brandy, gin, whisky, rum or balsamic vinegar, and seal up the parcel not too tightly, but sufficiently to see it doesn't leak. If you are doing fillets, put the seasonings directly on to them or sandwich them as described above.

Place the parcel over the heat source (or as close as possible if the heat is above) and allow the fish to sizzle in its silver paper. Make sure every part of the surface area of the fish comes into contact with the heat, so that it 'browns' evenly. I actually lower the lid of the Aga and 'iron' my fish. A 1.5-kg salmon would need to sizzle on the heat for 3–4 minutes and then 6–8 minutes on a rack in the top third of a very hot oven. A parcel containing fillets of Dover sole in a single thickness would need only a minute on direct heat and wouldn't need to go in the oven at all.

You may need to experiment to find the best combination of heat sources and temperatures to cook a fish this way, and be prepared to fail once or twice. So don't try this trick for the first time with a whole salmon or turbot on Christmas Day. You can obviously make separate parcels for individual servings once you have got the knack of this way of cooking. But whether you do a whole fish or several small parcels, always bring it to the table still sealed in foil. The aroma that escapes as the packet is undone is half the pleasure of the dish, and your guests, unless they have head colds, will swoon.

You can cook very thin cuts of meat and poultry like this, too, keeping in all the juices but adding lots of additional flavour. But restrict your experiments to cuts of meat that can be eaten underdone, or to sliced, boned bits of chicken and turkey – *paillard* of turkey or chicken breast is suitable.

CHUTNEY MARY'S SPICY LOBSTER BISQUE

This madly luxurious soup is given a thrilling new twist in this recipe created for their Christmas menu by Chutney Mary, London's Anglo-Indian restaurant. This tongue-tingling, palate-teasing version of a classic recipe is a good example of how Anglo-Indian cuisine was created in the first place and is a very economical use of lobster.

Serves 12

1 kg (2¼ lbs) live lobster (you can use 2 small ones)
2 sticks celery, finely chopped
1 medium carrot, finely chopped
1 leek, white part only, finely minced
50 g (2 oz, ½ cup) chopped mushrooms
4 cloves
2.5 cm (1 in) stick cinnamon
6 cardamom pods, crushed
½ tsp anise seed
4 bay leaves
5 litres (8 pints, 5 quarts) fish stock
200 g (7 oz, approx. 1 large) tomato, peeled, seeded and diced
100 g (3½ oz, ½ cup) rice
1 pinch saffron
3 Tbsp neutral-flavoured oil
1 large onion, sliced thinly
2 cm (¾ in) ginger, minced
5–6 cloves garlic, minced
1 Tbsp cayenne or red chilli powder
1 Tbsp ground cumin
1 Tbsp ground coriander seeds

To finish

100 g (3½ oz, just under 1 stick) butter
300 g (10 fl oz, 1¼ cups) single (light) cream
1 Tbsp almond flakes, toasted

Kill the lobster(s) by plunging them into boiling water or stab them in the back with a sharp heavy knife just where the head seems to meet the tail. Put it into a very large (more than 5-litre) saucepan and add the celery, carrot, leek, mushrooms, cloves, cinnamon, cardamom, anise, bay leaves and fish stock. Bring to the boil and simmer for about 8–10 minutes, or until the lobster is cooked. Retrieve the lobster and, when cool enough to handle, remove the meat and put the cracked shells back into the soup. (Bang them with a mallet if you haven't already smashed them up while taking out the meat.) Dice the lobster meat tidily and set aside for garnish.

Add the tomato, rice and saffron to the pot and continue to cook over a medium heat until the stock is reduced by about half – to about 2 litres (3½ pints). In a frying pan heat the oil and sauté the onions until light brown. Add the ginger and garlic and fry for a minute. Then add the chilli, cumin and coriander and fry for another half minute.

Scrape this mixture from the frying pan into the soup pot and simmer for 5–10 minutes. Remove the shells from the liquid and pass through a sieve, or process or liquidise in a blender. Just before serving, add the butter and cream and re-heat, but do not allow the soup to boil. Serve in individual bowls, each garnished with some diced lobster meat and a few toasted flaked almonds.

JENNY LO'S CLEAN-STEAMED FISH

Jenny Lo's family are Chinese Christians, living in Malaysia. Their family tradition is to have a Chinese meal. They sometimes start with fresh crabs steamed with ginger, spring onions, coriander, rice vinegar, garlic and chillies, and deep-fried chilli and garlic tiger prawns. Then soy chicken with dried and straw mushrooms; rice-wine chicken with coriander, spring onion and ginger; tofu and aubergines stuffed with pork, fish and shrimp; pig's trotters in vinegar with eggs simmered in ginger, rice vinegar and soy; a steamed fish, such as this one below; prawn and cucumber curry; white rice and chow mein for longevity, followed by Hangzhou fish-head soup with ham, parsley and pea shoots. Dessert is green mandarin oranges from China, local pomelo and crisp Japanese pears, with coconut and durian ice cream for the younger guests.

Serves 4 as main course, 8 as part of Chinese meal
1 whole fish, such as sea bass, grouper, carp or
    pomfret
salt
3–4 spring onions, shredded
60–100 g (2–3 oz) fatty smoked bacon or ham,
    shredded
6 dried Chinese black mushrooms, soaked, stems discarded and sliced
8 thin slices ginger
3 Tbsp peanut oil
1 Tbsp rice wine (or dry sherry)

For the sauce
1 tsp cornflour (cornstarch)
1 tsp salt
freshly ground black pepper
4 Tbsp chicken or fish stock or water

To finish
2 tsp sesame oil
fresh green coriander leaves

See that the fish is ready to cook. Scale and gut, if the fishmonger hasn't done this, and bone, if you wish (though it will taste sweeter if left on the bone). Dry the fish and rub salt all over and inside it. Place it on a plate that will fit inside the steamer, or on a trivet, or on a set of crossed chopsticks, in the wok.

Scatter the spring onions, bacon or ham, mushrooms and ginger over the fish, along with one tablespoon of the peanut oil and the rice wine, and steam on high heat for 15–25 mins, depending on the thickness of the fish. Drain off the juices and add them to the sauce ingredients in a saucepan and stir. Place the fish on a heated serving platter; heat the remaining 2 tablespoons of oil and pour over the fish and keep warm. Bring the sauce mixture to a boil and when thickened pour over the fish. Then spoon on the sesame oil and garnish with coriander leaves. Serve instantly, and let the guests pull the fish to bits as they eat it with their chopsticks.

FRANCES BISSELL'S TURKEY AND SCALLOP TERRINE WITH CORAL SAUCE

Makes a 450-g/1-lb terrine
Serves 4–8

As scallops are rarely available with their corals in the USA, cooks there will have to make the alternative tomato coulis instead of the coral sauce. It is equally good, I think. Frances Bissell says: 'This is an extremely delicately flavoured terrine and I would not want to serve too assertive a sauce with it. I like to accompany this dish with a coral sauce or with an unusual tomato coulis. I take a small piece of crystallised ginger, chop it finely and add it to the lightly cooked tomatoes, which I then blend and sieve. As a garnish I thinly slice and then cut into fine strips another piece of crystallised ginger and serve a little pile of this with each slice of terrine.'

170 g (6 oz) scallops with their corals
300 g (10 oz) turkey breast meat *plus* the 2 'fillets' removed whole from the breast
turkey liver and heart
6 Tbsp *crème fraîche* or double cream
1 egg
1 heaped Tbsp finely chopped coriander or parsley
150 ml (5 fl oz, ½ cup) turkey stock

Preheat the oven to 150–170°C (300–325°F, gas mark 2–3).

Clean the scallops, rinse them free of any sand, and pat dry on kitchen paper. Remove the coral and put aside, and cut the white part of the scallop into strips. Prepare the turkey by trimming any sinews from the breast and fillets, and trimming any fat or gristle from the heart and liver. Cut the giblets into strips and reserve, together with the fillets. Chop the breast meat into 2½-cm (1-in) chunks and put into the food processor bowl fitted with the steel blade. Season and process until smooth, using a third of the cream and the egg.

Lightly oil a 500-g (1-lb) loaf tin and put in a third of the processed mixture. Lay the turkey fillets on top of this – towards the middle – and cover with a little more of the mixture. Then press in strips of turkey liver and heart, down the length of the terrine. Spread some more of the processed mixture over the giblets, leaving about a third of the mixture in the bowl. Roll the scallop strips in the coriander or parsley, making sure they are completely covered in green, and lay them on the terrine leaving a border of ½ cm (¼ in) all around the outside of the terrine. Cover completely with the rest of the turkey mixture, and tap the bottom of the terrine firmly several times to settle the contents. Place in a roasting tin containing 2.5–5 cm (an inch or two) of water and place in the preheated moderate oven for an hour. Remove and allow to cool, then refrigerate until required.

It is vital to be absolutely certain that you allow enough time for the terrine to return to room temperature before serving. 'Few dishes are less appetising,' says Frances, 'than cold slabs of terrine straight from the fridge.'

To make the coral sauce, poach the reserved corals very gently in the turkey stock. Allow to cool and liquidise with the remaining cream and a little seasoning. Sieve before serving a puddle of sauce under or by the side of each slice of terrine.

LADY LOUSADA'S PIROZHKI

When Patricia Lousada was a ballet student with Balanchine, the big culinary festival was Easter. But at Christmas he handed these round with the drinks. You can use a huge variety of fillings – meat, fish or cabbage – so long as it is moist and well-seasoned. Lady Lousada says you can use puff pastry in place of the yeast dough, 'good, but not as authentic'.

Serves 8–12
For the dough
2 tsp dried easy-blend yeast
450 g (1 lb, 3½ cups) white flour
pinch salt
2 eggs
6 Tbsp warm milk
65 g (2½ oz, ¼ cup) softened butter

Stir the yeast into the flour and salt. Beat the eggs with the milk and mix into the flour, then add the butter and knead until smooth. Cover and leave to rise in a warm place until doubled in volume.

For the mushroom filling
½ large Spanish onion, minced
knob of butter
450 g (1 lb) brown cap mushrooms, finely sliced
squeeze of lemon juice
3 Tbsp soured or double or heavy cream
1 hard-boiled egg, chopped
3 Tbsp fresh coriander leaves, very finely chopped
salt and pepper
egg wash: 1 egg, 1 tsp water and a pinch of salt

Sauté the onion in butter until translucent. Add the mushrooms, lemon juice, salt and pepper, and cook, stirring, until the mushrooms start giving off their liquid. Then raise the heat to evaporate most of the liquid. Stir in the cream, hard-boiled egg and coriander. Taste for seasoning.

Preheat the oven to 200°C (400°F, gas mark 6).

Divide the dough into two and work with half at a time. Roll out thinly and cut into rounds with an 8.5-cm (3½-in) biscuit cutter. Roll out each round to make them thinner and larger, then place a tsp of filling in the top half. Brush the edge with egg wash and seal. Place on a baking tray. When you've used up the filling, glaze the pirozhki with the remaining egg wash and bake for 10 mins in the preheated oven.

SCALLOPED OR BAKED OYSTERS

The recipe used by my family called for spreading a well-buttered baking dish with a layer of saltine (or Jacob's cream cracker) crumbs, then a layer of oysters, seasoned with salt and white pepper, or a dusting of sweet paprika or a pinch of cayenne, along with bits of unsalted butter. Then you top with crumbs and make another layer, and so on, ending up with a layer of seasoned, buttered crumbs. Over this you pour all the carefully hoarded oyster liquor, and you cook it quickly in a hot oven until the crumb layer is just browning but the liquid has not bubbled up.

This is not the sort of recipe where quantities are relevant. In any case, nobody would dream of making it unless oysters were exceedingly cheap; or only available, as they were in my childhood, already shucked.

CHAPTER FOUR

Talking turkey

The poor old turkey has had a bad press since it was first domesticated. When we say 'he's a turkey', we are not only being rude about the third party's intellect, but we expect the second party, to whom we are talking, to laugh, and part of the joke is at the expense of the turkey, poor beast.

Turkeys are stupid, and highly strung, too. A loud noise or a bang will stampede them into the corner of their pen or barn, and they are perfectly capable of huddling together so tightly that the ones on top of the heap suffocate those under them. We speak of 'cold turkey', meaning coming abruptly off drugs or some substance on which we are dependent. We don't yet use the epithet 'turkey' to cast aspersion on a male's potency or virility; but we could do, because turkeys now have to be bred by artificial insemination. The turkey cocks, properly called stags, have been bred to be big-busted rather than stud-like. As a result they are too ungainly to copulate in the normal way, and tend to fall off the females' backs. We bred them to be big and ignored their eating quality. We should have seen it coming. As long ago as the 1930s one of André Simon's contributors to his *Encyclopedia of Gastronomy* wrote: 'A large turkey cock with sharp spurs is best stuffed by a taxidermist; it is an old bird to be avoided by all cooks.'

Dorothy Hartley's near-contempt for turkey (in her classic *Food in England*) was, she claimed, widely shared. She quotes an old saw, 'Turkeys heresays hops and beer/All came to England in one year.' (This country saying may be partly true. The first citation for 'hearsay' in the *OED* is dated 1532, when it was spelled 'here say', close to the time of the first appearance of turkey; but the controversy over hopped beer, when London brewers petitioned the Lord Mayor to forbid the addition of hops or herbs of any kind to beer, occurred in 1464.) The late Miss Hartley (1893–1985) dismissed the bird in so few words that she required a footnote to explain herself: 'Being a north-country woman,' she says, 'I have no enthusiasm for turkey.' In the appended note, however, she glosses herself: 'Northern farmers have chicken for Easter, duck and green peas for Whitsun, and a fine meaty goose for Christmas. Most northern farmers say that turkey is only like a big fowl.' Then, almost grudgingly, 'The best turkeys come from Norfolk.'

It was inevitable that the turkey, whose advantage over the better-tasting goose lies solely in his size and the ratio of his meat to his bones, would come to taste like boiled packets of blotting paper, at least in his most commercial manifestation. Turkey breeding and turkey fattening are now two distinct occupations.

The commercial breeder sees it as his job to provide chicks that put on weight as rapidly and cheaply as possible, and whose finished carcass has the appearance and weight desired by the Christmas and (now, in world terms more important) Thanksgiving market. The turkey stockman simply wants the bird that puts on the most weight for the lowest expenditure on feed. The customer, apparently, doesn't care how his turkey is reared or what his turkey tastes like, so long as it's cheap.

Just as this was bound to happen, however, it was also on the cards that a reaction would set in; that breeders would look back to older, tastier varieties, and that farmers would begin to farm their birds 'free range' and give them feed that would make their flesh more, rather than less attractive. The result is that we're living in the golden age of the turkey, where for a few pennies more per pound than the factory-farmed article, you can buy a turkey worth the eating. In Britain, and to some extent in France, the consumer can now choose from among turkeys of different races, and in the USA you can even eat wild turkey once again.

English turkeys simply were not cheap until Bernard Matthews came along, though the lower cost of imported birds made them much more accessible in the late Victorian era. To be sure, their price fluctuated. By 1555, C. Anne Wilson tells us, there were sufficient turkeys being sold in London for the authorities to fix the price, as they did that of other poultry, and the tariff was fixed at a massive six shillings for turkey cocks and two shillings eight pence for chicks. By 1572, she says, the price of cocks had dropped to three shillings four pence, and the hens, which always fetched a lower price, only one shilling eight pence. In 1898, J. A. R. Pimlott found (in *The Englishman's Christmas*, 1978) that native turkeys varied in price from five to 25 shillings per bird, and were in competition with turkeys imported from Ireland, Austria, France, Italy and Canada. Those from Italy could be had for as little as two shilling three-pence, and Canadian turkeys sold for only six or seven pence a pound, probably undercutting the cheapest English bird.

In the USA the statistics for turkey-eating are easy. No polls are needed to show that the percentage of the population that eats turkey at Thanksgiving is nearly one hundred. In Britain, however, gallopavo-phagy (turkey-eating) is not even now universal. In 1955 a poll showed that 41 per cent of people in Greater London, for example, had chicken for Christmas and only 38 per cent ate turkey. Since 1974, though, the balance has been reversed, reports J. A. R. Pimlott. From 1974–7 turkey sales remained steady at about ten million (which works out at one turkey per 5.6 people), whereas sales of chicken actually *decreased* at Christmas from the normal weekly figure of five to six million.

A poll conducted in November 1991 showed that 77 out of 100 Britons had the intention of eating turkey for Christmas. There was, unusually, no north/south divide on this matter; you were equally likely to be eating turkey if you lived in the south of England or in the Midlands or the north. But there *was* a class distinction: 82 per cent of socioeconomic group AB said they would be eating turkey. So if you are in one of the top professions, and are upper-middle class or an aristocrat, chances are you ate turkey for

Christmas 1991. (The poll was conducted for the British Turkey Information Service who, not surprisingly, do not give us the more interesting information as to what the other 18 per cent had for Christmas dinner.) Another poll, by Mori for *The Times*, asked respondents on December 27 what they had done at Christmas. Seventy-nine per cent said they had watched television, 72 per cent had stayed at home (rather than going home to Mum, or out to friends or neighbours) and 70 per cent spent Christmas Day 'having roast turkey'. Sixty-six per cent admitted that they had drunk booze.

Three varieties of turkey are reared commercially in the USA. The Bronze, with its rich gold plumage barred with white on the wings and edging the tail feathers, is the largest. An adult stag usually weighs 36 lb (16 kg). The Mammoth Bronze was, Raymond Sokolov says, 'the first truly American hybrid', bred at Pont Judith, Rhode Island. The White Holland is known in Europe as the White Austrian. Its plumage is pure white as its name promises, and the average weight of a stag is 28 lb (13 kg). The Bourbon Red is a handsome bird with rich red-brown plumage highlighted by the white wing and tail feathers, and an average weight for stags of 30 lb (14 kg).

Smaller birds are preferred in Britain, where the supermarkets experience a good deal of demand for turkeys weighing more than 14 lb (6 kg) but less than 20 lb (9 kg). The British consumer seemed to dislike the black pin feathers that speckled the carcass of the gamey-flavoured Black Norfolk, and it declined in popularity in favour of Bronzes and especially the (I think inferior-tasting) Whites. However, Blacks and Bronzes and various hybrids, with plenty of breast meat but leaner lines and more developed flavour, are making a comeback, especially with mail-order sales and speciality butchers.

It used to take about nine months to fatten a turkey for the table (before commercial feeds were available, and all turkeys ranged freely, chicks were hatched in late February and early March). Now day-old chicks are bought in late July or early August, and good farmers feed them on cereals and allow them to range as freely as is possible, so that they peck at grit, and eat flavour-making insects and plants. Turkeys are especially fond of stinging nettles, a plant introduced to Britain as a foodstuff by the Romans. The feed is, to my mind, the most important thing about a turkey, because you can taste the quality of the feed in the large amount of subcutaneous fat laid down by turkeys; if the bird has eaten fishmeal late in its life, it will taste fishy.

In America there is a demand for turkey all year around, in the form of roasts, escalopes and even sausages. The British eat a much smaller amount of these value-added products. One of the reasons for the higher US sales is the promotion of turkey as a particularly healthy meat, which, being lean and low in cholesterol, it actually is.

THE TURKEY CAN BE HANDSOME. THERE ARE GOLD glints in the plumage of the modern Bronze and Black turkeys, and I was surprised, on a visit to John Munson's turkey farm near Colchester, to see that the wrinkled necks of the Whites are a fetching Post-Modernist blue. Nonetheless, it remains a singularly clumsy bird, lacking the grace of the swan or peacock or the relatively streamlined shape of most game birds; turkeys are even less gainly than are chicken and geese.

Why 'turkey'? Naming this fowl has been difficult for mankind. We now know that turkeys have no more to do with the Levant than Apaches, Comanches and Blackfeet do with the Subcontinent. They seem to have arrived in Europe first in 1523–4 (says Reay Tannahill in *Food in History*) or in 1530 (says the contributor, H. W. Brand, to André Simon's *Encyclopedia*). Both agree that they were taken to Spain by Levant or Turkey traders, since Seville was a regular port of call as they plied between Spain and the eastern Mediterranean. The bird came from Mexico, where its Nahuatl name was *uexolotl*. Clearly, no Englishman could be expected to try to pronounce that; so the thing carried was given the name of the carrier and became the 'turkie cock'.

Still more confusion set in because, at precisely the same time, the Portuguese were bringing back the guinea fowl from West Africa, and Ms Tannahill thinks that the Turkish merchants picked up that bird as well, and brought it back to an England that had eaten it in Roman times but since forgotten it. Remember that the turkey we are talking about is the skinny Mexican bird, not the plump article we put on our present-day table, and you can see how the muddle arose. 'The guinea-fowl,' says Ms Tannahill, 'was not unlike a miniaturised version of the turkey in looks and in its reluctance to fly.' That is why turkey still bears the generic Latin name for guinea fowl, *Meleagris*, while Linnaeus also gave it the species name, *gallopavo*, showing still more confusion. Its first half means 'chicken' and its second 'peacock'.

This has led some historians to think that the turkey was an almost mythical beast, and that any 16th-century reference in English to 'turkey' really meant 'guinea fowl'. Not so, says Ms Tannahill. Cranmer's sumptuary laws, which he promulgated in 1541, and which forbade ecclesiastics to eat more than one of the 'greater fowls' at a single meal, 'classed turkey-cocks with birds of the size of crane and swan, not – as he would have done with guinea-fowl – with capons and pheasants'. Moreover there is another contemporary reference to a Sir William Petre, who kept his table birds in a pen in his orchard in Essex; and the inventory included 'partridges, pheasants, guinea-hens, turkey hens and such like'. There was even a grant of arms made in 1550 in which one of the heraldic devices was quite clearly a turkey.

One of those who made this error was E. D. Boulenger, whose *A Naturalist at the Dinner Table* (1927) was used by André Simon. Boulenger quotes the *First Part of King Henry IV* (Act II, sc.1, v.19), ''Odsbody! the turkeys in my pannier are quite starved' and goes on to say: 'One forgives Shakespeare for introducing a name that would have been quite unknown in the days of Henry IV, but one must not forget that he was referring to birds which we know as Guinea-fowls, two or more of which could be cooped in a pannier.' And, 'even later, in the 1633 edition of Dr Hart's *Diet of the Diseased* (p. 78), when we read "Turkies of a middle age and reasonably fat, are a good, wholesome, nourishing food, and little inferior to the best capon", it is obvious that the reference was to *Guinea-fowls*'. In his attractive pedantry, in fact, Boulenger has forgotten that the turkey increased in size very greatly from its introduc-

The Christmas Hamper by Robert Braithwaite Martineau (1826–69)

tion in Shakespeare's time, and that the bird in question was not a full-size modern gobbler.

Reay Tannahill has great fun pointing out that of the Old World nations, the Egyptians alone called the bird a turkey ('*dikrumi*, the "fowl of Turkey"') and she remarks that they were, after all, in a geographical position to have known better. We Anglophones were almost alone, too, in confusing it with a guinea fowl, with the most unfortunate exception of Linnaeus, who in his zeal to name *everything*, made the turkey's scientific name as opaque as its vulgar one.

But the bird was destined to cause linguistic misunderstanding. The French, Italians and Germans were never under the illusion that the bird had come from Turkey. They thought it came from India. So the French called it *coq d'Inde*. Eventually the creature lost its apostrophe and became *dinde* (the hen) and then *dindon* (the cock) and *dindonneau* (the poult). Italians baptised the bird *galle d'India*, Germans *indianische Henn*. Best of all, the Turks called the turkey *hindi*.

Aha, you might say: doesn't this actually show that the early 16th-century French, Italians, Germans and Turks actually knew the New World origins of the bird? After all, the Americas, as Ms Tannahill puts it, 'stubbornly remained "the new Indies" long after the error had been discovered'. Well, yes, except that the Germans, the Dutch and the Scandinavians actually got more specific about the fowl, and began to call it *calecutische Henn*, *Kalkoen* and *Kalkon*, all suggesting that it had come from 'Calicut, the place where da Gama first landed on the south-west coast of India. The Persians also had a contribution to make, calling the turkey the *filmurgh* or "elephant bird"' (by which they probably just meant that it was quite large).

In this nomenclatural comedy, the Indians themselves got much closer to the mark. In at least one of their languages they called it *peru*, which is, after all, only a few hundred miles wrong. It reached India, says Ms Tannahill, in the 1820s, where it was received as a novel and interesting food. It had probably come to India via the Philippines, which was then a Spanish possession governed from Mexico.

On the linguistic evidence, the Old World was quick to adopt the turkey for its table. The joke is, as Raymond Sokolov points out in his superbly scholarly and funny book *Why We Eat What We Eat* (1991),

that the turkey consumed in its millions by Americans every Thanksgiving is *not* the direct descendant of the native American wild fowl: 'The first domesticated North American turkeys were, in fact, imported from Europe.'

When the conquistadors reached Mexico there were only two domesticated species of livestock, the turkey and the dog. Turkey was thought nicer to eat. (I can tell you from my own experience that the Aztecs were right about this.) Some authorities claim it was generally cooked with a little chocolate, of which more, later. Meanwhile in the Jamestown settlement (1609), the first colonists, who were, by some accounts, bone-idle and dependent on the Indians for their food, don't seem to have been acquainted with turkey. But by 1620 in Massachusetts, the Pilgrim Fathers were already able to recognise turkey. Naturally they sowed confusion about its name; but it didn't matter because the native Indians obligingly called it *furkee* in their own language, though it isn't clear whether this refers to a wild or a domesticated bird, and we must assume that it differed from the domesticated Mexican bird brought to Europe by the Spaniards.

Now here's the good bit: it was English colonists who introduced the Mexican turkey to New England. Norfolk breeders had got to work, and scarcely a hundred years after the Columbian voyages, English settlers were taking to the New World a new, improved turkey. Both the Norfolk Black and the White Holland turkeys, Raymond Sokolov triumphantly tells his American readers, made their way to New England from old England where they had first been bred.

The English breeders were busy and enterprising. It is said, by Sokolov among others, that 'the English custom of the Christmas turkey was established in 1585'. It is certainly true that there are recipes for what C. Anne Wilson (in *Food and Drink in Britain*, 1973) calls 'the Christmas turkeys of late Tudor and Stuart days' (they were 'sticked full of cloves in the roasting'), and there is more than one Elizabethan recipe for turkey pie – but the same books give recipes for bustards, peacocks, cranes and swans. None of these was everyday fare. To quibble just a bit with this particular date, though, except for times when there was a glut of imported birds on the market, turkey mostly remained a rare and expensive delicacy in England until well after the Second World War; but it was true that it had become associated with Christmas on the tables of at least some of the landed gentry even during the reign of the first Elizabeth.

Indeed, in England it showed that it is possible to break down the general resistance of the English to novel foods, for soon after its introduction in the 16th century, when it graced the tables of the well-to-do, it, says Boulenger, 'displaced in a very short space of time the peacock, curlew, bittern, whimbrel and other fowls of the air and the sea, which figured on most bills of fare up to the beginning of the 17th century'. Mind you, it stayed on the tables exclusively of the well-to-do for several centuries. It was long a dish for great country houses, where there remained the need for a dramatic-looking bird that would feed large numbers of house guests. At first, there was little call for it in London except at the grandest tables where large numbers were regularly entertained. But by the 1650s the wife of Samuel Pepys was keeping her own turkeys in London, and in 1659 his diary notes that she dressed and served up leftover cold turkey for his dinner.

Turkeys were walked to London from Norfolk and Suffolk in droves of a thousand by the mid-17th century. The trip could take as much as three months, and so it often began in August at the end of the harvest. The roads were often muddy and hard-going, and the turkeys were sometimes shod, either in bags made of sacking, or with actual leather boots. Geese also had to be driven to market; but these sometimes ferocious animals will not tolerate shoes. (Hence the expression 'to shoe a goose' for a thankless task.) So their feet were dipped in tar, which was then sprinkled with grit. J. A. R. Pimlott, the pioneering social historian, relates a tale of two peers of the realm who, to settle a bet, staged a race between a flock of geese and a flock of turkeys from Norfolk to the Christmas market in London. Though the turkeys moved faster, the geese won by nearly 24 hours, as they ate while they walked and did not need to stop for the night. Despite this prodigious movement of birds, and that the middle classes of the time ate a protein-rich diet with what we should consider to be too much meat, turkey was still hardly an everyday item of food.

The supreme 18th-century use of the turkey at Christmas was in the famous Yorkshire Christmas pie, the last vestige of the medieval 'sotleties' ('subtleties'), of which the best-known example was the pie with four-and-twenty live blackbirds baked in it. In the recipe quoted by C. Anne Wilson in *Food and Drink in Britain* this begins with a boned turkey, into which is inserted a goose, stuffed with a fowl, in which is a partridge, and in it a pigeon. These go into a 'standing crust', sewn up to look like a whole turkey, and the sides of the pie are filled with chunks of hare on one side, and moor game or wildfowl on the other. Four pounds of butter are added before the very thick lid is laid on and the pie baked. The recipe concludes: 'These pies are often sent to *London* in a box as presents; therefore the walls must be well built.' Yorkshire goose pie is the same, but with the goose outermost, which means that the turkey, the second bird, must have been a small one.

The bourgeoisie really began to get a bite of the turkey around the time of Charles Dickens, and it was not until the 1890s that imported turkeys were cheap enough to grace the Christmas table of the average office clerk. In this century turkey was still smart in the era of the bright young things, smarter than chicken, anyway; and roast chicken was itself a very special treat for ordinary people in Britain until the 1960s, as the 1955 survey cited above showed. John Munson, an East Anglian turkey farmer whose family has been involved in the business for generations, tells me that he is certain it was not until 'well after the Second World War that most ordinary working men could put a turkey on their family's table'.

FRANCE WAS RECEPTIVE TO THE NOVELTY OF THE turkey and accepted it immediately, in contrast to the initial Gallic suspicion of the potato and tomato, for example. After its introduction to Spain from Mexico in the early 16th century, it spread rapidly throughout Europe. The first mention of turkeys found in her researches by Barbara Ketcham Wheaton (in *Savouring the Past: The French Kitchen and Table from 1300 to 1789*, 1983) was in November 1528. (Thus Grimod de la Reynière was simply wrong when he said that 'the first turkey cock to visit these shores arrived in 1570 and was dished up at the nuptials of Charles IX'; this passage, which misled historians for over 150 years, is quoted in Giles MacDonogh in *A Palate in Revolution*, 1987.) These earliest turkeys were six pairs kept as *pets*, by a 10-year-old princess, Jeanne d'Albret. She gave half their eggs to a nearby convent, so you can see why the number of turkeys grew so rapidly. At a banquet in Paris in 1549 for Catherine de Medici 66 turkeys were eaten; and by 1565 there are records of turkeys being bought in Toulouse for another royal banquet.

Clearly, in France it was also initially a bird for the well-to-do. Barbara Wheaton thinks that the reason for the rapid spread of turkey through Europe was that it could replace peacock as a roast for banquets, though she has never found a recipe in which turkey, as was done with peacock, was sewn back into its own skin and feathers to be served. But she thinks that turkey was enough like peacock that the latter could serve as a model for how to use the newcomer, which hastened its assimilation. One can see her point that as a luxury meat, turkey was a necessity at any ambitious banquet; never having tasted peacock, however, I cannot comment on the similarity of the two. But Charles Estienne, writing in 1564, wasn't so sure: 'It is very true that his [the turkey's] flesh is fine and delicate, but without taste and of hard digestion . . . And this is the cause why men use to powder them, lard them much, and season them with spices. There is much more pleasure and goodness in the flesh of a peacock.' (The English translation of his crie and furiousness when they are come to be great ones: or continuall cheaping whiles they be little . . .' This was merely the earliest of the turkey's bad press notices. About 1600, Mrs Wheaton discovered, Olivier de Serres complained that it was 'very frail when young, always greedy, and so stupid and brutish that it has not got the sense to avoid the depredations of men and beasts . . . Even the mothers kill their own offspring by walking on them.' By the next century, Mrs Wheaton points out, the poor turkey's silliness was so universally recognised that *dindonné* came to mean 'duped', like English 'gulled'.

Turkey was popular to eat, though; so popular that she found a 1557 menu in which turkey figured in two of the four courses of a triumphal banquet. It appeared boiled, served with oysters and cardoons, for the first course, and roasted and served cold for the third. The first recipes stem from the middle of the next century, and because the shape of the turkey lends itself to it, they usually incorporate a stuffing, most often a meat-based one. La Varenne's recipe from 1654 involves boning the turkey, leaving only the intact skin, with legs, wings and backbone still in place. The meat is chopped with that of some pigeons, plus veal, pork fat and egg yolks, to make a farce that you flavour with ground cloves and capers. The bird is reconstructed with the farce, then spit-roasted until nearly cooked. The cooking is finished by poaching the bird in a good bouillon with mushrooms, following which you make a sauce with the liquid and a chopped bacon and flour roux, made piquant with lemon juice and vinegar. Then, if raspberries are in season, you add them to the dish. Unfortunately, remarks Mrs Wheaton, the raspberries ruin whatever

In The Market (detail) by Victor Gabriel Gilbert (1847–1933)

Maison Rustique, or the Countrie Farme, quoted by Barbara Wheaton.)

Most of his complaints, though, had to do with the turkey's behaviour: 'Whatsoever he was that brought us these birdes from the island of India lately discovered by the Spaniards and Portingales, whether we call them cockes or peacockes of India, hath more fitted and provided for the tooth than for any profit. For they may rightly be termed coffers to cast oates into, a devouring gulfe of meate, and wherein there is no other pleasure to be taken, but only in their wine you drink. This recipe, incidentally, comes from La Varenne's chapter on simpler dishes for occasions when the cook does not have a completely equipped kitchen.

Other turkey preparations she has come across include little ragoûts made with the trimmings and giblets, and pies, such as one made with a turkey stuffed with young pigeons, the palate of an ox, sheep's kidneys and sweetbreads, cockscombs, artichoke bottoms, mushrooms and truffles. A 1767 *Dictionnaire Portatif de Cuisine* lists forty different ways of cooking turkey, roast, boiled and fricassée, and embellished with everything from anchovies to cucumbers. But by the late 18th century, the gastronomic supremacy of the truffled turkey was widely acknowledged.

Turkey eating *seems* to have been more democratic earlier on in France than in Britain. In the early 19th century, Brillat-Savarin (the lawyer and theorist of gastronomy whose dates were 1755–1826) said, in *La Physiologie du Goût*, his 'Meditations on Transcendental Gastronomy' published at his own expense the year before his death, that he regarded turkey as the biggest and, 'if not the most delicate, at least the most flavourful of our domestic birds'. He went on to say (in M. F. K. Fisher's translation) that 'it also enjoys the unique advantage of attracting to it every class of society'. As examples of turkey's classlessness he cites 'the vine tenders and the plowmen of our countryside', and by means of a rhetorical question claims that on a long winter night when these rustics want to treat themselves they roast a turkey over the kitchen fire.

When the hardworking mechanic or artisan gets a few friends together for a rare evening of relaxation, 'what is the traditional main dish of the evening he offers? A turkey stuffed with sausages or with Lyons chestnuts.' Finally, 'in our most renowned gastronomical circles', in those exquisite salons where even the discussion of politics must yield pride of place to considerations of food and philosophical conversation on the sense of taste, the most highly appreciated, eagerly anticipated dish of honour is always a truffled turkey. And in an arch aside, thought by his translator to be a boastful tease, Brillat-Savarin implies that if we could but read the entries in his 'secret diary' we would learn of the extraordinary aphrodisiac properties of the 'restorative juices' of the truffled turkey.

It is difficult to work out whether Brillat-Savarin was claiming that turkey was eaten often by all classes, which would imply that it was cheap; or whether he was simply saying that it is the meat of choice for celebrations in every class, which might mean that it was still very expensive. He actually gives the cost of a truffled turkey – 20 francs (this would be in the early 1820s in Paris, when a substantial meat main course in a good restaurant cost one or two francs) – but I should imagine that then, as now, the truffle cost more than the turkey.

Against this interpretation, Brillat-Savarin writes as though the 'fairly large trade' in turkeys is an important part of the national wealth because it is a valuable, expensive commodity. He says that raising turkeys makes it more easy for farmers to pay their land rents, and that young country women can increase their dowries by raising turkeys because 'town dwellers who want to treat themselves to a feast from this outlandish meat must give up their gold in return'.

Brillat-Savarin's speculations on how the turkey got to the French table echo Grimod's, which appeared in the 15 years between 1803 and 1818. Both writers were wrong about the date of introduction of the turkey into France, placing it far later than it actually was, and both attributed its naturalisation to the Jesuits. The order, said Brillat-Savarin, raised them in great quantity on a farm near Bourges, and that is why, he claimed, *jesuit* was common slang for a turkey. 'Nobody who likes baby turkey (and who in the world does not?),' said Grimod on the same subject, 'could possible hate the Jesuits; for it is said that we owe it to these good fathers (themselves no turkeys) for having introduced the bird to France . . . Ah! What in heaven does it matter where it comes from, as long as it is tender?' Grimod obviously had a thing about infant turkeys, though, as in another passage he mysteriously remarks: 'It is said that eating the feet helps you to sleep; but you sleep well anyway in the company of baby turkeys.'

Grimod commented sharply, however, that 'the turkey has become so common of late that no one dares serve it at table unless it has arrived directly from the Périgord and has been stuffed with several pounds of truffles'. Grimod, a scion of the nobility, could not tolerate this sort of snobbery, and said: 'True gourmands rise above prejudice . . . A simple turkey from the Gâtinais or from Orléans, when the flesh is good and white, young, tender and delicate, is in their eyes preferable by far to the Périgourdine, which is often dry and tough despite its rich sauce. It is thus,' continues the world's first professional food

critic, whose withered, claw-like hands made him physically repugnant to most women (though not to his long-standing mistress, Adelaide Feuchère, whom he married over his mother's objection in 1812), 'with a little common girl, who, when she is blonde and fresh, dressed in the simplest of clothes, will appear highly appetizing in the estimation of the connoisseur. She will always be a better bet than some rich old dowager, dripping with pride and brilliants.' (The translations are all from MacDonogh.)

Both Grimod and Brillat-Savarin appear to have been slightly obsessed by the subject of turkey, and each gave the bird a lot of space in their almost equally rambling reflections on gastronomy. Brillat-Savarin, though, does seem to have taken a genuine interest in how the birds were farmed, and hit upon a truth known to the modern turkey farmer. Rain is dangerous for turkeys, and they dislike it intensely, although not for the wonderfully imaginative reason he gives. His researches revealed that the survival rate for domesticated turkeys on French farms in the middle of the 18th century was only 50 per cent; whereas by the 1820s it was up to 75 per cent. 'Rainstorms,' he learnt, 'have always been the worst disaster for them: heavy raindrops, beaten against them by the wind, hurt their tender unprotected skulls and cause their death.'

Grimod, however, took turkey-lore to the furthest reaches. What could he have meant by this? '*Method of Knowing They are Young and Tender*: You should put your index finger into the anus of the animal and suck it immediately afterwards, at the same time breathing in heavily. This trick never fails.' (MacDonogh translation.)

Brillat-Savarin is a mine of information on the turkey, not least because he actually shot a wild turkey, in the course of his visit to Hartford, Connecticut in October 1794, but was uncharacteristically reticent on the matter of the recipe for wild turkey, which infuriated his translator. Mrs Fisher's gloss is, as so often, better than the text itself. She tells us that 'the only living human being I have known who could speak casually of hunting, cleaning, and then roasting a wild turkey, and all that in the state of Arkansas' told her that the wild turkey is normally stuffed with cornbread and butter. 'In general, this woman said to me, hoisting blue denim pants over her flat hip-bones and looking Chinese-like over her straight lower lids, in general wild turkey isn't thought highly of and people who cook them at all slice off the two breast-meat pieces and fry them in good hog fat. (*Filets de coq d'Inde sauvage*, I thought), and they sure taste damn near as good as steak, she said. But if they are roasted they take a lot of basting to keep from being dry, and yes they should be stuffed.'

Ranking high in the literature of turkey-eating, however, is Brillat-Savarin's tale of the gallopavo-phagic prowess of General Prosper Sibuet, first aide-de-camp to General Masséna, who died a hero's death on the battlefield in 1813. He was a countryman of Brillat-Savarin's, from near Belley, in the Ain. 'Prosper,' Brillat-Savarin relates, 'when he was 18 years old, and had that happy appetite which is Nature's way of saying that she is busy finishing off the creation of a fine sturdy man,' went as usual one night into the kitchen of the local inn belonging to Genin. It was the meeting place of the old men of Belley, who went there to eat chestnuts and drink *bourru*, which

The American Wild Turkey Cock by J.J. Audubon (1758–1851)

is what they, and the people of Chablis, too, call the newly fermented white wine. (I can tell you that *bourru* is a little cloudy, very fruity and delicious, and seriously laxative.)

There was a beautiful golden brown turkey which the landlord, Genin, had just removed from the spit, and its aroma was itself a temptation. The older men, no longer hungry, paid it no attention. Young Prosper's 'digestive powers', however, reacted violently to its smell, and he boasted that, though he had just arisen from the dinner table, he was capable of eating the entire turkey. His bluff was called, in the outlandish local dialect, by Bouvier du Bouchet, described as a 'fat farmer': *Sez vosu mezé, z'u payo*' – If you eat it all, I'll pay for it; but if you don't eat it all, you'll pay for the turkey and *I'll* eat what you've left.

Brillat-Savarin describes the contest: Prosper, 'the young athlete took off a wing very nicely, and swallowed it in two mouthfuls, after which he cleared his teeth by munching the neck of the bird'. To make a pause he drank a glass of wine. 'Then he attacked the leg, ate it with the same poise, and dispatched a second glass of wine, to prepare a passageway for what was still to come. Soon the second wing followed the same path: it disappeared, and the contestant, more and more active, seized upon the last of the four members, when the unhappy farmer cried out mournfully' (and in dialect) that he could see that the future general had won the wager, and that, as he was obliged to pay for the turkey, couldn't Prosper please leave a bit of it for him to eat himself. In fact, he not only restrained his appetite and left the table a little hungry and the rest of the turkey for the fat farmer, but had the good grace to pay for both it and the wine.

Alexandre Dumas *père* died in 1870, and three years later his *Grand Dictionnaire de Cuisine* was published. It is full of mistakes, but none so glaring, perverse or funny as those in his entry for turkey, in which the bird's name is almost the only thing he gets right. He leaned heavily on the accounts of Grimod and of Brillat-Savarin, whose turkey-obsession he shares. He disputes the earlier writers' turkey-lore, mostly; and he tells almost certainly spurious anecdotes about them – all in the course of this single entry. In the first place, he insists that turkeys were known to the Greeks, and that they called the birds *Méléagrides* after Meleager, King of Macedonia 'who brought them to Greece in the 3,559th year after the creation of the world'. (I am using Alan and Jane Davidson's excellent translation of 1978.) Dumas is perfectly aware that *Meleagris* is the scientific name for guinea fowl, but he says that those birds are misnamed, for Pliny (in book 37, chapter II) gives an unmistakable description under that name of turkeys. Moreover, in one of the lost plays of Sophocles, he insists, the playwright used the device of a chorus of turkeys to lament the death of King Meleager. Dumas accounts for the absence of any reference to turkeys in ancient Rome by blustering. Why is there no mention of them? Perhaps an epidemic wiped them all out. The Romans raised turkeys on small farms, he asserts, and it is just too bad that history doesn't tell us what happened to them; but we do know, says he, that turkeys became so rare that the Romans kept them in cages, as we do parrots.

Dumas's best turkey story is about Nicolas Boileau (1636–1711), the translator of Longinus and greatest literary critic of his age. Dumas prefaces the tale by saying (falsely) that turkeys react to the colour red as do bulls. Boileau, he says, was attacked by a turkey as a child; when the turkey saw the red of his jacket, he became so enraged that he 'so wounded the young Nicolas with his pecks that the latter, no longer capable of ever becoming an erotic poet, chose in consequence to be a satirical poet and to slander women'. This was also the cause, claims Dumas, of Boileau's 'secret aversion to the Jesuits'.

TURKEY RECIPES ARE SIMILAR THE WORLD OVER, as they are still uncommon birds except in Europe and the Americas. They do exist in the Middle East, says Claudia Roden in *A New Book of Middle Eastern Food* (1985), where they 'range very freely and are small and tough, more like game birds. So they are usually stewed rather than roasted.' Turkeys are not common food birds in China and Southeast Asia, though of course they can be bought in Hong Kong, Singapore and other cosmopolitan areas; and imaginative Oriental cooks such as Ken Hom have devised recipes for turkeys using oriental flavourings and techniques. Except in hotels and restaurants, ovens are rare, still, in this fuel-poor part of the world, and roasting is an uncommon cooking technique.

So it was, says Elisabeth Lambert Ortiz in her authoritative *The Book of Latin American Cooking* (1969), 'until recently when industrialization brought gas and electric stoves into the kitchens of Mexico to replace the charcoal stoves of the past'. In the home of the turkey, only breads and cakes were cooked in ovens except for roast turkey itself, usually with a hearty meat stuffing. 'I was a little taken aback,' she writes, 'the first time I encountered it; it seemed such a double richness, meat and bird.'

In fact, Mexico has been faithful to the turkey throughout its history, though Mexicans, like us, now eat a cultivated bird that is quite different from its scrawny, wild ancestor. Diana Kennedy, in the 1972 revised edition of *The Cuisines of Mexico*, remembered when she first went to Mexico, just before Christmas, seeing the traffic halted in Mexico City itself as a *campesino* drove his flock of turkeys through the great city, selling them door to door in the sidestreets. She also recalled hearing the sound of gobbling on the flat rooftops and even in the new high-rise apartment blocks, from then until Christmas Eve; for each household kept and fattened its own turkey on household scraps. Mrs Kennedy maintains that even before the arrival of the Spaniards, the wild turkey, *quajalote*, was already roasted (on a spit, of course), as well as casseroled with indigenous foods such as tomatoes, chillies and ground pumpkin seeds.

Turkey is still a food of importance in Yucatán (though not so much further north in the direction of Mexico City where *gallinas*, fat hens, are preferred), and Mrs Kennedy cites a single 'modest' regional Yucatán cookery book that gives 29 typical recipes for cooking turkey. She lists turkey *en escabeche oriental* (which she translates as an onion and chilli 'souse', in which a large quantity of onions, sliced, blanched and briefly marinated in vinegar, is added with chillies at the end of the cooking time to a turkey coated in a paste of garlic and spices, and poached in stock, before being coated again with the remainder of the spice paste and grilled); *en relleno blanco*, with a 'white' stuffing that is, in fact, not white at all, but the same beef and pork forcemeat used for *queso relleno*, the now-traditional Yucatán dish of a whole stuffed Dutch cheese; and *relleno negro*, the 'black' stuffing of minced meat with a paste of burnt dried chillies and spices.

But of course the most famous turkey dish of

Mexico combines the bird with the other native ingredient that is South America's most important contribution to the world's larder, chocolate. The French eat turkey and chocolate at Christmas, too, but not in the same dish, and it is always amusing to see the astonished look on the Frenchman's face when he learns that this is one of the earliest known recipes for turkey. I had the pleasure of being the first to tell Raymond Blanc, chef of Le Manoir aux Quat'Saisons, in my opinion Britain's best restaurant, about this most ancient of turkey recipes. He recovered his gastronomic composure immediately, by pointing out to me that using a little chocolate in a sauce for game is not unknown in Europe, 'and surely,' he replied with Cartesian rigour, 'turkey was originally a game bird.'

'No special festival,' says Diana Kennedy, 'is complete without *mole poblano de guajolote*. It is prepared with loving care, and even today, more often than not, it is the one dish that brings out the *metate*: chillies, spices, nuts, seeds, and tortillas are all ground on it.' (The *metate* is a sloping piece of volcanic rock supported on three thick legs, to which village women apply their *mano* or *metlapil*, or grinding stone, to pulverise corn, chillies, etc., very laboriously. Mrs Kennedy says that when she wanted to take it to New York with her, her Mexican removal men jokingly called it a *licuadora azteca*, or Aztec food processor.) For the village fiestas, each woman is allotted a task. Some kill and clean the turkeys, some toast and grind the chillies, some prepare the maize, which has to be soaked and cleaned to make the tamales, others grind the spices.

There are so many versions of this dish that not only does each village and municipality have its own

way of preparing it, each cook has a variation of her own. 'A few more *mulatos* here, less *anchos*, or a touch of *chipotle*,' says Mrs Kennedy, detailing the different chillies, 'cooked with the turkey; some insist on onion, others won't tolerate it.' Cooks in Puebla itself, the place the dish is named for, toast the chillies, sometimes using only *mulatos*, over an open fire and grind them until they're dry.

Mole comes from a Nahuatl word *molli*, which itself means 'concoction', or a sauce made from any of the chillies, whether sweet, pungent or fiery hot. 'It *isn't* a chocolate sauce,' Diana Kennedy insists. 'One little piece of chocolate (and in Mexico we used to grind toasted cacao beans for the *mole*) goes into a large casserole full of rich dark-brown and russet chillies.' Though people often think they won't like this dish, Mrs Kennedy has always found that her guests are surprised by how harmonious the sauce is without any spice or seasoning dominating – and I've never met anyone who could guess that the mystery ingredient is chocolate.

The origins of the dish are not known though some writers speculate that the Aztecs themselves were the first to combine turkey and chocolate. It is certain that they made a drink from chocolate, and Elisabeth Lambert Ortiz, whose authority is great in these matters, says it was a royal dish of the Aztec court. Because it contained chocolate, she says, it was not only forbidden to women, but reserved for the higher priesthood, the military nobility and royalty; and she says that Cortés, the Spanish Conquistador, was served turkey with chocolate at the court of the emperor.

Most writers think the recipe for *mole poblano*

(the name for the sauce; it can be served with chicken, pork and other foods, but is most often associated with turkey) was invented in the 17th century by a nun, Sor Andrea de la Asunción, sister superior at the convent of Santa Rosa in the city of Puebla de los Angeles. Diana Kennedy says the most often told version of the tale is that, wishing to thank the Archbishop for having built a convent for her order, she constructed a dish that combined the ingredients of the New World, chilli, chocolate, tomatoes, pumpkin seeds, maize and turkey, with the spices of the Old World, such as cloves, cinnamon, aniseed and sesame.

Elisabeth Lambert Ortiz doesn't think the nuns invented the dish, because she is convinced it was known to the Aztecs. 'All the same,' she concedes, 'I do think we owe the sisters a debt. They recorded the recipe, which might otherwise have been lost, and they substituted familiar ingredients for some of the more exotic herbs and spices used in the emperor's day. I'd be prepared to swear that in the past allspice (a native spice) was used instead of cloves and cinnamon brought by Spain from the East, but since the flavour is much the same, why fuss?'

Diana Kennedy gives another story of the origins of this greatest of all Mexican sauces, one that still attributes its invention to the convent of Santa Rosa. This time it was the Viceroy, Don Juan de Palafox y Mendoza, who was visiting Puebla and dining at the convent. The banquet was being prepared by Fray Pascual. 'Turkeys were cooking in *cazuelas* on the fire,' writes Mrs Kennedy, 'as Fray Pascual, scolding his assistants for their untidiness, gathered up all the spices they had been using and put them together onto a tray a sudden gust of wind swept across the kitchen and spilled over into the *cazuelas*.' This would account for the enormous variety of spices in the recipe. In Diana Kennedy's version *anchos*, *mulatos* and *pasilla* chillies are used with the turkey and its giblets, carrot, onion, garlic, peppercorns, green tomatoes, cloves, cinnamon, coriander seeds, aniseed, chilli seeds, sesame seeds, raisins, almonds, pumpkin seeds, tortilla, French bread and Mexican chocolate. Mrs Ortiz's recipe adds peanuts to that list.

In a way, the history of the dish hardly matters. As Alfredo Ramos Espinosa says in *Semblanza Mexicana* (quoted by Mrs Kennedy): 'Whether it was prepared for archbishop or viceroy, by the nuns or by the angels, the very thought of it makes your mouth water.'

However, as Raymond Sokolov points out in a different context to that of a cookery manual, it is very instructive that people have bothered to construct a pedigree for *mole poblano*. 'Puebla in the 17th century,' he reminds us, 'was a hub of novelty, just the sort of place where a refined nun would mix chocolate, chillies and imported ingredients such as cinnamon and coriander for a sauce to go with the great Aztec bird.' Others have noted, as indeed I have done myself, that the sauce that results from combining all these ingredients is reminiscent of Asian flavours; and Sokolov thinks it is even possible that 'our taste buds are hinting at an historical truth. Probably not, but the legend of *mole poblano* as an invented sauce concocted by a non-Aztec with non-Spanish and local ingredients is itself worthy of note. Even if the account is only a fable, it is a fable that shows how eagerly Mexicans embrace the idea of a mestizo or hybrid origin for the national cuisine.'

Harrods Food Halls, Christmas 1922

The points of worldwide culinary contact manifested in this one recipe are awesome. If you subtract the New World ingredients, you of course no longer have a Mexican dish. But the seasonings that are left, and some of the cooking techniques, such as thickening the sauce with rounds of stale French bread, would have been as familiar to the 12th-century Moorish cook in Seville as they would have been to the cooks at the court of King Richard I. As for the cinnamon, cloves and peppercorns, don't let us forget that it was in pursuit of these as well as gold that Columbus set out in the first place. The fact that he (and his successors) instead found chocolate and the poor old turkey turned out to be a bonus.

TALKING TURKEY
Cooking and Stuffing

I have come to the unhappy conclusion that a frozen turkey is a very poor second best to a fresh one. However, the worst aspect of freezing turkey is the effect the process has on its fat, and the less long a bird has been frozen, the less likely that its fat will taste or smell stale. So if you are obliged to have a frozen one, do try to make sure that it was only recently frozen and has not had ice crystals in it for six months or a year. Fortunately, most of the frozen birds sold in supermarkets are the current crop, and have only been frozen because of the inconvenient log jam that would occur if every single Christmas turkey had to be dispatched, plucked, drawn, delivered, displayed and sold in a two- or three-day period. Four to eight ounces (125–250 g) uncooked weight per person is a rough guide to the size to buy. Americans eat much more turkey than the British or French, who seem as interested in the trimmings as the meat. And leftovers are only to be expected, or desired.

If your turkey was frozen, the single most important thing to remember is that it must be thawed thoroughly and completely before you cook it. This is an elementary safety precaution, as turkeys are hospitable to salmonella bacteria. Salmonella is a surface organism, so it is easily killed on the outside of the bird, but less easily in the bird's cavity. So if you're worried, don't stuff your turkey, but cook the stuffing separately. Be careful, too, of cross-contamination, and wash all knives and forks that have come into contact with raw poultry in very hot water; and don't forget the cutting board. There is, of course, absolutely no danger if you check the temperature with a meat thermometer. When the breast meat registers 77°C (170°F), the turkey is safely and succulently done, whether it was stuffed or not. If you want to err on the side of caution wait until the thigh meat has reached 85°C (185°F); but the breast meat will then be a little dry.

Another precaution is to stuff the turkey only at the last minute before cooking it. Beware any recipe that tells you to stuff the bird the night before 'to allow the flavours to develop'. And of course, be sure your oven is working: it's a good idea to use an oven thermometer to take *its* temperature every once in a while.

There are two basic methods to roast a turkey, the fast and the slow. My mother, who never learned to cook, discovered that she could roast a turkey without thinking about timing or temperature by putting any size of turkey in the oven set at its lowest temperature at least a day before it was to be eaten. She was right, after a fashion; though sometimes the beast collapsed under its own overcooked weight and lost its shape. Certainly there was always enough gravy, as the roasting pan was invariably full up with the meat's juices. Of course the meat, having lost all its juices, tasted like boiled string.

My mother was of the extremely slow school of turkey cooking. The slow school preheats the oven to 165°C (325°F, gas mark 3) and cooks the bird for 33 mins per kg (15 mins per lb) if the turkey weighs less than 7.25 kg (16 lb); 26 mins per kg (12 mins per lb) if it weighs more, not forgetting to take the weight of the stuffing into account. Slow cookers generally start the bird breast down, and turn it right side up after an hour if it's a small bird, or 1½ hours for a larger one.

The fast school preheats the oven to 200°C (400°F, gas mark 6) for birds up to 6 kg (13 lb) and cooks them for 26 mins per kg (12 mins per lb). Larger birds go in at 180°C (350°F, gas mark 4) for 33 mins per kg (15 mins per lb). Don't forget to weigh the stuffing, too.

I use a combination of both

methods. I calculate the cooking time at 30 minutes per kg, and start the bird at 190°C (375°F, gas mark 5), for 15 minutes for a bird up to 6 kg, 30 minutes for a larger one. I then subtract that time from the total cooking time, double the remainder, and cook the bird for the resulting time at 140–150°C (175–300°F, gas mark 1–2). I am unable to be any more precise about the lower temperature because I cook on the Aga, and I start the bird in the hot top oven and then move it to the cooler bottom oven for the remainder of the cooking time. Naturally the temperature, especially of the bottom oven, varies a bit when the top oven is in use; but many people have reported success using this fast-then-slow formula to cook a turkey (or any other bird or joint) in gas and electric ovens.

In any case, the bird needs at least 15 minutes resting time in a warm place so that the juices return to the muscle tissue and the bird can be carved properly. I often give it 30 minutes, especially if the turkey is a big one. You can turn the oven off and leave the bird in it with the door slightly open, but I put the roasting tin on top of the oven, which is itself quite hot, cover the bird with foil, put a cloth over the foil, and cover the whole lot with a mixing basin or the stockpot. If you've cooked the turkey properly, this is the single most important step to ensure that the meat is succulent.

Another trick for making the carving more elegant is to remove the wishbone before cooking. This will give you lovely, even slices from the breast.

As the disparity between cooking times for the white meat and dark meat shows, cooking a whole turkey is not the ideal way to go about it. But if your family insists on seeing it in its glorious integrity, you're stuck with one of the methods above. If, on the other hand, they will only see carved turkey on a platter, take my advice. Be ruthless. Amputate the legs and thighs, and cook them at the same time, but by the side of the breast and back, not attached to them. Or compromise by almost but not quite severing the legs and thighs. Put the bird in the widest cooking vessel you can find, so that the semi-detached legs can cook splayed out from the body. Best of all, cook only the breast and wings, and save the dark meat to grill and devil later. (You do this by making a paste of olive oil, crushed garlic, Dijon mustard and cayenne, which you rub into the superficially slashed thighs and drumsticks before you grill them.)

If you're bold enough to do this, you might consider cooking the dark meat and light meat in two different preparations (see the recipes on page 100). Or you could bone the turkey completely, place it skin-side down on the cutting board, season it, roll it up into a sausage shape with the stuffing, and sew up the back. You can either leave it as a sausage or make it into a vaguely bird-shaped parcel.

THE STUFFING
Almost anything except chocolate bars or ice cream can be used to stuff a turkey, but it's not a very good idea. Tradition dictates that the stuffing should be based on something starchy, generally stale bread (but rice, wild rice, chestnuts or cooked potatoes are all possible), bound with egg, and incorporating something fatty (oil or butter), something meaty (the liver, sautéed just until stiff, then cubed; or ham, bacon, sausagemeat, wild or cultivated mushrooms, or oysters, which are best of all), something aromatic (onions, garlic), something crunchy (celery, walnuts, hazelnuts or pistachios) and some herbs (I like thyme best of all, and lovage or sage is very nice in small quantities).

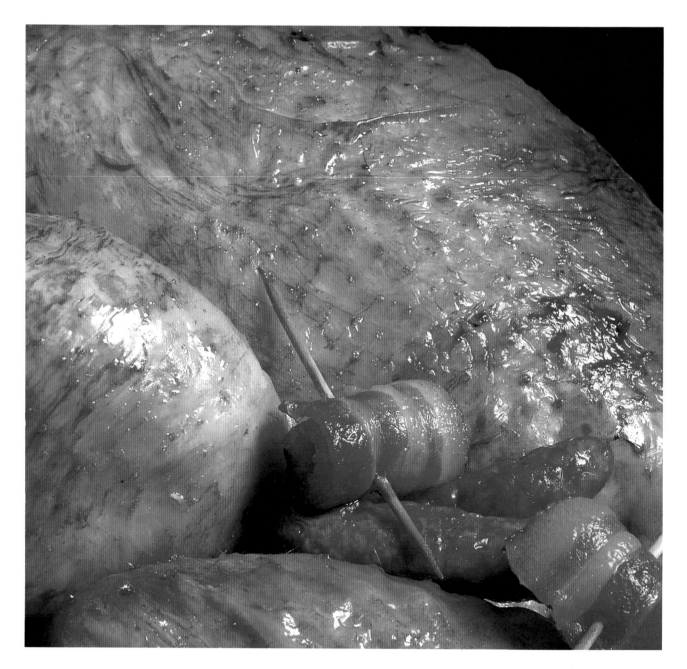

Fannie Farmer, author of the first standard American cookbook, says you will need about ¾ cup per lb or 9 cups of stuffing for a 12 lb turkey. These quantities are obviously untranslatable into metric or Imperial measures and, in any case, make very little sense unless you know the density of the stuffing. The most practical advice is to make up whatever quantity of stuffing you feel like making. If it is too little, that's fine, as it is imperative that the bird be stuffed loosely. If it's too much, cook the surplus separately in a buttered or oiled dish. You can stuff both the gut cavity and the neck cavity; and, of course, you can use two different stuffings, providing they are complementary in flavour.

Game birds such as pheasant often have a few packets of a soft white cheese such as *petit suisse* placed in the cavity with some salt and pepper. They melt and lubricate the bird very deliciously. Obviously you can do this with turkey, but you'll need a hell of a lot of cheese. It might be more sensible to do as the French sometimes do, and place a few *boudins*, previously blanched or stiffened briefly in butter, in the cavity. Both black pudding and white pudding are good; but I wouldn't use both, as the black ones will discolour the white ones.

I very often don't stuff the bird, but season the cavity and shove in a stick of celery, some garlic and onions and a sprig of thyme or rosemary, along with a lemon, orange or apple cut in half. The cooking time is thus reduced, and I think the result is somehow juicier.

THE GRAVY AND THE BREAD SAUCE

Roast the bird on a rack in a tin, or try this trick: slice some Spanish onions thickly, make a platform to rest the bird on and wedge it securely. You can vary this by putting coarsely chopped carrots, celery, shallots and garlic, sprigs of herbs, or even a properly constructed *mirepoix* of diced onion, garlic, carrot, celery and blanched bacon under the bird. Any of these will result in very superior pan juices, which can be served as is in a warmed *gras-maigre*, one of those sauceboats with two spouts.

Or you can make gravy (I never bother) by deglazing the roasting pan with wine, spirits, stock or water, and topping up the volume with more liquid. If you want thick gravy, add *beurre manié*, made by mixing together equal quantities of plain flour and softened butter. Add this a pinch at a time, and stir until your gravy is as you like it; then simmer for another 3–5 minutes so that the unpleasant raw taste of the flour disappears. Be sure you taste for seasoning before you put it into a warmed jug or sauceboat.

British cooks traditionally serve a dish of fried breadcrumbs and one of bread sauce with roast birds of every sort, including game. Bread sauce involves infusing milk with the flavours of a clove-stuck onion in a *bain-marie* for as long as possible. You then whisk in fresh breadcrumbs, usually white, in the proportion 90–125 g (3–4 oz, ¾–1 cup) to 500 ml (15 fl oz, 2 cups) milk, over the simmering water of the *bain-marie*. Jane Grigson advises adding more breadcrumbs if it is not thick enough (she says it 'should not spread very much when put onto a plate') or adding a little milk if it is so thick that the spoon will stand up in it. The traditional seasoning is mace and nutmeg, along with salt, white pepper and cayenne pepper. You finish the sauce by stirring in 2 Tbsp of butter or thick cream, and a sprinkling of cayenne over the top to mitigate its pale complexion. It's actually very good so long as you let the onion infuse long enough.

FRANCES BISSELL'S TURKEY IN TWO WAYS

Remove the breasts and thighs from the carcass, or get the butcher to do it, and bone and skin them. Cut the thigh meat (better than drumsticks, which are too sinewy) into regular-sized chunks and marinate overnight in a heavy plastic bag with olive oil, lemon juice and the rind of the lemon, crushed garlic, thyme, bay leaves, salt and freshly ground black pepper and some white wine. You can marinate the skinned and boned whole breasts in the same mixture, or slice the breast into thin steaks and flatten them further into the very thin *paillards*, and only marinate these for an hour or so, in the same marinade or merely in olive oil, lemon juice, salt and pepper.

Remove the thigh meat from the marinate, dry it, and brown it gently in olive oil, along with some aromatics, such as sliced onion or leek and celery. Then either stew briefly in the strained marinade, or in white wine. Add a bit of orange peel, if you like – and I should use a crushed dried and seeded chilli. As soon as the dark meat is done remove it from the heat and keep warm. If there is too much liquid, pour it off and reduce it separately so that the meat does not overcook. Add black olives, such as those of Nyons if you like them, in time just to warm through, and sprinkle with chopped parsley.

At the same time, serve everyone a grilled *paillard*, or thicker steak if you like, of the white meat. It looks wonderful if you heat a metal skewer to red-hot and make the *quadrillage*, the hatched grill marks on both sides of the meat.

KEN HOM'S ROAST TURKEY STEAKS

Cook the turkey in the usual way, anointing the breasts if you like, or putting butter between the skin and the meat (see Claudia Roden's Flavoured Butter, below). Allow the bird to rest in a warm place for 20 mins, or even half an hour if it is a big one. Then, working quickly, remove each breast (this is much easier if you have taken out the wishbone before cooking the turkey). Put it, skin attached, meat-side down on the cutting board, and slice off steaks about 2.5 cm (1 in) thick. As the idea is to save the carver's energy you will probably wish to joint, rather than slice, the dark meat, and then slice chunks off legs and thighs. Serve with *jus* or gravy made in the usual way. If you've cooked the turkey so that the white meat is still moist, this will give succulent steaks that are nicer to eat than thin slices.

TURKEY MOLE POBLANO DE GUAJOLOTE

There is a major difference in the recipes given for this dish by Elisabeth Lambert Ortiz and Diana Kennedy, in that the former first simmers until tender her 4-kg (8-lb) turkey cut up into serving pieces with onion and garlic, and then sautés it in 100 g (3 oz, ½ cup) of lard. Mrs Kennedy braises hers in the oven, without liquid, in 6–8 Tbsp of lard. Put the turkey aside and either save Mrs Ortiz's stock or, if you have followed Mrs Kennedy, make some with the turkey trimmings and giblets (except for the liver).

Serves 10

5–6 *ancho* chillies, stemmed, seeded and torn in pieces
6–8 *mulato* chillies, stemmed, seeded and torn in pieces
4–6 *pasilla* chillies, stemmed, seeded and torn in pieces
2 medium onions, chopped
3 cloves garlic, chopped
2 tortillas, broken up
3 medium tomatoes, peeled and seeded
20 almonds, unskinned
50 g (2 oz, ¼ cup) peanuts
75 g (2½ oz, ½ cup) raisins, fried in a touch of lard just until they swell
4 Tbsp sesame seeds
1 tsp coriander seed
½ tsp anise seed
2 cloves
1-cm (½-in) stick cinnamon
4 Tbsp lard
500 ml (16 fl oz, 2 cups) reserved turkey broth
45 g (1½ oz) tablet drinking chocolate (if you can't put your hands on that, substitute the same weight of plain chocolate, or better still, American Baker's unsweetened chocolate plus 1 Tbsp sugar)
2 Tbsp pumpkin seeds, hulled, unsalted

You make the sauce by steeping in boiling water to cover, the stemmed, seeded and torn chillies from 30 minutes to a maximum of 2 hours. Then process them and their soaking water with the onions, garlic, tortillas and the flesh and juice only of the tomatoes. Reserve this paste. Start again with a clean, dry food processor, and put into it the almonds, peanuts, raisins, plus 2 Tbsp of sesame seeds, the coriander seed, anise seed, cloves and a stick of cinnamon, all toasted lightly in the same frying pan. Whizz this up and combine it with the chilli paste you made earlier. Sauté this in the lard, using that left over in the turkey sauté pan, if there is any, for 5 minutes.

Now stir in the reserved turkey broth plus the secret ingredient, the tablet of chocolate, broken up. Cook over a low heat, stirring constantly, until the sauce is the consistency of double (heavy) cream. Add more stock if necessary, and don't forget to taste for salt. Simmer the turkey in this, covered, for 20–30 minutes.

In a small frying pan toast the remaining sesame seeds and the pumpkin seeds and sprinkle these over the turkey and its sauce arranged on a warmed serving dish. Accompany with tortillas, rice, fried beans and guacamole.

CLAUDIA RODEN'S FLAVOURED BUTTER FOR TURKEY

Make this up in quantities to the size of your turkey. This will do for a bird of 5 kg (10 lbs) or under; double the recipe for a larger bird, and treble it for a very large turkey. Separate the skin from the flesh using your fingers, as gently as possible so as not to tear the skin. (Sew it up if you do tear it.) Start by loosening the skin of the breast, and you will find that you can easily detach the thin membranes that join the flesh to the skin of the thighs. The skin is more difficult to detach from the membrane at the backbone and the ends of the legs. Simply massage the flavoured butter into the flesh, giving a thicker coating of butter to the breast, and roast the bird as you usually do. This is a slightly Middle Eastern butter, with sweet spices, and goes well with Claudia's dried fruit Turkey Stuffing (right). Almost any flavouring can be used, from garlic, parsley and grated lemon zest, to anchovy paste or finely minced black truffle, to flavour the butter.

115 g (4 oz, 1 stick) unsalted butter, softened
1 tsp ground cinnamon
1 tsp ground allspice
salt and freshly ground black pepper

Blend the ingredients well together with a fork.

CLAUDIA RODEN'S TURKEY STUFFING

This is taken from a recipe for Persian chicken stuffed with dried fruits. The quantity given will stuff a 5 kg (10 lb) turkey fore and aft, as you do not want to cram the bird to bursting. Double or treble the recipe as needed. It is also very good with goose.

2 onions, finely chopped
4 Tbsp unsalted butter
500 g (1 lb) prunes, soaked, stoned and chopped
500 g (1 lb) dried apricots, soaked and chopped
120 g (4 oz, ⅔ cup) seedless raisins
120 g (4 oz, 1 cup) broken walnuts
4 apples, peeled, cored and chopped
salt and freshly ground black pepper
2 tsps ground cinnamon

Sauté the onion in the butter until soft and golden. Add the chopped fruits, raisins and nuts and cook gently until they plump up. Season with salt, pepper and cinnamon, being certain to taste.

CHUTNEY MARY'S TURKEY NARANGI

This is an adaptation of a genuine recipe for lamb, which originated in the banqueting kitchens of the late Nizam of Hyderabad. This version was developed by the chef of Chutney Mary in London. This was, in fact, the way most Anglo-Indian dishes originated, with Indian cooks giving an interesting and always spicy twist to English recipes. Wild rice is the ideal accompaniment to this dish; and I found that, despite the strong orange flavours in the sauce, it was very good with a young, robust Italian red wine.

1 whole small (3.5–4 kg, 8–9 lb) turkey
1 bouquet garni

For the stuffing
1 large onion, finely minced
4–6 Tbsp oil
1 tsp each ground cinnamon, cardamom, cloves
200 ml (8 fl oz, 1 cup) single (light) cream
3–4 fresh green chillies, seeded unless you want some fire in your stuffing
150 g (5 oz, ½ cup) Indian *paneer*, for which you can substitute a packet of fine curd cottage cheese or dry curd cheese
150 g (5 oz, 1¼ cups) dried currants

For the marinade
4 heaped tsp chilli powder
salt
1 heaped tsp turmeric
100 g (4 oz, ¼ cup) fresh ginger purée, made in food processor *or* pounded in mortar and pestle

For the sauce
1 heaped tsp cumin seeds
2 heaped tsp ground coriander
450 g (16 fl oz, 2 cups) yoghurt
1 litre (1¾ pints, 1 quart) fresh orange juice, preferably from bitter Seville oranges, or made sour by 1 tsp lemon juice
2 Tbsp Orange Curaçao
6 oranges, peeled and cut into in tidy segments, with the grated zest of two of them

Joint the turkey into 4 pieces. Take off the wing tips, but keep the wing bone attached to the breast. Bone the legs and thighs and mince the dark meat. Put the bones into a stockpot with 5 litres (8 pints, 5 quarts) water and the bouquet garni. Bring to the boil and reduce to 1 litre (1¾ pints, 1 quart). Cool, strain and set aside.

Take each breast and wing joint and, holding the cut side towards you, make a slit in it lengthways so as to make a pocket to hold the stuffing. For the stuffing, sauté the onion until brown in 1–2 Tbsp of the oil. Mix this with the minced turkey and ground cinnamon, cardamom and cloves in the food processor with the steel blade fitted. Process to a paste with the cream, the green chillies and the *paneer* or cottage cheese. Add the currants and process briefly.

Spoon the filling into the slit in the turkey breasts and tie with string at regular intervals. Now smear the turkey breasts with a marinade made from 1–2 Tbsp of the oil, mixed with 1 tsp of the chilli powder, a big pinch of salt, ½ tsp turmeric and half the ginger purée. Allow to stand for 4 hours to absorb the marinade.

Roast in a preheated moderately hot (200°C, 400°F, gas mark 6) oven until the skin is light brown, about 45–50 mins. Then rest in a warm place while you make the sauce.

Heat the remaining 2 Tbsp of oil in a saucepan on medium heat and add the cumin seeds. Stir for 30 secs, and add the remaining 3 tsp of chilli powder; the remaining ½ tsp of turmeric and the ground coriander. After 10 secs add the rest of the ginger purée. Stir for another 30 secs and add the yoghurt; stir vigorously for another min. Now add the orange juice and enough turkey stock to make a smooth, flowing, thinnish gravy. Flavour it with the Curaçao, add the orange zest and simmer for 1 min longer. Off the fire add the orange segments to the sauce. Slice the turkey across the breast and serve with a generous amount of the sauce.

TRUFFLED TURKEY (EN DEMI-DEUIL)

Following the method on page 102 for inserting butter under the skin of the turkey, do so, with the addition of some brandy and finely chopped truffle to the butter. Then insert thin slices of black truffle under the skin as well, making as regular a pattern as your pocket will allow. Roast in the usual way, being sure to keep the breast covered with butter-soaked muslin. Rest before carving – at the table to show off your extravagance. And don't lose any of the precious truffle-flavoured juices, which should simply be served in a warmed sauceboat.

KENTUCKY HOT BROWN SANDWICH

This is the way we used up leftover turkey in Kentucky. The recipe was supposed to have been invented at Brown's hotel in Louisville, and perhaps it was. Good bread is toasted lightly, put into an ovenproof dish, topped with regular slices of turkey, usually breast meat only, and slices either of Kentucky ham or of crisp bacon. Over this open sandwich goes a cheese-flavoured white sauce, made by stirring either mature grated cheddar or a good grated Swiss cheese into a *béchamel*. A sprinkle of cayenne and a grating of nutmeg are both good ideas, and I'd be tempted to butter the toast lightly and smear it with Dijon mustard before placing the meat upon it. It goes under the grill till brown.

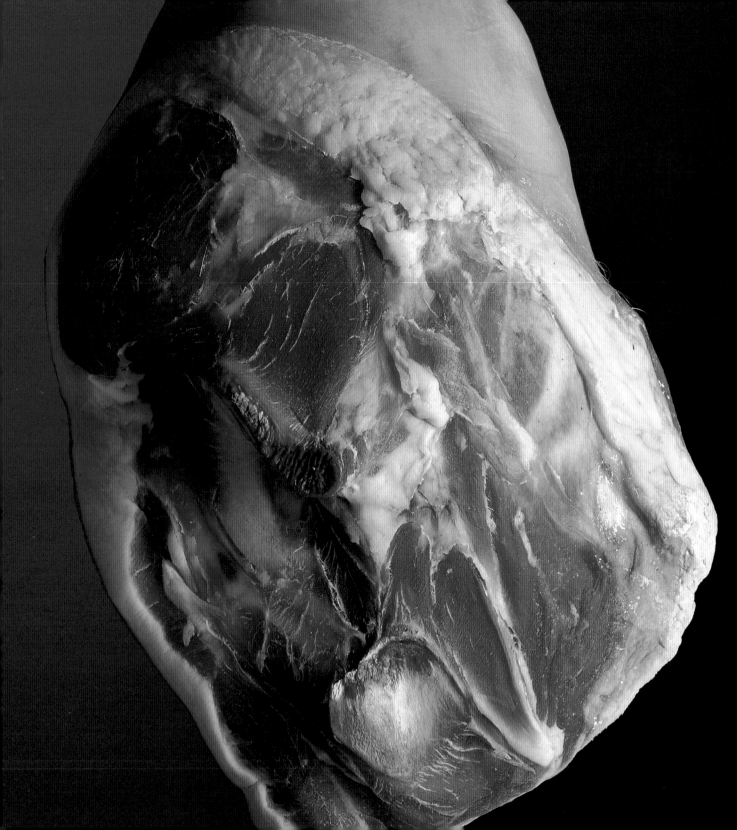

CHAPTER FIVE

Tired of turkey?

The Chinese say a duck is too much for one and not enough for two people to eat. Ultimately, this is the reason most of us now eat turkey at Christmas, for similar problems arise with the capon and the goose. None of the fat, succulent birds yields quite enough meat to cope with an extended family bent on gorging themselves.

Geese are not at their best at Christmas. 'A Michaelmas goose,' wrote Dr William Kitchiner in *The Cook's Oracle* (1820) 'is as famous in the mouths of the million as the minced-pie at Christmas; yet for those who eat with delicacy, it is, at that time, too full-grown. The true period when the goose is in the highest perfection is when it has just acquired its full growth, and not begun to harden; if the March goose is insipid, the Michaelmas goose is rank. The fine time is between both; from the second week in June to the first in September.' Whatever the time of year, the goose's own diet is of paramount importance to its eating quality. The first duty of a goose is to be plump.

The goose, in any case, was a make-do. The proper Christmas tradition was to eat a boar's head. Though it looked absolutely splendid, and could be accompanied to table with great ceremony and more than one version of a well-known song, the boar's head had its drawbacks, too. Your minstrels or varlets could sing:

> Hey! Hey! Hey! Hey!
> Hey! Hey! Hey! Hey!
> The boar's head in hand I bring,
> With garlands gay in carrying,
> I pray you all with me to sing
> Hey! etc.
> Lords and knights and squires,
> Parsons, priests and vicars,
> The boar's head is the first mess!
> Hey! etc.
> The boar's head is armed gay!

meaning it was properly decorated. Or they could sing the version in the Balliol MS, as the choristers of The Queen's College, Oxford, still do late every December, as they lead the procession bearing the now rare dish.

> The bores hed in handis I brynge
> With garlondis gay and byrdis syngynge
> I pray you all helpe me to synge
> Que estis in convinio

The bores hed I understand
Yo cheffe serwyes in all this londe
Where so ever it may be fonde
Servitur eum sincfio

The bores hed I dare well say
Anon after the xııth day
He taketh his leve and goth away
Exiunt tune di patria.

The reasons for the demise of the habit of eating a boar's head at Christmas are two. The first is a matter of taste, which Dorothy Hartley compares to 'cold boiled bacon, rather highly spiced'. (In fairness, though, I've tasted it myself, and brawn or normal French *charcutier*-made *fromage de tête* or *hure* is closer to the mark, which means you have to quite like crunchy and squishy bits of the pig as well as the meaty ones to enjoy it.) It is clear, though, from a passage found by J. A. R. Pimlott, that boar's head, at least in the form of brawn, was still an essential part of Christmas in 1745, when Thomas Gray wrote to Thomas Wharton, 'May you live a hundred Christmasses and eat as many collars of brawn stuck with rosemary.'

The second and more dramatic reason is that the boar's head was a remnant of earlier, pre-Christian winter solstice celebrations. It was an all too fleshly link with paganism and the Norse gods, in particular. Its associations with the older religions go back almost as far as possible, even to the ancient Egyptian religion. In *The Golden Bough* Frazer has pages and pages on the sacredness and sacrifice of pigs, and on the twin poles of those eastern rites in which the pig

was eaten and those, equal in number, in which eating pork was forbidden. The boar was certainly a sacred animal to many, and its sacrifice commemorated the death of Set, or Attis, or Adonis or Osiris. In short, the ritual killing of the boar was a substitute for the earlier rite in which a human being, a mock king, was sacrificed.

With the major exception of the Eucharist itself and the minor one of hot cross buns, Anglophone Christianity does not have many symbolic foods associated with its festivals. When you think about the practices of other religions in this regard, this seems a little surprising. At the Indian winter festival of Dewali, earthenware lamps are lit to show that, like Christmas and Hanukkah, this is a feast of light, sweetmeats are eaten and given as gifts. This profusion of sweets represents riches and wealth, for it is the festival of Lakshmi, goddess of wealth.

Jewish festivals are surrounded with symbolic food. At Purim, the feast of lots, observant Jews celebrate the defeat by Queen Esther of Haman's plans to annihilate the Jewish people by eating pastries baked in the shape of Haman's three-cornered hat. At the Passover, the original of the Last Supper, the celebration of which is itself a meal, Jews eat bitter herbs to remind them of their ancestors' slavery in Egypt, salt water to recall their tears, a mixture of nuts and apple representing the mortar used in their labours, and various other food and drink designed to remind the participants in the *seder* meal of the ten plagues that descended upon the Egyptians and the sparing of the Jews; above all, water-biscuit-like *matzo* is eaten, because the haste of the exodus meant there was no time for leavened bread to be baked. At the New Year, apples and honey are eaten in the hope that the year to come will prove as sweet as the food, and even the Sabbath meal, eaten by definition once a week, has its symbolic bread and wine, and a chicken or some other symbol of plenty – if not luxury.

At Hanukkah the symbolism of the food is even more straightforward. It must be cooked in oil, to celebrate the miracle of the single day's supply of holy oil that lasted for eight days. In eastern Europe, and in the English-speaking countries to which Ashkenazi Jews emigrated, the Hanukkah food is, in Yiddish, the latke, or *levivot* in Hebrew, the potato pancake (see page 118). It is made exactly as the potato *crêpe* of eastern France, or that of Germany or Switzerland, with coarsely grated potato, onion, egg, some starchy binder (matzo meal usually, but sometimes plain flour), salt and pepper, and sometimes a rising agent such as baking powder. Formerly latkes were fried in the saturated rendered chicken, duck or goose fat that has contributed so much to the heartburn folklore of Jewish cooking and shortened so many Jewish lives. Nowadays they are more commonly, healthily and accurately fried in vegetable oil.

The major question, really, is how the potato got from Peru to the latke. In *Why We Eat What We Eat* Raymond Sokolov dates the first encounter of Europeans with the potato in 1537 in northern Peru, and reckons it reached Europe only in the 1570s and was first cultivated in Seville. The story that Sir Walter Raleigh brought the first spud to England from Virginia seems just plain wrong, though Tom Stobart says he grew a not very useful sort of potato on his Irish estate at Youghal, County Cork. It soon

spread to Italy, and by 1739 was being grown extensively in Scotland though the French (and some other Western Europeans) were notoriously reluctant to eat it until it was popularised by Parmentier (1737–1818, whose name on a dish indicates the inclusion of potatoes in it). Irish immigrants took the potato back to America with them in 1719.

Sokolov has established that the chipped potato (or French fry) reached England around 1870 and that the potato chip (*anglice* crisp) recipe was published in America precisely in 1878. While that doesn't entirely sort out the latke situation, we are on safe ground, I think, in presuming potato cakes to have existed at least 50 years earlier. They seem to have originated in Russia, where, according to Faye Levy's *International Jewish Cookbook* (1992), Jews make latkes from all sorts of ingredients other than potatoes. She lists cheese, buckwheat flour and noodles.

The Russians had certainly worked out how to distill a liquor made from fermented potatoes, and by 1845 when the blight struck, the Irish had discovered most of the other uses to which the spud could be put. As the latke has several Irish cousins, you would think 1800 would be a reasonably conservative date for the first latke. Having said that, though, *The Jewish Manual* published in London 1846 and attributed to Lady Montefiore, and generally accepted as the first Jewish cookery book in English, has no recipe for latkes or any other Hanukkah food; the same is true of the *Jewish Cookery Book* by Mrs Esther Levy, published in Philadelphia in 1871, though she does give a recipe for potato fritters. They are, however, made from cooked potatoes and are sweet. Worse,

Edouard de Pomiane's *The Jews of Poland: Recollections and Recipes* (first published as *Cuisine Juive: Ghettos Modernes*, 1929) has the recipe, which uses virtually the same ingredients, for potato *kugel*, but none for latkes. This is a little disturbing, because it suggests that the tradition of latkes for Hanukkah may be of relatively recent origin. Or, to put it another way, as Raymond Sokolov does in another of his books, *The Jewish-American Kitchen*, 'since there were no potatoes available to any Jewish cook until the Spanish Conquest of Peru, some 1700 years later' than the re-dedication of the Temple by Judas Maccabaeus in 165 BC, 'it is definitely the oil that connects these tasty pancakes to Hanukkah'.

Sephardic Jews may just have an older tradition. Israel has adopted the Sephardic habit, now catching on in north London Jewish communities as well, of eating jam doughnuts, *pontchikes* or *ponchkiss*, at Hanukkah. This has been brilliantly documented by Nicholas Stavroulakis in his *Cookbook of the Jews of Greece* (1990) in which he points out that 'as the sentiments of Hanukkah are overtly anti-Hellenist, and as the Hellenised Jews who settled in Greece would hardly celebrate what was in fact their own defeat, it is not surprising that Hanukkah is not a major holiday in Greece as it is in the West. In addition,' he says interestingly, 'Hanukkah's proximity to Christmas might account for the stress placed on a Jewish festival in Western countries. In Greece Christmas has become a major holiday only in recent years.'

The chief Hanukkah food eaten in Greece is called *zvingous*, a version of what are called *boumwelos* or *bimwelos* in Ladino, the vernacular of the Sephardic Jews. They are fried balls of choux pastry, unless made with milk, when they are called *loukoumades*. In America they are called doughnut holes, because they look like the bit missing from the centre of the doughnut shape. The frying medium is, of course, olive oil, and this particular food is common to all Sephardim. Greek Jews, however, have one of the largest repertoires of Hanukkah foods, including *tiganites*, pancakes flavoured with ouzo, masticha or raki, served sprinkled with cinnamon and sugar or honey and ground walnuts, or a whole wheat version called *lalangites* by the children of Ioannina at the turn of the century. In Corfu and Zakynthos *tiganites* are made of rice flour, as are the slightly different *fritoles*. And in Salonika and Hania, types of halva are eaten at Hanukkah, though these alone of Hanukkah treats are not fried foods.

There is a confused medieval folk tradition that assimilates the Apocryphal story of Judith with Hanukkah. In it Judith is a Hasmonean princess who serves a salt-preserved cheese to the Greek commander. He then drinks too much wine and, in his stupor, she beheads him and saves the kingdom. Some say that cheese dishes are eaten at Hanukkah because of this. The general point is clear, though; like most of the Jewish festival foods, and unlike most Western Christmas foods, Hanukkah foods are all symbolic.

Moreover, there are other reasons for the association of the holiday with fat or oil. In the eastern Mediterranean Hanukkah comes near the end of the olive harvest, just as the oil is being pressed. It also coincides with the end of the fattening season for geese, so that Jewish kitchens would be occupied with rendering the fat to preserve it for future use. Above

The boar's head, 1855

all, though, as Oded Schwartz points out in *In Search of Plenty* (1992), a history of Jewish food, the association of Hanukkah 'with oil and light is probably very old and belongs to a pagan ritual of fire and lights for warding off the approach of winter darkness'.

TO RETURN TO THE BOAR'S HEAD. WHEN DOROTHY Hartley published *Food in England* in 1954, she could still say: '"Ye Olde boar's head" may be bought, handsomely prepared, at provision stores in the Christmas season.' I have a dim memory of having seen, one Christmas, an elaborately confected tusker in the window of Richards, the pork butcher, in Oxford's covered market, but I think it was there for show, rather than for sale. Miss Hartley thought that if it was made from a wild boar it was 'always justifiably expensive' but that made from a domesticated pig was homely peasant fare. She actually tells how to make it, warning that it is a lot of trouble, though it 'makes a very imposing dish at very small cost'.

To sum up the fairly grisly recipe, you get the butcher to prepare the head, splitting it into two halves, joined only by the skin at the top. (Jane Grigson's recipe for *hure* starts in the same way.) 'Eyes, ears, snout and all the bone at the back should be removed,' says Miss Harley, 'and the brains wrapped separately.' You then pickle the head in saltpetre, salt and spices for a week or ten days and cook it by boiling gently in vegetables and flavourings until the bones are loose, and truss it, with the skinned tongue, into a conical shape. Ears and snout go to make up a gelatinous glaze; when the cone-shaped head is cold, it is brushed with this jelly, though, for some reason, the last coating must be poured over the pig's head.

'Serve "hym",' says Miss Hartley, 'on a convenient carving board, laid on a clean, flat fir bough.' She suggests giving 'hym' split almond tusks, prunes for eyes and a necklace of holly. You carve it lengthwise and serve it with mustard sauce; she repeats for emphasis that it is a 'very savoury form of cold spiced bacon', which will come as a disappointment to anyone who imagined that the object carried in with such ceremony was steaming hot. André Simon gives a recipe for pig's head in imitation of boar's head, which involves leaving the ears and snout in place – I think, but he is not explicit about this. He is quoting Alexis Soyer's recipe, which is for an actual wild boar, and makes everything clear by ending: 'Have some very fresh tulips and roses, which stick tastefully in the ears, and some around, but leaving space to carve.' If you ever feel ambitious enough to attempt a boar's head, do use the recipe in Jane Grigson's *Charcuterie*, which though a labour for giants, does at least give quantities and measures.

From the cook's point of view, it was a happy day when, because of the influence of churchmen or just because it became fashionable to have a hot main course for Christmas, roast goose took over from the boar's head. The boar's head may look spectacular, but so can the goose; and the goose definitely does not taste merely of cold bacon. There is a passage in Zola's *L'Assommoir* in which the appearance of the goose upon the table, 'huge, golden and flowing with its own juices' reduced everyone to silence: 'We didn't attack it immediately. There was a wonderment, a respectful surprise', while everyone at the table simply looked at the bird.

Dickens summed up the real pleasure of the Christmas goose: 'There never was such a goose. Bob said he didn't believe there ever was such a goose cooked. Its tenderness and flavour, size and cheapness were the themes of universal admiration. Eked out by apple-sauce and mashed potatoes, it was a sufficient dinner for the whole family; indeed, as Mrs Cratchit said with great delight (surveying one small atom of a bone upon the dish), "they hadn't ate it all at last!" Yet every one had had enough, and the youngest Cratchits in particular were steeped in sage and onion to the eyebrows.'

Though the golden days of the goose are probably in the past, the bird is increasingly available at Christmas, even in the supermarkets in Britain and France, and specialist growers do far more business at this time of year than before Michaelmas, whatever Dr Kitchiner thought about the proper season of the goose. Tom Stobart, by the way, disagrees with Dr Kitchiner anyway, and thinks that the goose is at his best 'from the autumn through to February'.

Game, on the other hand, is in season at Christmas, with the exception of grouse, whose season ends on December 10 because it began, along with that for snipe, way back on the Glorious Twelfth of August. Partridge and woodcock may be shot until the first of February, pheasant until the day before that, and furred game until April 30 when the shooting of red deer stops. The tradition of eating game at Christmas goes back to the days of sewing the roasted peacock back in its own skin and feathers, and to the one-bird-stuffed-inside-another Christmas pies of the last chapter. While it is difficult to make much of a dramatic statement with game, in the absence of peacocks it is a very good solution to the problem of variety, if there are not too many people around the Christmas board.

In recent years, in England, anyway, the price of pheasant in particular has fallen so greatly that it is feasible to cook it for a large number. The only difficulty is that an oven capable of roasting a large turkey does not find it so easy to cope with the same weight of smaller birds, so it can be tricky to roast pheasants for large numbers of people. (Though pheasant being so much richer, the quantity needed for a single serving is less than of turkey.) One year Frances Bissell and I dealt with this small crux by using only the breast of the pheasant, which we marinaded the day before in pomegranate juice and seeds, and grilled while the guests were eating the earlier courses (see page 122). It was very successful.

With all birds, wild or domesticated, the stuffing question is bound to arise. For many people, the stuffing is more of a treat than the birds; especially when the bird is turkey. Oddly enough, years of experiment have convinced me that the bird is always moister when it is *not* stuffed. Pop a citrus fruit, anything from a kumquat to a grapefruit, or an apple into the cavity, which you have salted and peppered, along with an onion, peeled or not, as you fancy, or some cloves of garlic, and you will have added to the flavour and moistness of the bird. The point is a simple one, really: the cooking juices either run into the stuffing, or back into the flesh of the fowl. You can achieve some very interesting flavouring combinations if you are willing to forgo stuffing the bird and fill the cavity instead with things such as chilli, fresh limes and slices of ginger; or an orange and a sprig of rosemary; or thyme, bay leaves and garlic; or tarragon and a lump of butter; or rub the cavity with light soya sauce, and insert ginger, garlic and spring onions, or with Thai *nam pla* and use garlic, chilli, ginger or galangal and bruised, sliced lemon grass. Even game birds benefit from garlic, thyme and juniper berries, or a chunk of German *Speck* or French *petit salé*, preferably blanched before inserting it into the bird's belly.

Part-cooked *boudin*, either black or white, makes a wonderful unorthodox stuffing for pheasant or chicken, as do *petit suisse* cheeses. Both give off moisture rather than absorbing it. The same moisturising effect is achieved by using any fatty sausage or meat, from minced beef or pork to steak.

You can, of course, stuff a bird with anything, and good rules to follow are something starchy for comfort, something aromatic for flavour, something crunchy for contrast, and maybe something meaty for luxury because it's Christmas. The starch can be anything from cooked potatoes to stale bread, but couscous, cooked rice and buckwheat can be used to add new interest. Aromatics: I think members of the onion family are essential for their perfume; whole heads of garlic, blanched, have quite a different flavour to single garlic cloves, and are suitable if the bird is going to cook slowly for a long time. The crunch can come from celery or from nuts; I'm partial to both in a stuffing, and both can be useful for keeping the texture of a farce loose and open. The bird's own liver is usually a delicious addition to a forcemeat, and some people insist on a Christmas stuffing having minced veal or sausage. You may be happier, though, with the extra flavour imparted by a bit of chopped ham, or the extra unctuousness conferred upon a stuffing by fat bacon.

Or you could always eat the ham on its own and forget about the bird altogether. There is a good deal to be said in favour of this, for as Xavier Aubryet said in *La Cuisinière Poétique* (1877), 'The pig is simply a vast dish walking around until it is time to be served up at table. His pink skin, spotted with black, brings to mind a truffled galantine; his firm and well-padded rump is already in the shape of a ham.' A whole ham is a noble sight; it has the drama necessary to be the centre of a celebration meal. When served hot, the best hams have a melting succulence; when cold, enough flavour to provide the perfect gastronomic foil for pickles, chutneys and interesting salads. It is our habit to have a ham on Boxing Day, the feast of St Stephen, December 26, an adjunct to Christmas totally lacking in the otherwise satisfactory celebrations of both the French and the Americans.

Ham, a common main course for Easter lunch in Britain, often takes pride of place on the American Christmas table. Because the turkey is *de rigueur* for Thanksgiving, which is the last Thursday in November, many American families have had enough turkey to last them for the month until Christmas, especially in the south, where the regional 'country' hams are so good. The best known are Kentucky and Virginia hams. These appellations mean a little more than the '*jambon de Paris* and *jambon d'York*' that are ubiquitous in France, and indicate not the place, but the style of the cure.

Virginia hams should come from the razorback breed of hog, and these should be fed on peanuts and peaches. Cured over fires of apple and hickory wood

Mutton hams being cured at Ashdown Smokers

and kept in old-fashioned smokehouses until ready, this ham is much less common than the poor quality western soft pork ham that has usurped its name by being cured commercially in Virginia. Smithfield hams are something else again; the name comes from a small town in Virginia, and not from the old

London meat market. The hams are from razorbacks that subsist for their first nine months on acorns, beech mast and hickory nuts (so it is said, but I don't see how even a semi-wild razorback hog can crack a hickory nut; we had a tree in my childhood, and I found the nuts impervious to the heaviest hammer blows). They are then supposed to feed in the peanut fields before being finished on maize. Dry-salted and seasoned with cracked black pepper, Smithfield hams are heavily smoked over fruit and nut woods and oak, and aged at least one year. They are salty and American Chinese cooks find them an excellent substitute for the hams of Yunnan.

The hams of Kentucky, to which I retain my devotion, are from Hampshire hogs, and the piglets supposedly feed freely on beans, acorns and clover for almost the whole of their lives. They are only penned and finished on grain when their time approaches. Dry-salted for 30 days, they are smoked over apple and hickory for another month and then hung in paper wrapping to age for a year at least. We used to hang them in the cellar and keep them for two and, I think, sometimes three years. They invariably had a white mould on the surface, which was regarded as harmless and wiped off before soaking them for days and cooking them by simmering at a very low temperature for a very long time. The resultant ham was very chewy, like seriously overcooked roast beef, but with a savoury flavour I have never experienced in any other sort of food. It was rare to eat much more old Kentucky ham than a mere sliver on a buttered beaten biscuit. 'Beaten biscuits' are like particularly tough, round crackers. As children we used to wonder whether they were not older

than the ham, in fact petrified. Younger Kentucky ham can be fried in the slice, as can the Tennessee version of 'country ham' that is now commonly found in shops and supermarkets, even in Kentucky itself. Old Kentucky ham is so strong in flavour and so chewy that it is perhaps better used in small quantities to flavour dishes such as soups or slow-cooked green beans. (There is a version of this last dish made with kosher all-beef salami that is one of the world's great gastronomic curiosities; for, over the years, it has become a southern dish, and is more associated with black cooks than with the Jewish housewives who must, surely, have invented it.)

In Britain York and Wiltshire hams are enjoying something or a revival, though I have heard a rumour that there is only a single plant now doing the York cure. (No ham is cured in York itself.) It is a dry cure, with salt, saltpetre, juniper berries and pepper rubbed into the surface, which Jane Grigson says has 'a gentler, more prolonged effect' than a brine cure, to which sugar is often added to slow down the harsh rapid action of the salted water.

York ham is firm but tender. That is its chief merit, I suppose; but it is an attractive pink colour, and does have a pronounced flavour. Indeed, nowadays it is often sold with the equivalent of a health warning that some people may find it too strong for their taste. We have never had a complaint, and the ham is particularly good hot. York hams are cured for three to four months and can be smoked either lightly or heavily. Normally they should be soaked anywhere from six hours to a day, and cooked at the merest simmer for 30 minutes per kilo or 15 minutes per lb.

Wiltshire ham is supposedly milder than York.

This is because it is actually gammon, i.e., bacon — the leg is left attached to the whole carcass, which is all cured at once. Its keeping qualities are affected by this, and gammon does not last as long as ham. It is supposed to be 'milder' (which I gloss as 'less interesting in flavour') than true ham; but I find that a whole Wiltshire ham has a different and better flavour than the sliced gammon one buys at the supermarket.

Bradenham hams are the ones with the jet black outside layer. This is a feature of their six-month cure, which is done to a recipe from 1781 by the Bradenham Ham Company of Chippenham, Wiltshire and involved molasses, juniper berries and other spices. It has a distinctive sweet taste. 'Bradenham' is a trade mark, and each ham is branded with a horse rampant.

Ham must never boil when it is cooked, and the ideal cooking temperature is 77°C (171°F), at which shrinkage is minimised. Cooking times vary with the cure, but ham is perfectly cooked when a meat thermometer in the centre of the thickest part reads 65°C (150°F). Overcooking ham is a common failing, and a sin.

Whether it's turkey or game, ham or goose, or even a fish, the Christmas meal requires some vegetables. These are traditionally, to the horror of children all over Europe and America, Brussels sprouts. To get the major question out of the way, Harold McGee tells us in *On Food and Cooking* (1984) that the evil odours that characterise members of the cabbage family result from breaking down mustard oils and cysteine derivatives to form compounds that include the rotten-egg-smelling hydrogen sulphide, ammonia and mercaptans. These can react with each other to form even worse trisulphides. 'The longer

the vegetable is cooked,' warns McGee, 'the more of these molecules are produced, and the flavour of the cooked vegetables gets stronger, not weaker, as time passes.' You have been warned.

Why do we eat Brussels sprouts at Christmas? Gardeners will tell you that they and celery are the only vegetables that actually improve with being frosted. They are supposed to get crisper and sweeter after being exposed to freezing temperatures and, therefore, are the only vegetables that are actually better at Christmas than earlier on in the year. Hmmm. I grow at least three varieties of sprouts in my garden (one an Italian red variety that is quite spectacular); one of the green types is an autumn-eating one, and goes rank if you keep it too long.

If your family or guests don't like Brussels sprouts, try this trick: shred them with a sharp knife or in the food processor, and stir-fry them over high heat in a wok with olive or peanut oil, shredded garlic, ginger and fresh or dried chilli. It looks beautiful, the sprouts keep their crispness, and they are cooked too briefly to get smelly. They will look even more decorative if you simply quarter the sprouts, leaving a tiny bit of the root end to hold the leaves together. In fact, any rapid method of cooking them will avoid the sulphur stink. I sometimes steam shredded or quartered sprouts (but not whole ones, as that risks lengthening the cooking time unacceptably) or cook them for three to four minutes on full power in the microwave, in a microwave-safe clingfilm-covered dish with a scrap of garlic and some good, fruity olive oil.

Even if you *like* sprouts, do try the other, much nicer winter treat, and stir-fry celery, sliced on the bias so that it is almost diamond-shaped, in a hot wok with peanut oil. After a minute add a good sprinkling of salt, stir again, and then a few tablespoons of water. Cover the wok and lower the heat to medium for one or two minutes. Then remove the lid, raise the heat, and stir constantly until the liquid is reduced to a syrupy glaze, and the celery is shiny and still crunchy. This authentic Chinese recipe is refreshingly wonderful with poultry, game, ham and even fish. If you like celery, it's probably the ideal Christmas meal vegetable, as it has the effect of lightening the heaviest menu. Although it has to be prepared at the last moment, it is the work of an instant and it is equally good cold, which sprouts are most definitely not.

For me, however, the one absolute necessity with the Christmas meal, whether it is lunch or dinner, is a green salad (see page 137). In the first place, salad is needed to alleviate the heaviness of the feast, and for a contrast of texture. But, second, it's a question of morale. We need to be reminded at midwinter, as our ancestors could not be, that the world will again be fresh and green.

Finally, what are you going to drink with your main course? There are several schools of thought. One, very French, says that you ought to have a young, tannic red wine, such as a young claret, with turkey or goose. Others insist that it is the acid of the wine, whether its colour is red or white, that determines how well it marries with the flesh of birds. It is certainly true to say that a fatty bird, such as goose or duck, needs acidity to cut cleanly through its unctuousness; this is one reason why German wines go so well with goose, as even the higher grade, later-picked ones usually have such good acid levels. For the same reason, many Alsace whites are wonderful with goose or capon.

I confess, though, to prejudice. By this point in the meal, I want to drink red wine. So with the turkey we look for a wine that balances tannic firmness with a fairly high acid level, and, of course, as much fruit as possible. The solution we have hit upon is wines from the south of France. Not that we neglect claret and burgundy at our Christmas meal. If we have game, then red burgundy it must be, matching the barnyardy, earthy nose of the wine, and its raspberry or black cherry fruit, to the highly pronounced, equally earthy taste of the carefully hung pheasant. If not, we save the oldest, grandest red wine for the cheese (though not for the stilton).

LATKES

I am very reluctant to give quantities for potato pancakes. Everything depends on the potatoes, and it is quite impossible to say what quantity of liquid any potato will give off when it is grated – even if you know the variety. None of the dozen or so recipes I've consulted even says whether a waxy or a floury potato is preferable. At least in America the all-purpose Idaho potato relieves the cook from having to make that decision. I have used both sorts of potato, and come to no conclusion about their merits. The cleverest recipes for latkes are those that try to give a potato/onion/egg ratio; but even those have to guess at the amount of starch – flour or matzo meal – needed to bind the mixture.

So. Peel and grate coarsely (the food processor is a boon to latke-making) four large potatoes, weighing, say 250 g (½ lb) each and one large onion. Put them in a mixing bowl and drain off most of the liquid. Add a generous amount of salt and freshly ground black pepper, and one large, lightly beaten egg if the mixture gave off a lot of liquid, two if it seems relatively dry. Bind with 1–4 tablespoons of medium matzo meal or plain flour. Some cooks add a big pinch of baking powder at this stage, some

don't. Stir just enough to amalgamate everything. More liquid will begin to appear in the mixing bowl. Don't worry. The liquid will result in lacy, delicate pancakes.

Heat a neutral-tasting vegetable oil or rendered chicken, goose or duck fat, or a mixture of fat and oil, in a frying pan until a haze appears. The quantity of oil is up to you. I use only a thin film of oil; others deep-fry their latkes. You can make small pancakes by stirring the batter and dropping it in the pan from a tablespoon; I use a larger spoon and make only three pancakes in a 22-cm (9-in) diameter frying pan.

Like any pancake, it is ready to be turned when bubbles start appearing in the uncooked batter. Slide the spatula under and turn them, cooking for a few minutes – lift to see if the second side is getting crisp. Drain on kitchen paper. It is a counsel of perfection to say that the latkes should be eaten as they come out of the pan. Normally you will have to stack them up and keep them warm till the batter is finished up. They only get a *little* soggy.

Some families eat these with apple sauce, some with soured cream. They are, it almost goes without saying, divine with braised and boiled meat of every sort.

CLAUDIA RODEN'S BIMUELOS DE HANUKKAH (FRITTERS IN SYRUP)

This is the special Hanukkah food of the Jews of Turkey, Greece and the Arab world, fritters bathed in syrup, 'variously called,' says Claudia Roden, '*lokma, loukmades, aweimat, zalabia* (by us in Egypt) and *bimuelos* in Ladino,' which is the Sephardic vernacular, based on Spanish, and equivalent to the Yiddish language of the Ashkenazi Jews. In Ladino, they say Hanukkah is '*el buen dia a la tripa*', which means it's a good day for the stomach, though, in view of the amounts of fried foods consumed, says Claudia Roden, 'good in one way, maybe, but perhaps not for the digestion.'

Serves 6
For the sugar syrup
1 kg (2 lb, 5 cups) sugar
500 ml (18 fl oz, 2 cups plus 2 Tbsp) water
juice of half a lemon
1 Tbsp rose or orange-flower water (optional)

For the batter
500 g (1 lb, 3½ cups) all-purpose flour
½ tsp salt
1 pkt fast-action dried yeast
700 ml (1¼ pts, 3 cups plus 2 Tbsp) warm water (1
    part boiling to two parts cold)
light oil for frying

Make the syrup first. Put the sugar, water and lemon juice in a pan and simmer for about 20 mins until it is thick enough to coat a spoon. Add the rose or orange-flower water and simmer for only a few seconds longer, then chill.

For the batter, put the flour in a large bowl and mix in the salt and yeast, then stir in the water gradually and beat vigorously for at least five mins until smooth and elastic. Cover with a damp cloth and leave to rise in a warm place for at least an hour, then beat the batter once more and let it rise again.

Make the fritters in batches. Pour little balls of batter, by the teaspoon or tablespoon (they can be tiny or large) into sizzling (but not too hot) oil and fry until puffed up, crisp and golden, turning them with a slotted spoon to brown all over.

After a bit, lower the heat a little so that the fritters have time to get done inside before they are too brown. (If the oil is not hot enough to begin with the batter tends to flatten out.) You may find it easier to dip in oil the tablespoon with which you shape the fritters. The batter is light and produces irregular shapes.

Lift the fritters out with a slotted spoon, drain on kitchen paper and dip them in the cold syrup for a few seconds, or, if you prefer, let them soak up the syrup for longer. They are at their best hot, but are also good cold. Instead of dipping the fritters in syrup, you can serve them covered with warmed diluted honey or sprinkled with cinnamon and icing sugar.

SEPHARDIC HANUKKAH DOUGHNUTS

This recipe is adapted from *Cookbook of the Jews of Greece* by Nicholas Stavroulakis (1990). He calls these *zvingous*, and says they are the Romaniote (and also Christian) version of *boumwelos* or *bimwelos*, what Americans call doughnut holes. Despite having the same name – though a different spelling – as Claudia Roden's recipe, these are actually only fried puffs of choux pastry. In most parts of the world they are sprinkled with icing sugar, but the Greek recipe calls for pouring a well-chilled syrup over the still-hot pastries and sprinkling with coarsely crushed walnuts and almonds.

Makes 15–20
2 Tbsp olive oil
200 ml (7½ fl oz, ¾ cup) water
salt
170 g (6 oz, 1½ cups) flour
4 eggs, lightly beaten
450–680 ml (16–24 fl oz, 2–3 cups) olive oil for
    deep-frying

In a large, heavy saucepan bring the oil, water and a pinch of salt to the boil. Off the heat, rapidly stir in all the flour, whisking vigorously until you have a thick batter. Whisk in the eggs – the mixture will get quite shiny and glossy. The batter should be so thick and cohesive that it will not drop off the spoon by itself, but has to be dislodged with your finger. Heat the olive oil in another large and heavy saucepan until a haze appears. Drop in a tiny bit of batter; the oil is at the right temperature when the batter sizzles and swells up.

Dip a tablespoon in oil and take up a spoonful of the batter. Use your finger to push the batter off the spoon into the hot oil, but cook only a few at a time. They are done as soon as they swell and turn golden brown.

FRANCES BISSELL'S
PHEASANT BREASTS WITH POMEGRANATES

This recipe was devised by Frances Bissell one Christmas when I had decided that we would have pheasant, just to make a change from turkey. There were 20 of us, and I had meant to order 10 pheasants but, in a sort of culinary Chinese whisper, things went wrong. We had asked for the birds to be separated into legs and breasts, and the legs were going into the freezer to use later on for a pheasant cassoulet. It was when we counted more than 20 legs that we began to realise that we had not 10 birds, but 10 brace of pheasants. We actually ate the lot. This recipe is for the breasts of *one brace* of pheasants.

Serves 4
4 trimmed breasts from 2 pheasants
2 pomegranates
1 carrot, sliced into rounds
1 stick of celery, sliced
1 onion, peeled and sliced thinly
black peppercorns to taste, crushed
pink peppercorns (optional and I don't like them)
garlic, crushed (optional and quantity to taste)
8 Tbsp rich game, meat or chicken stock

Place the breasts in a single layer in a shallow dish, or into a strong plastic bag. Cut the pomegranates in half. Pick the seeds out of one half, and keep these for decorating the finished dish. Squeeze the remaining three halves in a lemon squeezer and strain the juice over the pheasant (or into the bag). Add the carrot, celery, onion, crushed peppercorns and garlic to the marinade.

Marinate for a few hours or overnight. Then remove and dry the pheasant, and strain the marinade into a small saucepan. Preheat the grill and cook the pheasant quickly over or under fierce heat, so that it is brown but not burnt on the outside, and still juicy inside. (Press the thickest bit with your finger; it is done when it still gives a little, but is not soft.) Put the meat in a warm place to rest while you finish the sauce.

Add the stock to the marinade and reduce until syrupy. Put a dollop of the sauce on each of four heated plates, place the pheasant breasts on top of the sauce, and scatter the reserved pomegranate seeds over them.

'Serve with a few steamed broccoli florets and a purée of celeriac, garlic and cardamom or wild rice,' says Frances Bissell, 'and, if you must, stir-fried Brussels sprouts.'

PHEASANT CASSOULET

For using up any surplus created by the recipe above.

Cook the beans separately. The best are gigantic *belles de Soisson*. I bring 2 kg (about 4 lb) of these back from France whenever I see them (usually in a shop selling health foods), and beg my friends to do the same; but they remain rare. So begin by soaking dried white haricot beans, according to their freshness – anything from a few hours to overnight but no longer – and then discard the soaking water. Bring to the boil with a generous amount of water, boil hard for 10 mins, and discard that water (with it will go some of the beans' flatulence-making properties). Cover with fresh water to 10 cm (4 in) above the beans, add a coarsely chopped onion or two, several peeled and smashed cloves of garlic, a chunk of unsliced bacon or *petit salé*, a sprig of thyme and some bay leaves. Simmer these, covered, until the beans are tender. I usually do this in an earthenware *marmite* (casserole) in a very slow oven. Add salt and pepper after the beans are cooked, as the bacon may have contributed enough salt.

For appearance's sake, brown separately, in a minimum of oil or rendered poultry fat or dripping, the pheasant legs and at least one spicy sausage such as a Toulouse sausage per person. I also like to use the big fat Lyonnaise sausages, about one for every 4 diners. The pheasant (or any other game, for that matter) is replacing the *confit* of duck or goose (preserved in its own fat).

Now assemble the dish. Put the beans, with thyme and bay leaves removed, in a flat oven-to-table gratin dish with a fresh sliced onion and a coarsely chopped tomato or two. (The tomato is optional, and a source of controversy, but a little of it helps the flavour enormously.) Cut the now-cooked bacon into chunks and tuck them into the beans, along with the pheasant and sausages. Sprinkle with more thyme, if needed, and freshly ground black pepper.

Strew breadcrumbs over the top of the gratin dish and dot with some sort of fat. As you have been very good and hardly added any fat to the dish apart from the meat, you could restore some of the traditional unctuousness to this dish by using deliciously flavoured rendered-with-onion duck, goose or chicken fat for this purpose. Cook in a hot oven until bubbling and push the breadcrumb crust down once or twice to thicken the dish, adding another layer of breadcrumbs.

This recipe only needs a *confit* of duck or goose in place of the pheasant to be authentic. But the gamy flavours also result in a healthier as well as a more delicious dish. It freezes all too well; we usually find ourselves eating up leftover cassoulet in late spring.

COQ AU VIN WITH CHINESE BLACK MUSHROOMS

Use your own favourite recipe for *coq qu vin*, but substitute dried Chinese black *shiitake* mushrooms for the mushrooms; they give an otherwise difficult-to-achieve depth of flavour. Soak them in water for 20 mins before using them.

We have lately had some huge chickens (one weighed more than 7 kg, 15 lb) from John Munson, and found this was the best way to deal with them; it is also a useful way to cope with a too large turkey. One of the best means of ensuring that the breast is perfectly cooked is to amputate the legs and thighs and cook them like this.

Joint the bird and, if it is large, chop it into serving portions with a Chinese cleaver. Dredge the pieces in seasoned flour if you like. Brown in olive oil with a knob of butter if you don't give a damn. Remove to a large, preferably earthenware casserole, and, in the same fat, sauté some *lardons*, rectangular solid 1 cm (½ in) strips of previously blanched bacon or salt pork or serious ham, if you have such a thing. (This is a good recipe for using up scraps of Bayonne and other raw ham, in which case, don't blanch or sauté, but put straight in the casserole with the browned bird.) In the same fat, quickly brown a sliced onion or two, some peeled, smashed cloves of garlic and a sliced stick or two of celery. Transfer everything to the casserole, and de-glaze the pan with a huge slug of brandy, which you can set fire to if it amuses you. At this point you add the soaked-in-water, stemmed and sliced best quality Chinese mushrooms, as many as you fancy and can afford.

Season with salt and pepper, a sprig of thyme and some bay leaves and cover the contents with *good* red wine. This is important, as you can taste the quality of the wine in the finished dish. No one uses Chambertin any more, naturally, but it makes sense to use a young fruity pinot noir such as you might get from the Hautes Côtes de Nuit or Hautes Côtes de Beaune. Stew the casserole in a moderate oven until the chicken is just done and all the flavours blended. If the sauce is too thin, which is quite likely, thicken it with a *beurre manié*, made by combining equal parts of softened butter and flour, rolled into little balls in your fingers, and dropped bit by bit into the simmering casserole. Stir and test the sauce for thickness.

Prepare separately the traditional garnish of button onions by peeling them and browning in olive oil or butter with a sprinkling of sugar to caramelise them. Add them to the casserole, with fried croûtons if you're really going for broke, and a scattering of chopped parsley.

NAMITA PANJABI'S DUCK MOLEE

This recipe comes from the Anglo-Indian community of Bombay, who eat it at Christmas. It is a dish made for occasions of celebration by Anglo-Indians all over Western and Southern India.

Serves 3–4
For the masala (the spice mixture)
½ tsp ground turmeric
1 tsp ground cumin
½ tsp freshly ground black pepper
8 cardamoms, seeds only
5 cm (2 in) cinnamon stick
8 cloves
2.5–3.5 cm (1–1½ in) fresh ginger
6–8 cloves garlic
8 dry red chillies, seeded
1 heaped tsp flour
300 ml (10 fl oz, 1¼ cups) cooking oil
4 medium onions, 3 finely minced, 1 finely sliced
6–8 green chillies, slit lengthwise, seeded unless you
    like it hot
3 large tomatoes, peeled and puréed
4 large potatoes, quartered
1 duck (1.5–2 kg, 3–4 lb) jointed into 6–8 pieces (in
    India fowl is cooked in relatively small pieces)
400 ml (14 fl oz, scant 2 cups) coconut milk, extracted
    from the grated flesh of 1 coconut, *or* a 400 ml
    tin of coconut milk, *or* made from half a 200 g (7
    oz) packet of creamed coconut
2 Tbsp vinegar
salt
fresh coriander for garnish

Grind the spices for the masala to a fine paste with the flour and 3–4 tablespoons of water and reserve.

In a pan large enough to sauté the duck and hold the potatoes as well, heat all but 3 tablespoons of the oil and fry the chopped onion to a brown colour over medium heat. The onions should be soft, not crisp; if need be, sprinkle with water a few times during the cooking.

Add the masala paste and stir-fry so that the paste doesn't stick; cook for 3–5 mins, until the oil separates from the spice mixture.

Now add the green chillies, tomatoes and potatoes and cook for 1 min. Put in the duck pieces and fry them in the masala for about 5 mins over medium heat. Add 100–150 ml (4–6 fl oz, ½–¾ cup) water and cook the duck until you think it is about ⅔ done. Stir in the coconut milk and simmer on low heat until the duck is tender. The consistency of the sauce should be that of a thick gravy. Add the vinegar and taste for salt.

While the duck is simmering, in another pan fry the sliced onion in the 3 tablespoons of oil until it is crispy brown. Drain on kitchen paper and garnish the duck with it and the fresh coriander.

CLAUDIA RODEN'S KEFTA TAGINE
(*Meatballs in Tomato Sauce*)

If you want to have a total alternative feast, Claudia Roden also suggested this dish, which can be either a first course, or a main course served after the stuffed peppers. The recipe is Moroccan, and is simply small spicy meatballs, usually made of lamb, simmered in an equally spicy tomato sauce, with eggs broken over them and cooked in the liquid and the steam.

Serves 6
For the sauce
1½ large onions, chopped
3 Tbsp oil
2 cloves garlic, crushed with a knife (not in a garlic press)
750 g (1½ lb) tomatoes, peeled and chopped
salt
1 tsp ground paprika
½ tsp ground cumin
½ tsp ground cinnamon
1 bunch parsley, finely chopped

For the meatballs
750 g (1½ lb) minced lamb or veal
small bunch of parsley, finely chopped
small bunch of coriander, finely chopped
a few mint leaves or 2 tsp dried mint
salt
1 tsp ground paprika
1 tsp ground cumin
1 tsp ground cinnamon
¼ tsp ground ginger

To finish
6 eggs

Use a wide flameproof gratin dish or casserole that you can take to the table.

To make the sauce, fry the onions in oil until golden, add the garlic, and when the aroma rises add the rest of the ingredients. Add 300 ml (½ pt, ⅔ cup) water and simmer for 15 mins.

While the sauce is cooking, make the meatballs. Mix all the ingredients together and work them to a paste with your hands. Wet your hands and roll the mixture into marble-sized balls. Drop them into the sauce and simmer for 15 mins.

About 10 mins before you are ready to serve, bring the stew back to the simmer and carefully break the eggs over the meatballs. The eggs will stay on the surface and the dish is ready as soon as they are set. Don't let them get hard.

FLORENTINE FENNEL

Can be trimmed, quartered and cooked in a covered microwave dish with chopped garlic or onion, a dribble of olive oil and salt and pepper. I find four minutes on full power will do 500 g (1 lb) of fennel so that it is still firm when you bite it, but not crunchy. You can do the same trick by putting it in a low-sided dish and steaming it. Broccoli can be treated in the same way, but will also respond well to the more powerful flavours of chilli and ginger.

NAMITA PANJABI'S SORPOTEL

A celebration dish of pork and pork offal from Goa, where there are large numbers of Christians, so this is frequently served at Christmas. The flavours and method of preparation are characteristically Goan. It is often made 2 or 3 days in advance and refrigerated for the flavours to mature.

Serves 4

2 tsp red chilli powder or cayenne
½ tsp finely ground black pepper
½ tsp ground cumin
1 tsp ground coriander
2–3 Tbsp sherry vinegar
120 g (4 oz) pig's liver, in large dice or strips
1–2 Tbsp oil
120 g (4 oz, ¾ cup) finely chopped onions
1–3 cm (½–¾ in) fresh ginger, peeled and minced
2–3 cloves garlic, finely minced
450 g (1 lb) lean pork, in 2.5 cm (1 in) cubes
tamarind juice, made by soaking a 2.5-cm (1-in) diameter ball of tamarind pulp in 2–3 Tbsp hot water and discarding seeds and skin
½ tsp sugar
salt
1 tsp garam masala (mixed Indian spices)

Mix the first 4 spices with 1 tablespoon of the vinegar and reserve.

Boil the pork liver in water to cover until partly cooked. Then drain, reserving cooking liquid, pat dry with kitchen paper and dry-fry the liver over medium-to-high heat in a nonstick pan until light brown. Stir constantly to prevent it sticking.

Heat the oil in the cleaned nonstick frying pan or in another pan large enough to hold all the remaining ingredients. Fry the onions over a low–medium flame until golden brown. Add the ginger and garlic and fry for another ½ min. Then add the vinegar-steeped spices and stir constantly to keep the mixture from sticking.

After 2–3 mins you should see the oil separating at the sides of the mixture. Add the pork and the liver at this point and fry over medium heat for 3–5 mins, stirring constantly so that nothing burns. Add the tamarind juice, sugar, salt to taste and garam masala. Cook until the meat is fork-tender, adding a little of the liver stock if it appears to be drying up. Finish the sauce, which should have the consistency of a thick gravy, with the rest of the sherry vinegar. Reheat when you want to serve, and eat either with white Basmati rice or with bread, such as naan.

CLAUDIA RODEN'S KEFTA TAGINE

(Meatballs in Tomato Sauce)

If you want to have a total alternative feast, Claudia Roden also suggested this dish, which can be either a first course, or a main course served after the stuffed peppers. The recipe is Moroccan, and is simply small spicy meatballs, usually made of lamb, simmered in an equally spicy tomato sauce, with eggs broken over them and cooked in the liquid and the steam.

Serves 6

For the sauce

1½ large onions, chopped

3 Tbsp oil

2 cloves garlic, crushed with a knife (not in a garlic press)

750 g (1½ lb) tomatoes, peeled and chopped

salt

1 tsp ground paprika

½ tsp ground cumin

½ tsp ground cinnamon

1 bunch parsley, finely chopped

For the meatballs

750 g (1½ lb) minced lamb or veal

small bunch of parsley, finely chopped

small bunch of coriander, finely chopped

a few mint leaves or 2 tsp dried mint

salt

1 tsp ground paprika

1 tsp ground cumin

1 tsp ground cinnamon

¼ tsp ground ginger

To finish

6 eggs

Use a wide flameproof gratin dish or casserole that you can take to the table.

To make the sauce, fry the onions in oil until golden, add the garlic, and when the aroma rises add the rest of the ingredients. Add 300 ml (½ pt, ⅔ cup) water and simmer for 15 mins.

While the sauce is cooking, make the meatballs. Mix all the ingredients together and work them to a paste with your hands. Wet your hands and roll the mixture into marble-sized balls. Drop them into the sauce and simmer for 15 mins.

About 10 mins before you are ready to serve, bring the stew back to the simmer and carefully break the eggs over the meatballs. The eggs will stay on the surface and the dish is ready as soon as they are set. Don't let them get hard.

FLORENTINE FENNEL

Can be trimmed, quartered and cooked in a covered microwave dish with chopped garlic or onion, a dribble of olive oil and salt and pepper. I find four minutes on full power will do 500 g (1 lb) of fennel so that it is still firm when you bite it, but not crunchy. You can do the same trick by putting it in a low-sided dish and steaming it. Broccoli can be treated in the same way, but will also respond well to the more powerful flavours of chilli and ginger.

KEN HOM'S CHRISTMAS ROAST DUCK, PEKING-STYLE

The Chinese-American cookery teacher and television presenter wrote this recipe for me for the *Observer*'s 1990 series. It's awfully good, and you can use the recipe for goose as well.

Serves 4–6
1 duck (1.8 kg, 4 lb)
675 g (1½ lb) green apples, such as Granny Smiths
juice of one lemon
4 Tbsp finely chopped fresh ginger
4 Tbsp finely chopped spring onions
2 Tbsp finely chopped fresh coriander
salt and freshly ground black pepper

Basting liquid
1 litre (2 pints, 4 cups) water
3 Tbsp dark soy sauce
2 Tbsp honey

Peel, core and cut the apples into thick slices. In a large stainless-steel bowl, combine the apples with the lemon juice, ginger, spring onions and fresh coriander. Season with salt and pepper to taste and reserve.

Thaw the duck completely if it is frozen, and dry inside and out with kitchen paper. Season the inside with salt and pepper, and fill the cavity with the apple mixture. Secure with skewers tied lengthwise with string, and one band of string across the bird's middle to truss the wings. Put an S-shaped meathook into the neck end of the duck, or make an arrangement with a wire coat-hanger.

In a medium-sized pot, combine the ingredients for the basting liquid and bring to the boil. While still simmering baste the duck several times with the hot liquid. Hang the duck up to dry or dry it on a rack in a cool place in front of an electric fan for 2–3 hours. When the duck is properly dried the skin will feel like parchment paper.

Preheat the oven to 240°C (475°, gas mark 9). Place the duck, breast-side up, on a rack inside a roasting pan. Pour in 300 ml (½ pt, a generous cup) water. Roast the duck for 20 mins, then turn down the heat to 190° (375°, gas mark 5) and cook for 40 mins longer. Finally, return the heat to the higher temperature and roast for another 10 mins.

Take the duck from the oven and allow it to rest for 15 mins. Remove the skewers and string, scoop out the apple stuffing and serve separately, and carve the duck as handsomely as possible.

HAM WITH CHABLIS AND MUSTARD

The best way I know to serve leftover ham hot. Place thickish slices of good ham in a gratin dish you can bring to the table. Cover it with a *béchamel* sauce made from a roux using equal quantities of flour and butter, to which you add as much good dry white wine (not really chablis) as you feel you can afford. Make up the remainder of the sauce with milk or cream in the usual way, seasoning with a pinch of cayenne and anything from 1 teaspoon to 1 tablespoon of Dijon mustard, added at the least minute to keep its flavour. You probably won't need salt because of the ham. Cover with the sauce and flash under the grill or brown in a hot oven.

KEN HOM'S SINGAPORE-STYLE LETTUCE FRIED RICE

To go with Ken Hom's Christmas Roast Duck (see page 128), or on its own for supper after a lunch of too much turkey.

Serves 4

5–6 Chinese dried mushrooms
2 Tbsp peanut oil
4 shallots, sliced
3 cloves garlic, crushed
long-grain rice to the 400 ml (15 fl oz, scant 2 cups) level in a measuring jug, then cooked in the normal way
50 g (2 oz, ¼ cup) fresh or frozen peas
3 Tbsp finely minced spring onions
2 fresh chillies
2 eggs, beaten lightly
3 Tbsp light soy sauce
½ tsp salt
¼ tsp freshly ground black pepper
225 g (8 oz) iceberg lettuce, shredded
2 Tbsp finely chopped spring onions, as garnish

Soak the dried mushrooms in warm water for 20 mins, squeeze out liquid, discard stems and cut the caps into small dice.

Heat a wok or large frying pan and add the oil (after the wok is hot – this is important in Chinese cooking). When almost smoking add the shallots and garlic and stir-fry for 30 secs. Add the cold, cooked rice and stir-fry for 1 min; then add mushrooms, peas, spring onions and chillies (chopped if you want the dish to be hot; whole if you want only to flavour the dish, in which case, remove before serving). Continue to stir-fry for another 3 mins. Stir in the eggs, soy sauce, salt and pepper and stir-fry for a further 2 mins or until the eggs have set.

Finally add the lettuce and mix thoroughly. Turn out on to a warmed serving plate, garnish with the spring onions and serve at once.

THE EASIEST VEGETABLE RECIPE THERE IS

Take whatever member of the squash family is available – Turk's cap, butternut, patty pan, a small pumpkin – pierce it several times with a skewer or knife blade, and microwave it on full power until you can smell it. It's done. When you can handle it, cut it in half and discard the seeds, season and serve. Or scoop out the flesh into a gratin or soufflé dish and season with butter, cream, olive or nut oil, and sweet spices such as grated nutmeg, ground cinnamon or cardamom – or with ground cumin and coriander seed. Don't forget salt and pepper.

You can do this in a conventional oven as well, but you need to oil the skin of the squash, and open the oven door from time to time for a good sniff.

FRANCES BISSELL'S WILD RICE WITH WILD MUSHROOMS

Cook the wild rice according to the directions on the packet using three volumes of liquid, either lightly salted water or stock, to one of rice. Check its progress. Some people like it with a little crunch left, others prefer it when each grain has exploded fully.

Clean and slice whatever wild mushrooms you can acquire. Ceps are wonderful, so are golden *girolles* and black *trompettes de la mort; pieds de mouton* are fine, and oyster mushrooms will do when there's nothing more interesting. They can all be supplemented with good cultivated mushrooms, and sometimes the chestnut-coloured ones have more flavour than some in the list above. I shouldn't bother with fresh shiitake mushrooms, but reconstituted dried ones are excellent.

Sauté the mushrooms apart from the rice, in olive oil, butter or a mixture of both, with or without some diced onion, shallot or garlic, as the mood takes you. Combine this with the cooked rice and serve with a generous dusting of minced parsley or green coriander.

KEN HOM'S RED-COOKED WINTER VEGETABLES

With the duck and the Lettuce Fried Rice (see pages 128 and 132), plus a light dessert, this would make a complete Chinese-style Christmas dinner, but it can be served Western-style and will go well with a spicy white wine or a young, fruity red.

Red-cooking is a technique usually employed for cooking meats, simmering them in a rich, red sauce of Chinese spices, and you can easily adapt the recipe for meat, poultry or even a very sturdy fish. Ken Hom discovered, though, that it works equally well with vegetables, making a quick, tasty stew. You might like this after the Christmas binge, with a bit of grilled chicken or meat, and a green salad.

Serves 4
450 g (1 lb) carrots
225 g (8 oz) turnips
1 Tbsp peanut oil
2 cloves garlic, peeled and crushed with a knife (not in a garlic press)
2 tsp coarsely chopped fresh root ginger
2 Tbsp hoisin sauce
1 Tbsp dark soy sauce
2 tsp sugar
150 ml (5 fl oz) water

Peel and cut the carrots into 2.5-cm (1-in) pieces. Peel the turnips and cut into 2.5-cm (1-in) cubes. Heat a wok or large frying pan. Add the oil, then the garlic and ginger. Stir-fry for 10 secs and add the carrots, hoisin sauce, soy sauce, sugar and water. Cover and cook over high heat for 8 mins. Then add the turnips and cook for another 3 mins or until the vegetables are tender but not mushy. There will be very little sauce left. Turn on to a hot platter and serve.

BAKED BEETROOT

Take fresh, scrubbed but not peeled beetroots and put them in a double thickness of foil, with as many cloves of peeled garlic as you like. Add salt and pepper and drizzle over olive oil. Seal the foil parcel loosely, and cook exactly as you would bake a potato. It's done when it gives a little to the touch, or a skewer goes in easily. Peel the beetroot while still it is warm, slice and eat with the golden-brown garlic. Or dress with olive oil, a squeeze of lemon and salt and pepper, scatter the garlic about with some chopped parsley or chives, and eat at room temperature as a salad or first course.

CLAUDIA RODEN'S PIMIENTOS REYENADOS
(Stuffed Peppers)

Despite its Spanish-sounding Ladino name this is actually a Turkish dish, and is usually made with smallish green peppers; but Claudia Roden suggested this in my *Observer* Alternate Feasts series, for those who are 'tired of turkey'. It makes a splendid vegetarian main course, and if you make it with both red and green peppers you can see its visual relevance to Christmas. It is always served cold – at room temperature – and so is the most obliging dish imaginable for the cook.

Serves 6
6 large or 12 small sweet (bell) peppers
2 large Spanish onions, finely chopped
150 ml (¼ pt, ⅔ cup) olive oil
2 Tbsp pine nuts
250 g (8 oz, 1 cup) short-grain rice, washed and drained
2 Tbsp currants
salt and freshly ground black pepper
1 Tbsp sugar
bunch of mixed herbs, parsley, mint and dill, finely minced

Cut a small slice around the stem end of each pepper and remove the core and seeds. Reserve the top.

For the filling, fry the onions in 5 Tbsp of the oil in a saucepan until golden. Add the pine nuts and when they begin to colour, add the rice and stir well until it becomes translucent. Then add the currants, salt, pepper and sugar, and pour in 450 ml (¾ pt, 2 cups) water. Let the stuffing cook with the lid on for 15 mins, then stir in the herbs. Preheat the oven to 190°C (375°F, gas mark 5).

Cool the filling a little and pack it into the peppers and cover with their tops or, if you prefer, follow the Turkish custom and cover them with slices of tomato.

Place in a baking dish so that the cut side is up, and pour in about 150 ml (¼ pt, ⅔ cup) water plus the rest of the oil. Cover with a lid or a sheet of foil and bake in the preheated oven for 40 mins. Then remove the cover and bake for another 20 mins until the peppers are soft. Leave to cool.

You can use this filling for other vegetables such as tomatoes, aubergines (eggplants) and courgettes (zucchini), also to be served at room temperature.

SALADS
Christmas Crunch

One thing I cannot bear to be without in the winter is fresh green salad. When green vegetables are at a premium or out of season altogether, and we eat meals that are heavy with meat and dried beans, we all need a little crunch in our lives.

Christmas is not a bad time of year for finding salads in the shops. Radicchio comes into its own just about now, and there is always the delicious frizzy chicory. The greengrocers' shops only start to become dreary after the New Year – but that, I think, is when the human body most needs what they no longer have for sale.

So I try to grow salad in my garden all year around. This can be done almost anywhere. If lettuce will grow in summer, there ought to be some salad plant that you can grow in the winter, although you might need the protection of a cloche or small plastic tunnel. I have to admit, however, that we have recently had our first-ever failure in this regard. We had sharp, severe frosts just before Christmas last year and, to my surprise, there was hardly anything left in the garden at Christmas by way of salad stuffs. The only survivors were two rows of cultivated French sorrel and, very oddly, a row each of chervil and coriander. This does not quite amount to a salad – though they make very welcome additions to the Chinese leaves in the shops in winter.

On the other hand, we did take our annual precaution of growing Witloof chicory. If you dig up the carrot-thick roots and plant them thickly in large pots with potting compost, and cover and keep these in a cool dark place, you will be rewarded with *chicons* for using in salads. Dress with nut oil, such as walnut or hazelnut oil, dribbled into rather more olive oil, plus salt, freshly ground pepper and the juice of an orange, especially a blood orange or, though you are unlikely to see one of these much before Christmas, a bitter Seville orange (which will need a pinch of sugar).

Normally, even in late winter, we would have a crop of *mesclun*, salad leaves for cutting. You can plant a mixture, under the name 'saladini' or something similar, or sow seed separately. One of the hardiest parts of this mixture is, to my taste, the best – rocket. A salad of rocket, dressed only with salt, pepper, good olive oil and lemon juice (or a drop or two of real Balsamic vinegar from Modena if you can afford it) is the ideal chaser to too much turkey, and the best imaginable balance to rich goose or game. Like a dish of watercress or a mixed green salad dressed in this simple way, it will cleanse the palate and give you and your guests renewed appetite.

American land cress is another salad survivor, and there have been years when radicchio and Treviso chicory lasted through the winter. There are several varieties of lettuce such as Lobjoit's green cos, Valmaine and Winter Density that will flourish in a cold frame or unheated greenhouse, and several of these will struggle along in the garden itself, especially with a little protection from a cloche.

Another useful ruse is to dig up a clump of chives just as they are dying back in early winter, pot them up and bring them inside. They are easy and quick to force back into growth for the salad bowl. I also put up a plant or two of parsley; and if you can spare a root of French tarragon, that will come up very early indoors as well.

To go into this subject properly, if you are interested, buy a copy of Joy Larkcom's *The Salad Garden* (published by Frances Lincoln in the UK and Viking in the US) and for more exotic, but very hardy salad stuffs, consult her new *Oriental Vegetables* (John Murray, UK and Kodansha, US).

137

CHAPTER SIX

French leave

The most crowded place I've ever been was Philippe Olivier's cheese shop in Boulogne on Christmas Eve. Of course the French eat cheese every day of the year so at Christmas it has to be something special, and the housewives and *fins becs* of Boulogne jam themselves into this best but tiniest of all cheesemongers. While the floor space of the shop may be limited (though it has recently doubled), the place where the real business goes on is not so small. For Philippe Olivier is an *affineur*; he does not just sell cheeses, he ripens and matures them in his own cellar. They only make an appearance in the shop when the cheese is perfectly ready to eat. If you want a Pont l'Evêque for the day after tomorrow, the shop assistant will not sell you one from the current display; she will descend into the *cave d'affinage* and choose one for eating precisely when you have specified.

Most of the customers left with a small, round wooden box containing a Vacherin du Mont d'Or, for that is the Christmas cheese of France, equivalent to the British habit of buying stilton at this time of year. This very seasonal cheese comes from the Franche-Comté, on the Swiss border. The only disagreeable story I have ever heard about that otherwise blameless but mysterious land, where military service and nuclear-bomb shelters are universal and prices so high that a cup of coffee can consume a normal day's food budget for a visitor from less economically advanced countries, has to do with this cheese. For the Swiss not only purloined the French name, but sullied it, as Patrick Rance says in *The French Cheese Book* (1989).

In the 1980s the Swiss began pasteurising the milk used to make their version of this cheese. Pasteurisation of milk intended for cheese is *always* a bad idea from a gastronomic point of view. This is a point that does not even need arguing, at least on grounds of taste and texture. And, as the following tale shows, it is not even certain that there are any health or hygiene grounds for the practice. During the winter of 1988/9, when Britain and much of the rest of Europe were seized by *Listeria* hysteria, it was revealed that at least 37 people had died of listeriosis since 1983 and that they had all consumed vacherin cheese. That winter the French vacherin makers had to destroy their cheeses because the market for them had collapsed, and there were none on the Christmas table. In Britain stocks of it were recalled. The panic was increased, because the French did not pasteurise the milk for their cheese.

It turned out that the raw-milk French vacherin was apparently resistant to *Listeria monocytogenes*;

every single case of listeriosis was associated with the Swiss *pasteurised*-milk cheeses. But the damage was done. Or was it? Everyone knew that the Swiss version was gastronomically inferior to the French one anyway, and, so far as I can see, consumers have learnt to discriminate between the two and give the Swiss cheese a miss. The new appellation names for French vacherin called for it to be labelled as simply 'Le Mont d'Or' or 'Vacherin du Haut-Doubs'. It is still easily recognisable because of its wooden box and the band of spruce bark that encloses the cheese itself. The surface of the cheese is a gold or even pinky-yellow colour, and it looks as though there is something soft and undulating under its pillow-cover crust. As indeed there is. The inside is a very pale creamy yellow in colour, with a profusion of tiny, pin-prick holes. It can be so runny that it is best spooned on to the plate, or firm enough to slice. The outside of the cheese, where the bark is attached, can be bright orange, and the scent of a mature specimen is pungent.

Patrick Rance advises that you cut your portion, gently pull it away from its spruce-bark wrapping and, 'to enjoy the texture and savour to the full, slice the cheese in strips up to a quarter of an inch thick, and lay it, do not spread it, on thick crisp-crusted bread'.

I sometimes wish that we consumers could band together to teach a lesson to the bureaucrats and boycott all cheese prepared from pasteurised milk. Unfortunately, were we to do this, we should never again taste stilton, the cheese that is – or was – the glory of the English table. I think there is almost a case for saying that stilton is extinct, that it no longer exists. That is to exaggerate, but only a little.

In the same bleak midwinter, that of 1988/9, the Colston Bassett Dairy, which was in fact a cooperative of farmers located five or six miles to the southeast of Nottingham, panicked and bought expensive pasteurising equipment. There were rumours about stilton and listeria, and they were afraid of losing their business, especially with the very exigent English supermarket buyers. They were then the last makers of unpasteurised stilton in the world.

Though the proud cylinder of stilton in its starched white napkin, sitting on a silver salver next to the crystal decanter of port and the jug of celery, is the very symbol of what is best about English gastronomy, it's all been a con for years. Stilton is an industrial product, made in dairies and creameries. No farmhouse stilton has been made since the 1930s, when the Watson family gave up after four generations of making stilton on their own farm. They were the last; most did not survive the First World War. Stilton had been made in factories since 1870, and by the time of the Second World War it was entirely made in factories. If you see someone selling 'farmhouse stilton' they're breaking the law.

This is a terrible fate to befall a cheese that has been celebrated since the early 18th century, a cheese whose fame has been spread by Daniel Defoe and Charles Lamb, one of the few gastronomic glories of the country. I am surprised there was not a greater outcry when Colston Bassett gave up the struggle; it seems to me that their cheese was a national monument, part of the national heritage and its disappearance on a par with the destruction of a great building. I hope we should make more of a fuss if someone threatened to pull down Blenheim or Castle Howard

– but the point seems to me to be the same one.

Still, all is not lost. Stilton no longer has the deep, rich flavour and distinctively creamy texture that was the hallmark of unpasteurised Colston Bassett, but I have tasted a post-pasteurisation Colston Bassett, and it is still an interesting cheese, worthy of a place on the Christmas table – just. Long Clawson stilton is acceptable as well. But I don't think I'll ever again buy a whole large stilton, as we always used to do. A two or three pound chunk (about 1½ kg) is quite enough now.

There are only three things to remember if you do buy a whole stilton. First, prepare it by cutting off a 6mm/¼ in lid, which you replace when you store the cheese in the coolest place in the house that is not your fridge. (Your fridge will dry it out unless it has a special cheese-keeping compartment at its bottom.) Second, to serve, slice it across horizontally. Do not let your guests cut vertical wedges out of it, unless you have first made a horizontal cross-section, which you serve separately on a plate, or balance on top of the remainder of the whole cheese. The object is always to keep the cut surfaces smooth and to the minimum. If anyone gouges the stilton, ask him to leave the table. Don't mash up the leftover stilton with port – unless neither the stilton nor the port has any merit on its own.

Stilton has never been made at Stilton, which is in what used to be Huntingdonshire (now part of Cambridgeshire), though the cheese was sold there, at least in the early 18th century, at the Bell Inn, where Daniel Defoe ate it in 1722. But cheddar certainly was made in Cheddar, Somerset, at least once upon a time. In 1980, however, the residents of the village opposed a plan to resume making the cheese there, on the grounds that the dairy would smell. In the event, local opposition was overcome, and cheddar cheese is once again produced at Cheddar. The name, of course, has been degraded; in the British way, it was not protected, and even in its own country, cheese not fit to bait a mousetrap can be called cheddar.

Originally, as was the case everywhere in the south of England, the West Country was grazed by sheep, and the first cheeses of the region must have been made from sheep's milk. By Tudor times, though, cheddar was already produced from cow's milk. These were usually made cooperatively, with each farmer getting back the proportion of finished cheese that he contributed in milk. The cheeses were gigantic, and could take several years to ripen. Patrick Rance speculates (in *The Great British Cheese Book*, 1982) that the cheese must have differed in height rather than diameter, as there must have been a limit to the variety of moulds available.

By the 17th century, cheddar was a luxury cheese, selling in London for two to three times the price of cheese from Cheshire; and it maintained its relative position in the cheese marketplace through the next century. At some point cheesemaking began to be done on individual farms, but until 1914, Major Rance tells us, some village dairies continued to make the cheese. Unfortunately, in the aftermath of the Second World War, most of the cheesemaking farms that had survived the First were swept away, and cheddar began to be made in factories, in huge blocks rather than cloth-wrapped truckles, and from pasteurised milk. That could easily have been the end of

Sausage & cheese sellers, fresco, Italian school 15th century

cheddar, but the combined efforts of Patrick Rance's research, plus his retail shop at Streatley, which was, before long, joined by other shops specialising in cheese, as well as selective buying by the Foodies of the 1980s and the shouting of food journalists, have kept the craft of making farmhouse cheddar alive.

The cheese is as good as ever – probably. It is just possible that the long-maturing, enormous cheeses,

such as that made for an 18th-century Lord Wey-
mouth that was said to be large enough to contain
a 13-year-old girl, tasted better, and explained why
Daniel Defoe wrote that 'without all dispute, it is the
best cheese that England affords, if not that the whole
world affords'. And Rance quotes, to telling effect, Dr
J. G. Davis saying: 'English *real* Farmhouse Cheddar,
English factory Cheddar, New Zealand Cheddar and
Canadian matured Cheddar may differ more among
themselves than do the common French unripened
soft cheeses which bear distinctive names.' (For those
readers too young to have known them, before the
English cheddar revival the best available were
long-matured Canadian cheeses, often wrapped in
black wax.) In other words, there may be a greater
difference between a proper artisanal cheddar and a
factory-made one than between a brie and a camembert. This is by no means silly or even shocking, for
the manufacture of the French cheeses in question is
chiefly a question of the size and shape of the mould.
The basic recipe for brie and camembert is identical,
much though they differ in taste: the shape and volume of the cheese determine how and to what extent
flavour-conferring organisms penetrate and colonise
the cheese, and thus how it tastes and smells.

'Sweet and sharp, moist and hard' are some of the
adjectives Patrick Rance used to describe cheddar. I
prefer it to smell and taste nutty, with a sweet first
note followed by tanginess, a real bite. I can see merit
in a creamy, moist texture, but equally in a firmer,
crumbly one. I now know that what a cheddar needs
to please me is age. So every Christmas we buy a
small truckle, weighing from five to seven pounds or
so (about 3 kg), keep it in the cellar and turn it care-

Stiltons ripening at Colston Bassett

fully until it is time to decapitate it for Christmas, in
the same fashion as that described above for the stilton. When we buy the truckle, it is at least 10 months
old, and we usually manage to mature it for another
month before attacking it. (It is sometimes possible
to buy an even older cheese but, naturally, the more
popular the cheese, the younger it tends to be when
it is sold.)

Last Christmas's cheddar came with a hand-
written label attached that gave its birthday as February 2. On March 2 the little there was left of it was

Stiltons at Melton Mowbray market at the turn of the century

still nutty and delicious. It came, as our cheddar now always does, from Mr and Mrs Keen and their sons at Moorhayes Farm, Wincanton, Somerset. It is, of course, made of the unpasteurised milk of the cows of their Friesian herd, which graze on grass grown on valley and higher sandstone, and, writes Major Rance, 'achieve a butterfat level of 4.1 per cent'. Keen's cheddar is made in traditional clothbound truckles, normally cylinders weighing 60 lb (27 kg). I have tasted other unpasteurised, matured farmhouse cheddars, but never one that I liked better than Keen's. Perhaps this is because they have an unfair advantage. 'Cheddar,' says Rance, 'has been made on this farm for as long as anyone can remember.'

We also have a cheese from the northwest of England on the table at Christmas, a cheshire, the oldest named cheese in Britain – older, Rance thinks, than the Romans, whose extensive experience with cheese and dairying must have improved cheshire cheese. The cheese gets a mention in the *Domesday Book*, and was praised by Thomas Fuller in 1601, and Celia Fiennes almost exactly a hundred years later.

Though it's made for most of the year, the best cheshire cheeses are those made in autumn. They used to be left unwaxed to dry out for 18 months, which is really the ideal age for eating cheshire, though it is very rare to find one that old nowadays. I buy Appleby's cheshire, made by Abbey Farm, Hawkstone, Weston-under-Redcastle, Shropshire, where the cheese is made by Mrs Appleby. Their cheeses won the Supreme Championship and several other prizes at the Nantwich Show in 1980, the last time the cheeses of this region have been judged on such a grand scale.

Most farmhouse cheshire is now matured in wax, which coats the natural cloth binding. This is deplored by Lance Appleby, none of whose cheeses is waxed; and Rance says his opposition to waxing ought to give pause for thought to the other producers. Appleby is convinced that waxed cheeses tend to sweat, says Rance, 'a long-standing worry of cheshire cheesemakers . . . Most cheeses are now waxed and graded for eating young, a deprivation for lovers of mature rich cheshire.' Count me in. That is why we try to buy a small truckle of Appleby's cheshire and mature it ourselves – a simple matter of standing it in a cool, dry, well-ventilated place and remembering to turn it at least once a week.

Note that Major Rance warns that 'genuine farmhouse cheshires are stamped with the number of the farm, together with the date of making and "superfine" or "fine" grading. Waxed cheeses not so marked may not be sold as farmhouse Cheshire.' The Appleby's number is 125.

There has been an almost more remarkable renaissance of farmhouse cheesemaking in Ireland, which is not restricted to traditional varieties, but includes many cheeses that have analogues in France, such as blue cheeses and washed-rind cheeses. If you see Milleens, Gubbeen or Cashel Blue, buy it. In America, it is very worthwhile experimenting with the new cheeses made in the Pacific Northwest; I sampled some sensational examples being sold in Seattle. There are also a large number of goat cheeses made by artisans

The cheese fair at Islington Dairy Show, October 8, 1878

in Britain and Ireland, though I have never tasted any so good as those made by Laurie Chenel in California. But goat cheese is not at its best at Christmas, so we don't include it on our cheeseboard. Its season is April to October, and beware of buying any later than November. There should be no fresh milk available then, as the nanny goat's kids should be taking it all.

Red wine is not always better with cheese than

white wine. In fact, some cheeses savage red wine. Stilton is a good example, for almost all blue cheeses are temperamental in this regard. It is famously well known that the best combination of wine and cheese is sauternes and roquefort; but several other white wines, including all the *viognier*-based ones of the Rhône, and many of the wines from Alsace, stand up well to roquefort's aggression. Few reds survive the encounter at all; though one of our strange findings in our tastings was that Bouzy rouge, the red version of the pinot noir usually vinified white for blending in champagne, is superb with roquefort.

All these whites are better with stilton than most reds, though we found some merit in matching it with powerful older rhônes. It will not do any favours for the claret or for fuller red burgundies, though light, fruity pinot noir comes out of the conflict relatively unscathed, which points to a pinot noir d'Alsace, perhaps, or a red Sancerre. Best of all, though, is the Englishman's traditional answer to what to drink with stilton: port. Vintage port usually has the guts to deal with the cheese bully; but I think I prefer the nuttiness of an older tawny. One year we had some Taylor's Twenty-Year-Old Tawny with the Colston Bassett. I can still remember the combination.

Port is also glorious with the cheddar and the cheshire, as it is with the vacherin, if you happen to have any to hand. It is with the hard English cheeses, though, that good claret and burgundy come into their own. The wine is flattered by the cheese (as claret, especially, is by old Gouda – look out for three-year-old, if you've got a bottle of great claret to show off); the rich, warm flavours of mature cheese are brought out by good red wine.

FROMAGE FRAIS AUX HERBES

Sometimes, either because you feel you've binged, or because you need to eat something that reminds you of summer, you want a really light dish after Christmas, on Boxing Day or New Year's Day. Buy a carton or two of *fromage frais*, which comes with percentages of butterfat from zero to slightly, but not very, rich. Whisk it with a fork and incorporate whatever chopped fresh herbs you can find. Chives are the most desirable but most rare at that time of year, so use the green tops of spring onions sliced terribly finely. Add a bit of minced garlic, salt and pepper, and stir in a drizzle of the fruitiest olive oil you can find.

If the mixture is not stiff enough to stand up on its own (possibly because you've used 0 per cent butterfat) either serve it as a dip with crudités, or mix in enough low-fat cottage cheese to give it the consistency that allows you to eat it with a fork. Served, for example, with a tomato salad made simply by slicing good tomatoes thickly stem-end down, salted and peppered (and sugared if their flavour is insipid), with oil and no vinegar, scattered with herbs including basil if possible, it will give you the illusion of having lunch on the beach somewhere in the Mediterranean.

POTTED STILTON (OR ANY OTHER CHEESE)

Instead of ruining leftover stilton with port, mash it, or any other really good hard cheese, with ⅓ of its volume (or weight) of unsalted butter. A pinch of cayenne is a very good idea, and a scraping of nutmeg not a bad one. If you must use the port with stilton, add it now – as much as it will absorb. Sherry goes very well with cheddar or cheshire, too. Pack the cheeses into individual ramekins or small soufflé dishes and cover with fat-safe clingfilm. Store in a cool place or the bottom of the fridge, and always bring back to room temperature before serving as part of or instead of the cheese course.

Cheese in moulds in the press room at Appleby's of Hawkstone

CHEESE SOUFFLÉ

This is the obvious way of using up leftover cheese of any sort, including the 'cooked' Swiss cheeses, washed-rind cheeses and goat's cheese (though goat's cheese is not in season at Christmas so you really shouldn't have any leftovers of that). To make any soufflé, begin with a flour and butter roux, with equal amounts of each. Make this into a *béchamel* sauce with hot milk, or a mixture of milk and cream if you have no interest in your cholesterol level. Pop a whole peeled onion in to melt into the sauce and flavour it, add some bay leaves if you like, a pinch of cayenne and a grating of nutmeg, but no salt yet. Fish out the flavourings before using, if the onion hasn't actually dissolved.

Now you have an interesting choice. You can leave the sauce to cook for an hour in a *bain-marie*, then add the flavourings and the eggs, and finish by cooking in a flat gratin dish for 10–15 mins in a moderately hot oven, which gives you a deliciously crusty and runny but not very puffed-up soufflé. Or you can proceed in the normal way, by taking the *béchamel* off the heat and stirring in the flavouring ingredients.

These can be anything, including cooked spinach, cubes of ham or smoked salmon scraps. But mainly it's a vehicle for leftover cheese. The golden rule is to use enough cheese to flavour and make the inside of the soufflé gooey, and a drop of Worcestershire sauce is usually a good idea, too. Once the main ingredient is incorporated (and melted, if it's cheese), add the egg yolks, one per serving, and beat them in off the heat. Whisk the egg whites separately (save old ones,

they hold more air), with a pinch of salt or cream of tartar if you like, to the soft peak stage. Use at least one more white than yolks – the more the better.

Stir a few blobs of egg white into the egg yolk mixture to lighten it before you dump the whole lot of egg white in and fold with a metal spoon. You do this with a deft touch, so as to incorporate all the white, but without knocking the air out of it. Spoon the mixture into one large or several individual soufflé dishes, prepared by buttering them and coating with ground parmesan (if appropriate), and fixing a collar of silver foil around the rim, if you're making one large soufflé. Bake in a moderately hot 190°C (375°F, gas mark 5) oven until risen and puffy, 10–20 mins for individual soufflés, 20–45 mins for large ones.

Soufflés are really very good-natured once you've grasped the principles involved in their production. If they're too liquid when cut into, I sometimes spoon out and serve the cooked bit, and put the rest back in the oven.

CHAPTER SEVEN

The sweet conclusion

It is only yesterday, as it were, since the traditional ending to the Christmas feast has become a flaming plum pudding, decorated with a sprig of holly, and containing a silver coin and other charms hidden within its hemispherical shape. From Tudor and Stuart times, right down to the Edwardian era, the Christmas pudding was only one among many of the sweet conclusions to the great spread. Nowadays, instead of having a table laden with flavoured creams, fruit jellies and light, frothy puddings, we have a single plum pudding (which, though it has a good deal of dried fruit, may contain no plums at all), served with hard sauce or brandy butter. If Christmas dinner is served at lunchtime, in Britain at least, this is likely to be followed, at all too short an interval, by mince pies served at tea-time, accompanied by Christmas cake, an all-too-rich fruitcake encased in a layer of marzipan under a shell of rock-hard royal icing adorned with a sprig of holly.

America is not addicted to Christmas pudding, and the French, on the whole, shudder at the thought of it, while adhering loyally to their sticky, rich, often gooey chocolate *bûche de Noël*. I was astonished, when doing the research for the television programme associated with this book, to discover several shops in Boulogne that sold *le plum pouding*. It transpired on close questioning that it is not the taste of the residents of the Pas de Calais for steamed puddings that is responsible for its presence in these shops, so much as their proximity to the English Channel. On the whole, the French attitude to this apparently medieval dish is to say that, as a nation, they have also lost their taste for feudalism, *droit de seigneur* and eating with the hands from wooden trenchers. More about the medieval aspect in a moment.

One firm, Matthew Walker of Derby, manufactures almost 40 per cent of the Christmas puddings eaten in the world, including virtually all those sold under their own labels by the British supermarkets. There are 120 different recipes currently in production, so each product is genuinely different from each of the others. Still, for Christmas 1992 they hoped to sell 8 million puddings. Incidentally, the French market has trebled in size recently. It could just be that this is accounted for entirely by British expatriates buying them at Fauchon in Paris; but I suspect the existence of a French underground of plum-pudding eaters.

Let us note that in some parts of America, particularly the south, though plum pudding is seldom on the Yule menu, nut-laden fruitcake, heavily laced with spirits, often is. At Thanksgiving, Americans have a prescribed dessert in pumpkin pie; but just as Christmas is the less important feast in the United States, so the rules for making up the meal are more relaxed.

Not only the ingredients and method of cooking, but the very ritual of making the Christmas pudding seems antique. Stir-up Sunday, the first Sunday before Advent, which is itself the Sunday before St Andrew's day, is when, by tradition, the whole family gathers around the mixing bowl. Each member from youngest to oldest stirs from east to west in commemoration of the journey of the Magi in the same direction, while silently making a wish. Though this could easily be a custom stretching back to 1066 and beyond, it actually originated in the 19th century.

Indeed, it is only since 1836 that plum pudding has been called 'Christmas' pudding, says Maggie Black in her finely researched Women's Institute *Calendar of Feasts* (1985, reprinted in Davidson's *On Fasting & Feasting*). Though George I had a plum pudding on his first Christmas in England in 1714, it was not then a dish exclusively associated with Christmas. Indeed, over a hundred years later, William IV had a plum pudding to celebrate his birthday.

It is commonly known that our modern, solid Christmas pudding originated in a thick liquid dish; what is startling is that the solid version and the more primitive liquid one co-existed for over two hundred years. The first reference to a solid Christmas pudding, a recipe only recently published, is as early as 1604; the latest recipe for a liquid one seems to be 1841.

Christmas porridge or broth sounds very odd to modern ears and not very attractive to modern palates. (The terms 'Christmas porridge' and 'plum porridge', 'Christmas broth' and 'plum broth' and 'Christmas pottage' or 'plum pottage' are all interchangeable.) But many Scandinavians even today eat a sweetened rice porridge as their Christmas Eve first course, which was also the position in the meal occupied by the British Christmas porridge. The hardship of a meal begun in this way is mitigated by the fact that a charm – a blanched almond – is hidden in the rice pudding, and its recipient gets a present.

Though a recent article in the press (in the *Observer*, 22 December 1991) repeats the old saw that the Christmas pudding 'is said to be derived from the time of William the Conqueror, when it consisted of a thick soup containing beef, raisins, currants, bread and suet', the first trace of the recipe, says C. Anne Wilson in *Food and Drink in Britain* (1973), is actually in the early 15th century, when it was called 'stewet beef to potage'. The recipe then had chunks of beef seethed in water and a lot of wine with minced onion, herbs, bread for thickening, a red colouring agent, seasonings of cloves, cinnamon and mace and, most importantly, currants. The point about this recipe, which was not then especially associated with Christmas, is that it is one of the few of many meat and dried fruit pottages of its type that survived into Georgian times, by which era most 'such compositions had lost their appeal and were rarely eaten', according to Anne Wilson.

In its Elizabethan version it acquired prunes, along with the raisins and currants. The prunes, a Tudor touch, were imported; they had already been added to meat pies, but were only now added to stews. They made such an impact on Tudor cooks that, says Anne Wilson, the name 'subsequently became a token of the other dried fruits; so that plum cake and plum porridge were confections containing some dried fruits, but not necessarily prunes'. In *English Bread and Yeast Cookery* Elizabeth David made the same point about figs, as well. 'Figgy' pudding very often contained raisins and currants, but no figs. By the time of Gervase Markham's 1615 *The English House-Wife*, his 'ordinary stewed broth' had lost its herbs but was otherwise identical. Then by 1660, with the publication of Robert May's *The Accomplisht Cook*, it had become a celebratory dish appropriate – still as a first course – for All Saints', Christmas and New Year's Day. Finally, by 1673, William Rabisha first called it a special Christmas dish, and soon after it was commonly called Christmas broth or Christmas or plum porridge. It was most often spiked with alcohol – claret and sack are the most frequently mentioned sorts – and could be made in advance and stored in earthenware pots. So the question of whether it's a medieval dish depends on what view you take of when the Renaissance started in England.

Along with mince pies, plum porridge became a particular horror to the Puritans in their campaign against Christmas. J. A. R. Pimlott quotes an anonymous rhymester of the 17th century saying, 'Plum broth was Popish, and mincepie – oh, that was sheer idolatry', and Sir Thomas Overbury caricatured a Puritan who attacked the Pope by refusing to eat the Christmas broth he was offered. Curiously, the heirs of the Puritans, the Dissenters, also bore plum porridge a grudge. Sir Roger de Coverly expressed surprise and pleasure that a strict Dissenter who had Christmas dinner at his house ate up his serving of plum porridge.

'When exactly plum pudding ousted plum por-ridge is a mystery,' wrote Mr Pimlott in 1978, 'which it must be left to later research to resolve.' The strange answer, as hinted at the beginning of this chapter, is, in historical terms, the day before yesterday. Pimlott himself quotes several authorities that appear to show that Christmas broth reigned supreme during the 18th century: '"Everyone from the King to the artisan eats soup and Christmas pies," wrote de Saussure in 1726. "The soup is called Christmas-porridge, and is a dish few foreigners find to their taste."' In David Garrick's 1774 *Christmas Tale* he says that it is indigestible to the foreign palate. An earlier reference is the Rev. W. Vickers writing to his correspondent in 1717 that, 'We can't come up to your country fare plumb por-rage, but must be content with onions and garlic.'

Writers of recipes also confirm the position of plum porridge in the 18th century. Hannah Glasse's 1747 *The Art of Cookery* gives 'Plumb-Porridge for Christmas': 'Make a beef broth with 8 gallons of water', the recipe begins, and continues with the familiar bread, prunes, raisins, currants, wine and spices. Hannah Glasse also has a 'boiled plumb pud-ding', but it has no connection with Christmas, and is less rich than her plum porridge. Even so, it is recognisably related to our own plum pudding, as it's made from suet, breadcrumbs, eggs, currants, raisins, nutmeg and ginger. Though there's an ambiguity about the date in his text, Pimlott seems to think that by the end of the 18th century 'an unnoticed revolution had taken place, and the plum-pudding had almost universally replaced its odd predecessor on the Christmas table'.

He cites in support of this a Mr Brand, who ate plum porridge at a dinner with the royal chaplains in

1801, and remarked that he did not know that it was still eaten. Even so, Pimlott found an exception. In 1841 Benson E. Hill's *Epicure's Almanac*, says Pimlott, 'gave recipes for both dishes, with the interesting difference that the porridge was to be made on 22 December and the pudding on Christmas Eve.' This must be the last such recipe, for the latest Anne Wilson found was Margaret Dods in 1826 who cited it as a Scottish recipe. Perhaps, says Anne Wilson, 'it lingered longer in Scotland than in other parts of Britain. Elsewhere the meatless plum pudding had already prevailed.'

We can agree that the porridge still hadn't quite disappeared by the mid-19th century. What is odder is that Hilary Spurling has found a recipe for the solid pudding that is earlier than anyone suspected. Lady Fettiplace (c.1570–c.1647) lived in an age that was a small time-pocket of female literacy. Under the influence of the Queen herself, well-bred girls learned to read and write for a brief period of 20 years or so. By the time of Elinor Fettiplace's death, under the Commonwealth, female literacy was once again discouraged. It is our good luck that Lady Fettiplace seems in 1604 to have written down a number of her own recipes. Mrs Spurling has published these as *Elinor Fettiplace's Receipt Book* (1986), where she says: 'We tend to think of Christmas pudding as a Victorian speciality, if not a 19th-century invention, but Lady Fettiplace made hers from virtually the same ingredients – eggs, breadcrumbs, suet, dried fruit and spices – in the same hospitable quantities as Mrs Beeton.' Mrs Spurling has told me that though the recipe is not explicitly linked to Christmas (none of Lady Fettiplace's recipes has any commentary attached to it), she is convinced that it was meant for use at Christmas, especially since the Christmas festivities in Lady Fettiplace's household went from November to Twelfth Night, and the pudding is clearly a midwinter dish.

The recipe must, of course, have been current and used in this form or another by hundreds or even thousands of Elizabethan cooks. The difference is that Lady Fettiplace could write it down. Her pudding is cooked in a sheep's paunch, like a haggis. It says: 'Take twelve eggs & breake them, then take crumbs of bred, & mace & currance & dates cut small, & some oxe suet small minced & some saffron, put all these in a sheepes Mawe, & so boile it.' Mrs Spurling glosses this as 2 lb (1 kg) of breadcrumbs and of suet, 5–6 lb (about 2½ kg) of dried fruit and 8–10 hours of boiling. As she points out, interpolating the quantities from Dorothy Hartley's recipe, which is said to be that used by the royal family since the days of George I, Lady Fettiplace's recipe would feed anywhere from 40 to 56 people. The saffron is an unusual ingredient, and makes one think of much older, properly medieval dishes.

In 1604 the pudding had to be boiled in an animal's stomach because, says Maggie Black, the pudding cloth was only invented in 1617. She thinks that the porridge mixture got richer and thicker until it became a candidate for boiling in a bag or cloth, but, as we have seen, the eggy pudding had already existed for at least a decade. I suspect, in fact, that it's a very great deal older than that – perhaps even as old as the porridge. But cleaning an animal's paunch was just as messy a job in the Middle Ages as it is today and, until the pudding cloth was invented, it must

The Cavalier is toasting not the Christmas pudding, but Margery, who is carrying it

have been far easier to serve porridge for Christmas than the more solid pudding. Even so, we shouldn't forget that the two dishes served different purposes – one was a first course, the other a final course.

The porridge had perhaps always had alcohol in it. The solid pudding did not, at least in Lady Fettiplace's version. The one served to George I, however, contained a large wine glass of brandy, and Mrs Maria Rundell's 1806 Common Plum Pudding had wine in

it. By 1816 Dr William Kitchiner, says Maggie Black, had created a plum pudding with brandy as a (one imagines unorthodox) Lenten dish and the circle was complete: the solid pudding had become associated with Christmas and then moved away again to become a dish associated with feasting in general.

As Maggie Black astutely observes, the Christmas pudding was a unifying dish, a democratic dish. As it 'could be boiled in a pot over the family fire', it was economical with fuel, and its relatively inexpensive ingredients must have been a welcome supplement to many a 'poor man's usually meagre beef or goose. It was in this role,' Maggie Black continues, 'that Charles Dickens saw it. Good journalist that he was, he wrote it up as the central symbol of Christmas cheer and plenty, and found a receptive audience. The new urban middle class was seeking to recreate what they believed had been medieval Christmas revelry.'

Their belief wasn't quite accurate, as we've seen. But the Christmas pudding acquired its central position as the symbol of Christmas feasting by ousting another culinary rival. It took over and transformed the ingredients of the Christmas porridge, but it literally captured the charms of the Twelfth Night cake.

In my family we try to remember, but usually forget, to put a silver coin in the Christmas pudding before it gets its second boiling. (We save a no-longer-legal-tender silver sixpence for this purpose – other families still guard a silver threepenny piece – but, of course, can never remember where it is so carefully kept.) Some families actually insert in their Christmas pudding the full panoply of charms: a thimble whose recipient will remain a spinster, a button for a bachelor, a ring for a wedding, a tiny horseshoe bringing good luck, as well as the coin bringing good fortune. These tokens were transferred directly from another institution, the Twelfth Night cake, and their transference marked its demise in England. Naturally this shift could only be accomplished when Christmas pudding has assumed its solid form: porridge eaters would be in danger of choking on concealed charms.

The Twelfth Night cake has survived as a recipe in Britain, where it has become Christmas cake; and as an institution in France, though the recipe has changed utterly. We shall discuss the French Twelfth Night cake later.

The disappearance of the Twelfth Night cake began in the 1850s. Its demise was brought about by the change in attitude noted by the writer in an 1850 special Christmas supplement in the *Illustrated London News* (quoted in Bridget Ann Henisch *Cakes and Characters*, 1984, which is the definitive book on this subject). The writer pointed out the difference between the appearance of the grocer's shop on Christmas Eve and the confectioner's shop as Epiphany approaches: 'It is the first only which produces the real national excitement.' Whereas in the past the Twelfth Night cake would have been the centre of every kind of interest and appetite, its appeal is now 'confined to the sense of sight. Fine combinations of saccharine splendour for the eyes; Kings and Queens, ill-formed but gorgeously gilt and frosted for the eyes; pippin-paste involved into curious scrolls – all for the eyes. But the interest of the Grocer's Shop on Christmas Eve penetrates far more deeply into the soul of the surveying crowd. Many, many of them, far beyond the limits of twelfth-cake consumers, hope to share practically in the boiled luxury. While the twelfth-cake is a more aristocratic type, the plum-pudding is a national symbol.'

Here is the nub of the matter. Christmas pudding has become democratic: 'It does not represent a class or a caste, but the bulk of the English nation. There is not a man, woman, or child raised above what the French would call *prolétaires*, that does not expect to taste a plum-pudding of some sort or other on Christmas Day.'

What about the charms? Originally they bore a direct line of descent from Saturnalia, for they began as a single bean. Its recipient was the King of the Bean, the temporary Lord of Misrule, the Master of the Revels. Sometimes there was a pea concealed in the cake as well, and the lady who got it became Queen; sometimes the King awarded the pea to a lady of his choosing. The power of the bean and the pea as fertility symbols was not lost on the revellers.

Twelfth Night festivities were so important that Shakespeare as well as Ben Jonson and Inigo Jones drew on the traditions of the masque; Kings diced at their courts, and gambling was licensed where state lotteries were organised; Samuel Pepys gave a new-fangled Twelfth-Night party where people assumed theatrical roles in a charade dictated by stock characters written on slips of paper and drawn out of a hat; and Thackeray wrote a 'book of Twelfth Night characters'.

The evolution of the Christmas pudding charms, then, was from the original bean, via the character cards, which by Pepys's time were no longer strips of paper concealed in the cake but a separate pack. By the mid-19th century these were types such as 'Park's New Twelfth-Night Characters' and included the violent, knife-wielding and melancholy Dicky Daggerwood and Mrs Daggerando; the bolters, Mr Benjamin Bounce and Countess Fly Away; the dandy, Swellerando and the fashion plate, Lady Low Sleeve; the boring, pipe-smoking Lord Dumble Dum Dreary; Lord Flirt Away and Lady Languish; the musical Lady Warble and Madame Mandoline; and the dancers Georgie Galloppara and Fanny Fandango. You assumed the character of the name you drew, consulting the illustrations in the book, and played him or her in the charade established by the host or the Bean King.

The Christmas pudding charms represented a simplification of these characters, now reduced to the stereotypes of the Spinster, the Bachelor, the Bride, the Gambler and the Rich Man. In most households the charms long ago disappeared altogether except for the silver coin – and even that is usually wrapped in a tiny parcel of greaseproof paper to make it more difficult for the recipient to swallow it.

The French maintain the Epiphany cake tradition assiduously, bean and all. The antiquity of the ceremony of *tirer le roi*, or choosing the king, is shown by the fact that the bean is a *fève* or fava bean, the one bean that is of old world and not American origin. Nowadays the bean is often replaced by a china replica-bean, or by a teeny-tiny porcelain Baby Jesus, or by a metal charm meant to become part of a girl's bracelet after the cake has been consumed. I recently burnt my fingers on a miniature Les Invalides in a cake just out of the oven, part of a series of the *Monuments Historiques de Paris* designed for pâtissiers to bury in their *galettes de Rois*, as the French cakes are called, in honour of the three kings, the Magi.

The *galette* is now nearly always the Paris recipe with flaky pastry, though there are still a few regional differences in Twelfth-Night cakes. In Savoy they eat brioche or fruitcake and in Vervier it has cinnamon and sugar candy. Originally the Epiphany cake was made by the bakers, the *boulangers*. But the *pâtissiers* lobbied the French parliament on the grounds that the recipe used butter and eggs, and not just the ingredients of bread. The bakers won, though, and continued to sell Twelfth-Night cake right up to 1914. Now you usually find them for sale in the pastry shops, starting just after New Year's Day. They come with a gilded cardboard crown, to be worn by whoever finds the charm. As it is usually an occasion for having close friends to dinner, the custom has grown in some places that the person who is king one year must buy the cake (and usually the champagne, too) for the next year's celebration.

Twelfth Night had a reputation for excess. In *Simple French Food* Richard Olney quotes Prosper-Montagné citing a 17th-century tract condemning the debauchery of the period: 'Large groups gather (on the Twelfth-Night) to elect a king; he chooses his cabinet members and then the celebration begins, continuing for days with the festivities multiplying until all purses are empty and the creditors arrive.' 'Nowadays,' says Olney, 'the game is an innocent excuse for friends to gather together and drink a couple of bottles of Champagne; it is apparently still great fun, for hardly is everyone recovered from celebrating the advent of the New Year than people begin gathering to *tirer les Rois* and it goes on throughout the month of January, the person crowned being designated as the next to receive; quite distinguished company is apt to turn loud and bawdy in the joyous atmosphere.'

Returning to the Christmas meal itself, there is the practical problem that not everyone likes plum pudding, and while you feel you must have it, if only for the sake of tradition, it is nice to have something enjoyable to eat; otherwise the Christmas feast takes on some aspects of those rubber-chicken dinners politicians and charity workers are obliged to eat so often. At our house we have solved that by instituting an alternative tradition.

It was Claudia Roden's idea to have a Moroccan pastry 'snake' for Christmas lunch, and she always makes it herself, from her own recipe. It has some affinity for (and some of the same ingredients as) pastries such as the Christmas fish of Lecce, described by Patience Gray in her *Honey from a Weed* (1986). Most of all, it is a large and impressive confection, suitable for a feast, but made from ingredients most people like – almonds and filo pastry. It is scented with orange-flower or rosewater, which makes it reminiscent of dozens of English dishes dating back as far back as Richard II. Having the snake at our own table reminds us that English food at that time, as revealed by the recipes in the first cookery book in English, *A Forme of Cury*, was indistinguishable from much that is eaten, even now, in the Middle East. There is a similar recipe in Lady Fettiplace's book, for a breadcrumb-thickened almond pudding cooked in a sausage casing. Not only is the shape similar to the snake, but the flavour is the same combination of almonds and rosewater, which of course goes back to the Arabs.

Cooking with scents such as orange-flower water or rosewater was very common in the 16th- and early 17th-century English kitchen, presumably because of the connection with the Arabs that went back to the Crusades. But Hilary Spurling makes the very good point that though rosewater is used in a great many of Lady Fettiplace's recipes, it is a 'a self-effacing ingredient', its elusive scent and flavour scarcely noticeable in the strong-smelling and strong-tasting company it often keeps. She remarks that it is very often used as the basic moistening element in a recipe, and that it must therefore be employed in lieu of 'dubious, muddy, polluted, twice used' ordinary water, which nobody at the time would even have considered drinking. Rosewater was distilled, and whether bought or made at home, came in clean, stoppered jars.

So though it may appear idiosyncratic, our new practice of eating the 'snake' at Christmas has a sound historical grounding. Equally 'medieval', and much more authentically traditional at Christmas, is mincemeat. Christmas pie was always mincemeat, and though the mixture of meat and dried fruit sounds self-evidently medieval, mincemeat is first documented in the 16th century. Thomas Tusser puts mince or 'shred' pies on his 1557 list of foods that were standard at Christmas.

One of the most interesting discussions of mincemeat is in Hilary Spurling's edition of Lady Fettiplace's recipes. Elinor Fettiplace's quantities are unusually precise for the period, so one can get a very good idea of what her mince pies tasted like – and they are nothing at all like modern ones. 'They turned out,' says Mrs Spurling, 'to be in fact little savoury pies, rich and fruity but not at all sweet, and quite

'The glutton' by Thomas Rowlandson (1756–1827)

unsuited to tea time.' They are far from our ordinary mince tarts, and much more like samosas 'and other dry, mildly spiced meat pasties of the Middle East', or like Latin American *empanadas*. The fruit is used in equal quantities with the meat (boiled mutton in this case) and suet (beef suet is specified) and the sugar used is only twice as much as the salt, which of course gives a savoury balance. Indeed, sugar is here used, like salt, as only a seasoning. The other ingredients are orange peel, raisins, rosewater, ginger, mace, nutmeg and cinnamon.

This must have been one of the last such recipes to show such a strong Middle Eastern influence, as Gervase Markham's mince pies, only a dozen or so years later, contain no salt at all. Mrs Spurling points out that the proportion of sugar rose as the quantity of meat was reduced, until the present, when English mincemeat contains no meat at all. (In fact, says Mrs Spurling, modern English mincemeat recipes are greatly improved in texture by the addition of a little minced tongue, beef or mutton.)

A Frenchman, M. Henri Misson, a translation of whose memoirs of his travels in England was published in 1719, approved of English 'Christmass Pye', as he did not of most English food: 'It is a great Nostrum the Composition of this Pastry; it is a most learned Mixture of Neats-Tongues, Chicken, Eggs, Sugar, Raisins, Lemon and Orange Peel, various kinds of Spicery.' The recipe hasn't changed much in America, where it still contains meat, and the chief alteration to the British recipe is the addition of ardent spirits in place of Lady Fettiplace's distilled rosewater. Mrs Beeton's ordinary mincemeat recipe contains 1 lb (½ kg) of lean beef and a pint (generous ½ litre) of brandy, whereas her superior offering called 'Excellent Mincemeat' (see page 165) contains no meat and a larger proportion of brandy to suet and fruit. Mincemeat had acquired its alcohol at least by the time of Sir Kenelm Digby's 1668 recipe, which calls for a little sack or sherry.

The Puritans hated mince pies even more than they disliked plum porridge. The Puritan figure in the dramatist Fletcher's 1656 *Christmas Day* apostrophises the pie thus:

> Idolatrie in crust! Babylon's whore
> Rak'd from the grave, and bak'd by hanches, then
> Sew'd up in Coffins to unholy men;
> Defil'd, with superstition, like the Gentiles
> Of old, that worship'd onions, roots and lentiles!

But the mince pie continued, as it does today, to be associated with Christmas. In England it was regarded as an indigenous, unfancy food. In 1754 the *Connoisseur* decried what it found to be the recent neglect of the 'solid, substantial, Protestant mince-pie', which was as much a part of Christmas as pancake to Shrove Tuesday or goose to Michaelmas.

This was the tradition taken over by the American colonists, and accounts for the fact that the American recipes are food fossils, much less evolved than their British counterparts. This statement is true despite the rule-proving exception of James Beard, who put strawberry jam in his mincemeat (see page 164).

Like all the Christmas foods we have examined, neither Christmas broth, Christmas pudding, Christmas cake nor Christmas pie has any symbolic connection with the festival. They all have an historic reason for their association with the feast, but nothing that apparently reflects anything to do with the meaning of the celebration.

In parts of France, however, the final course is laden with significance. The 13 desserts of Provence stand for Jesus and the twelve Apostles, and even some of the foods that make it up have their own, individual meaning. The fruits, nuts, sweetmeats and pastries that compose the *treize desserts* are sometimes not put out until the *réveillon* after the return from midnight mass; but they are always left on the table until Twelfth Night, and usually replenished as needed. The ingredients of course vary from place to place, and even from household to household. But they have in common that everyone tries to use as many foodstuffs as possible from the region itself, and this is always interpreted as narrowly as possible; so if your village has a special sweetmeat, for instance, its inclusion in the *treize desserts* is *de rigueur*.

Richard Olney thinks the whole Christmas Eve supper, of which this series of desserts is the conclusion, is a sort of Provençal Thanksgiving, which is why the dishes, like the 'lavish-sounding' desserts, are each chosen for 'its humble and homely character'.

It is not often remarked, but many of the fruits and nuts featured are common to the Mediterranean, and so are found in the Holy Land as well as Provence; and some of the sweetmeats have their counterparts in Middle Eastern confections. The essentials are the four 'beggars', the fruits and nuts representing the colours of the habits of the mendicant orders of friars. Thus white dried figs for the Franciscans, almonds for the Carmelites, hazelnuts for the Dominicans and black raisins for the Augustines. Fresh fruit comes, if possible, from your own property – which means saving some bunches of grapes if at all possible, though in most places it comes down to apples and pears. In the Vaucluse there is often melon, and the expensive whole candied melon that is the speciality of Aix-en-Provence is on the tables of those who can afford it. In the hill-villages of the Maures there are the chestnuts, the processing of which is one of the few local industries.

Tangerines, oranges and dates have always had to come from North Africa, though some of the citrus fruits will grow on the French Riviera. Almond-paste sweets called Calissons d'Aix are another expensive addition to the desserts; and many families still have the ritual of making their own nougat, by adding grilled almonds and bits of sugar to bubbling hot honey. It is invariably so hard that it has to be smashed with a small hammer. And there must be *pompe à l'huile*, the flat cake made of olive-oil-enriched bread dough. These are served with *vin cuit*, a homemade sweet wine made by boiling grape juice to concentrate it and then topping it up with neutral spirits.

The *pompe à l'huile* has many points of gastronomic contact with other Christmas foods. In the village in the Var that my family frequents, it is usually transmuted to *fougasse*, which is normally sold by the baker in its savoury form, with cheese or particularly fat bits of bacon. In its sweet manifestation, also called *fouaces*, it can be made with orange-flower water, flavoured with anise, or, as in the Niçoise *fougassette*, with saffron and candied fruit.

The symbolism goes even further in some households, for the 13 desserts are set out on the table with the *santons*. These modelled clay idols have evolved from the figures of the *crèche*, the Christmas crib, St Francis's *presepio*. The Provençal figures, influenced by the Portuguese practice of adding realistic secular figures to those of the Holy Family, the Magi, shepherds and animals, are representatives of the workers, peasants, artisans and craftsmen of Provence. There is the fisherman and the woman fishmonger; the garlic-seller and the wild-mushroom gatherer; the shepherd in his smock, the baker in his whites and the peasant housewife in her Provençal print apron.

The *santons*, sometimes life-size, are now found in Christmas *crèches* in homes and in churches as well all over France, not just in Provence. How, we have to wonder, did these very profane images acquire the right to be displayed in sacred surroundings? In Sicily there is a group of very large, carved stone idols dedicated to the cult of Cybele, and dating from the 5th century or so BC. They are called the *Santoni*. It really does make one wonder.

One last matter. What should one drink with the Christmas dessert course? If, like us, you've chopped and changed and drunk several wines already, the dessert wine really has to be something to make any impact at all. It makes perfect sense at this point to go back to something fizzy (or to have something fizzy for the first time if you have had only still wine so far). Probably the best choice for this slot in the meal is a low-alcohol (which is a great merit at this point), peachy-sweet Moscato d'Asti. With its gentle mousse and gentle price, it's hard to beat – and goes equally well with Christmas pudding, or the snake, or ice cream, come to that.

Sauternes, or a Barsac, is a dearer alternative, but you need one with a lot of 'noble rot' or botrytis character to face up to Christmas pudding. Andrew Quady's California oddities, his orange muscat Essencia and his red Elysium, have what it takes to partner plum pudding, too. But a fortified wine has much to commend it, and this might be the time to experiment with Australian 'stickies', such as the coffee-coloured Galway Pipe or one of the several Brown Brothers' dessert wines. If you are having port, and drinking it with the cheese, why not carry on with the dessert? Or – my most original idea – try an old, sweet sherry. In my own cellar I have Valdespino Solera 1842 Oloroso Viejo Dulce, and three choices from Gonzales Byass: Amontillado del Duque, Apostoles Oloroso Abocado and Matusalem Oloroso Muy Viejo. At one time or another I have tasted them all, and I cannot think of anything they would marry with half as well as Christmas pudding.

FRANCES BISSELL'S CHRISTMAS PUDDING

Serves 8–10; fills a 1.75-litre (3-pint) pudding basin

230 g (8 oz, 4 loosely packed cups) fresh wholemeal breadcrumbs

230 g (8 oz, 2 cups) *each* of roughly chopped muscatel (black) raisins, sultanas (yellow raisins) and dried apricots

60 g (2 oz, ¾ cup) crumbled almond macaroons or amaretti

60 g (2 oz, ¾ cup) chopped almonds

60 g (2 oz, ½ cup) ground or flaked almonds

1 grated apple

1 Tbsp grated orange zest

1 tsp ground cinnamon

1 tsp ground mace

½ tsp ground cardamom

½ tsp ground cloves

½ tsp ground allspice

2 Tbsp orange marmalade or candied orange peel

juice of 1 orange

4 medium free-range eggs

6 Tbsp or 1 miniature bottle of Cognac

140 ml (5 fl oz, scant ⅔ cup) fortified muscat wine, port, marsala or rich *oloroso* sherry

Put all the dry ingredients in a large bowl and mix thoroughly. Put the marmalade, orange juice, eggs, brandy and wine in another large bowl, or in the blender or food processor, and beat until well blended and frothy. Pour the liquid over the dry ingredients. Mix until moist. Cover and let stand for a couple of hours at least and, if possible, overnight to let the spice flavours develop.

Oil or butter the pudding basin and spoon in the mixture. As it contains no raw flour, it will not expand very much during the cooking, so you can fill the basin to within 1.25 cm (½ in) of the rim. Take a square of greaseproof or waxed paper, oil or butter it, and tie it over the top of the basin with string.

Place the filled pudding basin in a saucepan, with a long triple-folded strip of foil under it and coming up both sides. This is to help you lift the boiling hot basin out of the saucepan once it is cooked. Pour in boiling water to go halfway up the pudding basin, cover the saucepan and bring it back to the boil. Then lower the heat and keep the water at a steady simmer so that the pudding steams for 5 hours. Keep the water level topped up with boiling water.

When the time is up, remove the pudding from the pan and allow it to cool completely before wrapping it, still in its basin, in fresh greaseproof paper plus a layer of foil. Store in a cool, dark place.

On Christmas Day, steam the pudding for a further two hours. Then decorate it with holly, warm some brandy or rum in a ladle and anoint the pudding with it. Remember to turn off the lights before you bring it into the dining room. We prefer to eat it with only a blob of *crème fraîche*. Brandy butter rather undoes the good of this pudding, which has no fat except for the egg yolks and only the sugar of the dried fruits and the tiny bit of marmalade.

JAMES BEARD'S 'FABULOUSLY GOOD' MINCEMEAT

Americans continued to use real meat in mincemeat well after it dropped out of English recipes. This is a slightly toned-down version of James Beard's famous recipe from his *Delights and Prejudices* (most recent edition, with a new foreword by Barbara Kafka, 1990). (Beard adds a pint, about 500 g, 1 lb, of strawberry preserve, which makes it a bit sticky–sweet for my taste; and I find his original recipe a bit underspiced, considering the huge quantities of dried fruit. If you think I've overspiced it, subtract ¼ tsp or so from each of the spices.) Beard used to make it a year in advance in huge earthenware crocks, and not even put it up in jars until it was four months old. The quantities given here are so generous that he must have used it more frequently than merely to make mince pies for Christmas. You can actually eat it after a month or so.

Makes about 10 kg (22 lb)
1.5 kg (3 lb) lean brisket or rump of beef
1 ox tongue weighing about 1.5 kg (3 lb), not pickled or brined
750 g (1½ lb) beef suet, finely shredded
1 kg (2 lb) seedless raisins
1 kg (2 lb) sultanas
1 kg (2 lb) dried currants
250 g (8 oz) shredded and diced candied citron
250 g (8 oz) shredded fresh orange peel, with as much white pith removed as possible, diced
125 g (4 oz) lemon peel, treated the same way
125–250 g (4–8 oz) chopped figs or dates
500 g (1 lb, 2 cups) sugar
1 Tbsp salt
2½ tsp freshly grated nutmeg
1 Tbsp ground cinnamon
1½ tsp ground allspice
1 tsp mace
¼ tsp ground cloves
750 ml (one bottle) medium to sweet sherry
about 1.5 litres (two bottles) brandy

Cover the brisket and tongue with water and simmer until tender, 2–2½ hours. Let the meat cool, remove any remaining fat from the brisket, peel and trim the gristle off the tongue. Then put through the coarse blade of the mincer or chop by hand; it's probably not a good idea to use the food processor, as you must on no account end up with a paste; but you could process chunks of the meat with large dice of the dried and candied fruit – carefully, and in short bursts. Put the minced meat and all the remaining ingredients except the brandy (but including the strawberry jam, if you like the idea of it) into a deep earthenware crock that you can cover with a lid, and mix thoroughly. Now add the brandy. Stop when you've got a loose but not wet mixture. James Beard says to check it every week to see if it needs more sherry or brandy.

MRS BEETON'S EXCELLENT MINCEMEAT

From *The Book of Household Management*. Mrs Beeton says to make it about the first or second week of December. She gives another recipe that involves 375 g (1½ lb) of lean beef; this one, however, contains suet but no meat.

Makes 2.5 kg (5 lb)
3 large lemons
3 large apples
500 g (1 lb) seedless raisins
500 g (1 lb) dried currants
500 g (1 lb) shredded suet
1 kg (2 lb) 'moist' (i.e. brown) sugar
30 g (1 oz, about 1 heaping Tbsp) each shredded candied citron, candied orange peel and fresh lemon peel (with pith removed)
250 ml (8 oz, 1 cup) brandy
2 Tbsp orange marmalade

Grate the rinds of the lemons; squeeze out the juice, strain it and boil the remainder of the lemons until tender enough to pulp or chop very finely. Bake the apples in a preheated 180°C (350°F, gas mark 4) oven until very soft, 30–45 mins. Remove the skin and cores of the apples and add their pulp to the lemons. Add the remaining ingredients one by one, and, as they are added, mix everything very thoroughly together. Mrs Beeton says to store the mincemeat in a stone jar with a closely fitting lid for a fortnight before using.

LADY FETTIPLACE'S MINCEMEAT

Lady Fettiplace's 1604 recipe used cooked, minced mutton, but leftover tongue or beef will do as well. The quantities are Hilary Spurling's. You simply mix the whole lot together and use it as soon as you wish. Remember that Mrs Spurling found that it made a savoury rather than a sweet mincemeat.

Serves 10–12; 1 large or 48 tiny pies
250 g (8 oz) leftover meat, minced
250 g (8 oz, 2 cups) beef suet, shredded
250 g (8 oz, 1½ cups) dried currants
250 g (8 oz, 1¾ cups) raisins
1 big pinch each powdered ginger and ground mace
½ level tsp freshly grated nutmeg
1 level tsp ground cinnamon
1 heaped tsp salt
2 heaped tsp sugar
peel of 1 orange, finely grated, or slightly less of a Seville orange
6 Tbsp diluted rosewater, made up to strength according to whether it is double or treble distilled

You need 375 g (1½ lb) puff or shortcrust pastry, rolled very thin, for tiny tarts, and half that amount for a large, two-crust pie.

CLAUDIA RODEN'S M'HENCHA

(Moroccan Almond Snake)

Originally this would have been made with the Moroccan pancake pastry called *ouarka*, but bought filo pastry is just fine.

Serves 30
1.5 kg (3 lb) ground almonds
1 kg (2 lb) caster (fine) sugar
2 Tbsp ground cinnamon
200–250 ml (7–8 fl oz, up to 1 cup) orange-flower water or diluted rosewater
500 g (1 lb) filo pastry
75–125 g (3–4 oz, up to 1 stick) butter, melted
2 egg yolks

To garnish
icing (confectioner's) sugar
1 Tbsp ground cinnamon

Make the filling simply by mixing the ground almonds, sugar and cinnamon with your fingers and adding orange-flower water until the mixture feels like moist sand; work into a paste, using your hands. Preheat the oven to 180°C (350°F, gas mark 4).

Keep the sheets of filo stacked and covered with a damp cloth; they dry out quickly, so remove only one sheet at a time. Brush the top sheet of the stack lightly with butter. Take balls of the almond paste, roll them into thick fingers and place them end to end so as to have a line of paste as thick as a fat thumb; place this about 2.5 cm (1 in) from one of the long edges of the filo sheet.

Roll up the pastry tightly over the almond filling. Press the ends of the roll towards the centre, like an accordion, so that it becomes crinkled (this ensures that the pastry does not tear when you curve it round). Carefully lift up the roll and place it on a large sheet of foil on a large baking tray. (The foil will make it easier for you to remove the finished pastry from the tray.)

Starting from the centre of the tray, curve the almond-filled roll into a tight spiral. Repeat with the rest of the filo, until all the filling is used up. Place each new roll at the end of the spiral until you have made a long, coiled snake.

Brush the top of the pastry with a wash made of the egg yolks beaten with 1 Tbsp of water and bake in the preheated oven for about 45 mins or until crisp and brown.

Dust with icing sugar and sprinkle lines of cinnamon in the shape of a cross – or whatever motif you like. You can serve the snake hot, but Claudia Roden thinks it's better at room temperature.

HELGE RUBINSTEIN AND SHEILA BUSH'S CHRISTMAS PUDDING ICE

Ice cream made with some of the ingredients of Christmas pudding is a deliciously light alternative to the Real Thing, one that is much appreciated when the meal has been composed of several rich courses. I shouldn't recommend serving this ice cream in a blaze of brandy; but if there are only three or four guests, and if you are serving it in flameproof dishes, there would be no harm in warming some brandy or rum in a ladle, taking a match to it, and pouring just a little flaming alcohol over each serving. This dish bears a strong resemblance to what we used to call Nesselrode ice cream. The same ingredients were made into a syrupy sauce and poured over vanilla ice cream, or incorporated into an ice cream parfait.

Serves 4–6
175 g (6 oz, 1¾ cups) mixed dried and glacé fruits, such as currants, raisins, sultanas, orange and citron peel, marrons glacés, roughly chopped. You could make up part of the quantity with pecans, if you like them.
4 Tbsp light rum
300 ml (10 fl oz, 1¼ cup) single or light cream
5 egg yolks
140 g (5 oz, ½ cup) caster (fine) sugar
2 heaped Tbsp unsweetened chestnut purée (from a tin or a tube)
100 g (4 oz) Chocolate Menier or bittersweet chocolate
300 ml (10 fl oz, 1¼ cup) double or heavy cream, whipped until thick

Put the fruit to marinate and swell in the rum. Heat the single cream until almost boiling – when the surface trembles a little. Whisk the egg yolks with the sugar in a bowl, and pour the near-boiling cream over them, whisking constantly. Return the egg, sugar and cream mixture to the saucepan, and whisk over a very gentle heat until you have a thick custard. Be careful or you will have scrambled egg. If you don't trust your nerves, do this step in a *bain marie*, with a metal bowl suspended over, but not touching, the simmering water in the saucepan below.

When you're happy with the thickness of the mixture, whisk in the chestnut purée and then the chocolate, in small pieces. Stir until the chocolate is melted completely and the texture is smooth. Taste for sweetness. If the chocolate is particularly bitter, you might need a little more sugar. Leave to cool.

Now incorporate the plumped-up fruits and nuts (if used), and fold in the whipped cream.

If you like, you can freeze the ice in a pudding basin, and decorate it with a sprig of holly when you turn it out for serving. To do this, line the pudding basin in foil or fat-safe cling film. Pour in the mixture and freeze. If you can be bothered to give it a stir when it's half frozen, it will improve the texture marginally. Turn it out of the basin at least 1 hour before you mean to serve it. In fact, after a day you can turn it out, replace it in the freezer, and reclaim the pudding basin for another use.

Alternatively, you can freeze it in individual ramekins or soufflé dishes, or bung the whole lot into an electric ice-cream maker or sorbetière. But it should be allowed to 'ripen' for at least 1 hour in the fridge before you serve it.

MIDWINTER SUMMER FRUIT SORBET

Inspired by Jane Grigson's rule-of-thumb recipe for sorbet in her *Fruit Book*, we pick the glut of raspberries, *fraises des bois*, redcurrants, blackcurrants and gooseberries in late June and early July, and flash freeze them loose on trays. Then we tip the frozen pellets into polythene bags and keep them in the freezer. They are often most wanted in winter, when a sorbet is the only tolerable pudding after a heavy, warming meaty or fatty meal.

If you have an electric sorbetière – our Gelato Chef is the second most-used kitchen machine, after the food processor itself – you can do the trick I learned from Michel Guérard, and make the sorbet only as you sit down to dinner. A fruit ice is at its freshest twenty minutes after it's been frozen. The texture changes dramatically the longer it stays frozen.

Take any quantity of soft fruit, alone, or in interesting combinations, such as redcurrants and raspberries or redcurrants plus blackcurrants, from the freezer and allow to thaw. Process them and sieve carefully – important for annoying raspberry pips.

For each 500 g (1 lb) of puréed or liquidized and sieved soft fruit, add alternately a dollop of lemon or orange juice (to sharpen the flavour) and a slug of sugar syrup (to sweeten the flavour and give a good texture).

The syrup is made by boiling steadily for 5 minutes 150 g (5 oz, 2/3 cup) white sugar in 300–500 ml (8–12 fl oz, 1–2 cups) water until you have a limpid but sticky syrup. Jane Grigson advises varying the quantity of water in the syrup with the intensity of flavour in the fruit you mean to use the syrup with: more water for blackcurrants, less water for wild strawberries.

You can add the syrup to the fruit either hot or cold. If it is hot, you will get a very slightly cooked fruit flavour, whereas cool syrup will preserve the raw freshness of the fruit. (Some people do not appreciate raw currant flavours.)

This is the mixture you freeze. If you're using a sorbetière, you can add some alcohol now. Eaux de vie such as kirsch, framboise and myrtille add interesting flavours, and a little alcohol makes the texture smoother. This is the time to use up the crème de cassis and other sticky liqueurs at the back of the drinks cupboard. A Tbsp or two per pound of fruit is quite enough, though.

If you are freezing your water ice in an ice cube tray or in a bowl in an ordinary freezer, as soon as the sorbet is firm and icy at the rim and still liquid in the centre, tip it into a mixing bowl and beat it with an electric beater on full speed, incorporating lots of air and dissolving all the ice particles. Add the booze now. Return to the freezer, and repeat the whole performance one more time if you like. Jane Grigson thinks two beatings is as much as a sorbet can endure, and that more make no difference to the final texture.

An alternative to beating your sorbet is to wait until it has just gone firm, and then crunch it up in the food processor fitted with the metal blade. 'It makes a dreadful noise at first,' says Jane Grigson, 'and thumps about', but it gets beautifully smooth. It pays to leave this step until just before you want to serve the sorbet, as the resulting texture is so nice. But it takes nerves of steel, as an extra thirty seconds in the whizzer will liquify the whole mixture, and you have to start all over again.

KENTUCKY BOURBON FRUITCAKE

The quantities for this recipe, which are the closest I've ever seen to the fruitcake Rhoda, our family cook, used to make months in advance of every Christmas, are similar to those of Rose Levy Beranbaum, in *The Cake Bible* (1992).

Fills a 2-litre (3½-pint, 8-cup) baking mould or a 15 x 10 cm (6 x 4 in) cake tin

120 g (4 oz, 1 cup) diced mixed candied fruit, including glacé cherries
100 g (scant 4 oz, 6 Tbsp) candied peel
100 g (scant 4 oz, ⅔ cup) dried currants
60 g (2 oz, ½ cup) broken pecans
200 ml (8 fl oz, 1 cup) Bourbon whiskey
130 g (4½ oz, ¾ cup) unsifted plain flour
½ tsp ground cinnamon
pinch each of ground nutmeg and ginger
¼ tsp bicarbonate of soda
½ tsp salt
230 g (8 oz, 2 sticks) unsalted butter, softened
120 g (4 oz, ½ cup) dark brown sugar
2 size 2 egg (= 6 Tbsp beaten egg)
160 g (4 fl oz, 4 heaping Tbsp) unsulphured black treacle (Rhoda used molasses)
4 Tbsp milk

Dice the candied fruit and soak it with the candied peel, currants and nuts in half the Bourbon. You can do this a day in advance, so that the currants swell. Whisk the dry ingredients together. In a large mixing bowl cream the butter and sugar, and beat in the egg. Add the flour mixture a bit at a time, followed each time by adding a bit of the treacle and a bit of the milk, until everything is used up. Then beat in the fruit and nuts together with the Bourbon in which they steeped. The cake mixture will curdle slightly, as it contains so little flour. Don't worry.

Turn it into the greased-and-floured mould or cake tin and bake at 160°C (325°F, gas mark 3) for at least an hour, or until the cake has just begun to shrink from the sides of the tin and is springy to the touch. A skewer inserted in the middle will come out clean. Let it cool in the tin for 10–20 mins and sprinkle it with ⅔ of the remaining Bourbon. Rose Levy Beranbaum has the clever idea of putting a large piece of clingfilm on the work surface. Then take a new but washed tea towel or piece of muslin large enough to hold the cake and moisten it with half the Bourbon that remains. (Rhoda soaked her cloth in Bourbon.) Put the cloth on the clingfilm and turn out the still-warm cake on to it. Use up the Bourbon to swathe the cake in Bourbon-impregnated cloth, and wrap around this the clingfilm. When it cools, cover tightly with foil and store in a tightly closed tin. Rhoda would open the tin and the foil once a week or at least once a fortnight before Christmas and soak the cloth with Bourbon before re-sealing it.

RICHARD OLNEY'S POMPE À L'HUILE

This recipe, taken from one in *Simple French Food*, can also be the basis of *fouaces* or *fougasses*. In Provence they sometimes add orange-flower water to the liquid, and in Nice they add saffron to the dry ingredients. I sometimes make a savoury version, leaving out the sugar and lemon peel, and substituting some thick-cut chopped bacon or bits of ham or crumbled cheese. Olney says *pompes* are traditionally cut into large rounds of 15 cm (6 in), but he prefers a more manageable 10 cm (4 in). In our village in the Var they are not rolled out so thin, but simply made into large ovals and slashed across three times with a razor, which produces something more like a bread than a pastry.

1 pkt fast-action dried yeast
750 g (1¾ lb, 5½ cups) bread flour
¼ tsp salt
200 g (6 oz, 1 cup) brown sugar
4 tsp grated lemon zest
8 Tbsp olive oil
about 300 ml (½ pt, 1 cup plus 2 Tbsp) tepid water
2 medium eggs

In a mixing bowl or in the food processor fitted with the plastic blade, combine all the dry ingredients, the sugar and lemon zest, and mix thoroughly. Add the olive oil and mix or process briefly, then add the water and process or mix until the dough forms a solid mass and leaves the sides of the bowl cleanly. If it is too sticky, add a little more flour. If still crumbly, a tiny bit of water. Turn out on to a floured board and knead well until the dough is elastic. Put it in an oiled stout plastic bag, or back into the mixing bowl, covered, and put it in a warm place to prove until it doubles in volume.

Cut the dough in half. Knock each half down again on the floured board, knead lightly (but not so much that it becomes difficult to roll out); flatten with the heel of your hand, turning it repeatedly to keep it floured, until you achieve a thickness of ½ cm (¼ in).

Olney now uses an opened tin can or a bowl 10 cm (4 in) in diameter to cut out rounds; but you can make 2 large *pompes* with each half of the dough. If you cut out rounds, put them on an oiled baking sheet. Collect the scraps, make them into a ball, 'roll' them out again with the heel of your hand, and cut into another round or just press into an oval. Olney slits the surface of each 10 cm round with two razor slits each way in a criss-cross.

Leave the dough on the trays in a warm place, covered with tea towels, for an hour or so; they should only increase in size by about a third. Beat the eggs with a little water to make egg wash and brush on the dough. Bake in a preheated 200°C (400°F, gas mark 6) for about 20 mins. They should be a rich, crusty brown. Cool on a rack, and serve as part of the 13 desserts.

EXOTIC SUN-DRIED FRUIT SALAD

This dessert was specially created for Christmas by the chef at Chutney Mary Restaurant in London. It has an opulent feel about it, but in fact is relatively light and refreshing.

Serves 6

100 g (4 oz) each dried apricots, figs, prunes, black raisins (or use in whatever proportions you prefer)
50 g (2 oz, ⅓ cup) dried currants
200 g (7 oz, 1 cup) sugar
10 cm (4 in) cinnamon stick
5 cm (2 in) fresh ginger, crushed
60 ml (2 fl oz, ¼ cup) each rum and brandy
50 g (2 oz, ¼ cup) shelled pistachios
50 g (2 oz, ½ cup) blanched almonds
300 ml (10 fl oz, 1¼ cup) whipping cream
1 tsp ground cinnamon

Soak the fruit in cold water for 24 hours. Drain, but reserve 300–450 ml (10–15 fl oz, 1–2 cups) of the soaking water. Simmer this in a saucepan with the fruit, the sugar, the cinnamon stick and crushed ginger until you have a thin syrup. Off the heat add the rum and brandy and cool. Add the nuts and allow to steep for a day in the refrigerator. Serve with a dollop of whipped cream sprinkled with ground cinnamon.

LADY LOUSADA'S MASCARPONE SAUCE FOR PANNETONE

The Italian Christmas cake, *pannetone*, is a feathery light yeast-cake. Patricia Lousada recommends it with this sauce and a glass of *vin santo*.

Warm about 250 g (8 oz, 1 cup) mascarpone cheese with a few tablespoons of double (heavy) cream in a *bain-marie*. Serve as is, or add a dash of rum or a few spoons of praline. To make praline, use a small heavy saucepan to heat equal amounts of unskinned almonds and sugar. Caramelise the sugar well, then pour on to a lightly oiled surface. Leave to cool and harden and pulverise with a rolling pin.

CAKE AND PUDDING
Stirring Up

Making the Christmas pudding can be great fun. Stir-up Sunday is 22 November in 1992 and 21 November in 1993, as Advent is calculated as the first Sunday before St Andrew's Day, which is 30 November, and Stir-up Sunday is the Sunday before Advent. The idea is to give the pudding time to mature and for the flavours to mellow. It is as well to make the Christmas cake at the same time. Don't forget the ritual, which, so far as I am concerned, is the only point of making Christmas pudding at home. When all the ingredients are in the large mixing bowl, each member of the family should give it a stir, and silently make a wish.

Normally mincemeat is made between early October and mid-December and put to store in a cool place. Some cooks, Josceline Dimbleby, for instance, prefer a fresher tasting mincemeat and only make it two weeks before Christmas. Store-bought mincemeat can be cheered up by grating some apple and orange rind into it; and as it never has enough acid, a squeeze of lemon will improve it immensely. A little more alcohol, rum, brandy or even whisky, probably won't go amiss, either. If you are going to bother to

make your own, why not use one of the recipes given on pages 164–165 that incorporates some meat? These versions taste remarkably like the meatless ones, but are more subtle.

The reason I don't make my own Christmas pudding is that Anton Mosimann's is now fairly easily available, and I've never tasted any so good. Moreover, Frances Bissell's recipe is now made commercially and offered by *The Times* to its readers. *And*, in a tasting done at Christmas 1991, with Anton Mosimann forming part of the panel, we found that virtually all the own-label supermarket Christmas puddings were very good indeed. (This could be because they are all manufactured by the same firm – Matthew Walker of Derby – though each recipe is different from the others, it is claimed, and certainly the taste and texture of each one was different.)

The same is true of Christmas cake. The bought versions are so good that I should take a lot of convincing that home-made was any better. American fruitcakes are very like British Christmas cake, but without the marzipan and royal icing, which I, in any case, am not crazy about. When I was a boy in Kentucky we did make

our own fruitcake (or rather, our extremely accomplished cook did). Even if you buy in an American-style fruit cake, it will be improved by the treatment ours received. On to the cloth-wrapped fruitcake (see page 170) you pour as much as it will absorb of a bottle of bourbon whiskey. This you do at regular intervals, putting the lid back tightly on the tin. Highly recommended. With this we – even the children – drank heavy cream-rich egg-nog laced with bourbon, and little country ham sandwiches made with beaten biscuits.

These southern Christmas food traditions are of special interest chiefly, I think, because America as a whole has so few specific Christmas foods. The proximity of the Thanksgiving feast, diminishes the national importance of Christmas. True, Americans of Dutch, German and Scandinavian descent bake Christmas cookies, and Polish Americans make *kielbasa* sausage and the stew called *bigos*. However, with the exception of southerners, Americans by and large celebrate Christmas with food that reflects what was eaten in the original 13 colonies – the 18th century British menu of foods that share their season with Thanksgiving.

CHAPTER EIGHT

Preserves

In America whenever turkey is on the table, so is some form of cranberry sauce, relish or preserve. The British and French do not have the habit of always eating something sweet or fruity with the turkey, at least when it is served hot. Other birds, however, such as goose, duck (think of sauce *à l'orange*, although it is at its best when it is a *bigarade* sauce made with bitter Seville oranges) and game often have a fruit element incorporated in their cooking. Because the acid note is as important as the sweet one, cranberries are particularly good with poultry and game birds as well, and they have the merit of not having to be prepared much in advance: cranberries will set to a gel on cooling. Beware, however, their effect on wine; cranberries are not kind to red wine, and I shouldn't plan to serve my best burgundy or claret with the turkey if its garnish includes cranberries.

If a fruity note is wanted, think of putting it in the stuffing. Claudia Roden's Middle Eastern fruit stuffing, for which the recipe is given on page 102, is compatible even with great wine. Dried raisins and currants do little harm to wine, especially if it is they that provide the sweetness, replacing sugar.

Another reasonably harmless way of introducing a sweet note is to use a sweet wine, especially port or madeira, in the sauce or gravy. Just as fruit in stuffing is kept under control by the starchy (bread, rice, couscous, etc.) and aromatic (onions, garlic, celery, etc.) elements, the savoury portion of the sauce or gravy, contributed by onions, garlic or meat stock, will tame the sweetness of the fortified wine. Its alcohol will, of course, be driven off when it is heated, and so will not interfere with your enjoyment of the wine in your glass.

On the Franco-Britannic table, then, the main use of fruit jams, conserves, preserves, pickles and chutneys is to liven up the cold turkey, not to assassinate the wine served with the hot turkey. (You get around the wine problem of cold turkey and its fruit accompaniments by serving a white wine such as an alsace or a gutsy Australian chardonnay or New Zealand sauvignon blanc, or a more robust, even young and tannic red, anything from a beaujolais to a young rhône, or a fruit-packed New World cabernet sauvignon.) If you are having a ham, you'll almost certainly want a selection of fruit preserves or chutneys for serving it cold; though my own idea of perfection with really good ham involves only Dijon mustard.

The French are sometimes horrified by the British habit, barbaric to gallic eyes, and repulsive to gallic palates, of eating redcurrant jelly with meat, though the French are not averse to incorporating it in a sauce for lamb; and they know all about cooking duck, in particular, with blackcurrants. The blow to the

French palate can be softened a little by combining the fruit jelly with savoury herbs. Thus we have, in the past, made quite successful jellies of gooseberry with sage, or with thyme or rosemary, and we have made a happy combination of the last two herbs with red-currant jelly. If you're lucky enough to have access to quinces (I chopped down a clapped-out pear tree and was rewarded by a new tree shooting from its grafted quince rootstock), their perfume is wonderful with all meat, poultry and game, either as a jelly or as a fruit butter. Hedgerow jelly is another great user-up of oddments that goes well with the dark meat of poultry and game. Into it go the crab apples left on the tree after the crab-apple jelly has been made, blackberries, any wild sloes or bullaces the children find, and, in some years, the pregnantly swollen rosehips.

Though we are great preservers in my household, we seldom do anything special for the midwinter holidays. Instead, we are generally engaged, when putting up preserves, in some form of rear-guard action. Courgettes (zucchini) that are overlooked and allowed to turn into marrows are then transmuted into a wonderful chutney. We chose the recipe (see page 181) for the strange reason that it contains asafoetida, the smelly Indian spice, that I particularly like. Gluts and horticultural accidents, however, are not the only occasions for our bringing out the preserving pan. Last year we could see that the figs on our trees were not going to ripen, so we searched for, and found, a recipe for green fig conserve.

When we can't deal with the vast quantities of French green beans, green chilli peppers, shallots or green tomatoes that nature has decided to provide us with all at once, we make up a batch of the brine we use for pickled dill cucumbers (see page 180), and pop any or all of them in with the cucumbers – or just bottle them on their own. They are an amazing addition to the Christmas or Boxing Day table, as well as to the Hanukkah spread; and as every Russian peasant knows, their liquid is essential on New Year's day, as it is a sure-fire hangover cure. In those years when they just will not ripen, green tomatoes make one of the best chutneys.

As for the ripe tomatoes, a purée of them keeps nicely in jars, and is a good vehicle for the basil crop. But ripe tomatoes for cooking can be frozen whole and used still frozen; they rapidly pulp down in the saucepan, and can be sieved if you object to the pips and skins. It requires a special machine in our northern climate, but we dry about a quarter of the tomato crop, and our own taste every bit as good as the sun-dried tomatoes we buy. The secret of successful tomato-drying is to cut them in half and salt them with coarse salt for a day before drying them; the salt keeps them supple. Before I learned this trick our dried tomatoes had the texture of poker chips. Once dried, pack them in jars covered with olive oil, and add garlic or basil if you like. The oil in which they are stored is as valuable a flavouring agent as the tomatoes themselves – for dressing salads, anointing pizza dough or flavouring bread such as *fougasse*.

I try to make sure that there is a basil glut every year; and we generally manage to keep a few plants on the go in the house until well after Christmas. There is nothing like a *soupe au pistou* redolent of garlic and basil, or a tomato salad scattered with shredded basil leaves to remind you in December that it's only six months till summer. My best trick is to

Roman Saturnalia, as imagined by J. R. Weguelin in 1885

make the basil into demi-*pesto*, using the olive oil and pine nuts but leaving out the garlic and cheese, and freeze the slush in ice-cube trays before turning it out into plastic freezer bags. You add the garlic and parmesan cheese when you defrost the *pesto* cubes. Use one cube per person to make pasta sauce. The same applies to coriander and walnuts or parsley and hazelnuts. When you get tired of giving them freezer space, dump the whole lot into a soup made with stock and leeks and potatoes. But do remember to segregate the flavours, as basil and coriander make tedious companions.

We make one exception to the no-bottling-for-Christmas rule. The marmalade-making season, of course, comes just after Christmas, which means – or used to mean – that we had always run out of our wonderful, dark, chunky, bitter-sweet breakfast treat just in time for Christmas. We have now found the solution. When the Seville oranges appear in the market in January and February we now buy 20 lb (9 kg) of them. Ten pounds are immediately used to make marmalade (see page 178); the other ten pounds go – just as they come – into the freezer. They come out in September or October, depending on when we feel a marmalade crisis coming on, and are turned into a confiture that is deliciously ripe and fragrant in time for the holidays. In double-blind tastings, no one can tell the difference between marmalade made from fresh and that made from frozen Seville oranges.

Many families make a *Rumtopf* with the summer fruits, by adding currants, cherries, plums and even strawberries to an earthenware glazed pot with some sugar and some *eau-de-vie* or rum. I have never had a success with this, and am not even sure that I really like the result. But I can see the attractions of spooning your own summer fruits over some homemade vanilla ice cream in the middle of the winter. So I bought some unflavoured *eau-de-vie* last time I was in France, and this summer I shall try to beat the birds to the morello cherries, and we shall see.

There are, incidentally, a few other preserves that I should advise you to buy, and not even attempt to make yourself, though you might regard them as essential – if not to the feast, then to its seemingly unending aftermath. One of the very best leftover perker-uppers is the jewel-like Italian fruit mustard, *mostarda di Cremona* or *mostarda Venezia*. While I feel sure I've seen a recipe for this somewhere, it is where I personally draw the life-is-too-short-to-make-this-at-home line.

HAZEL'S MARMALADE

Our own marmalade is the best I've ever tasted; it is made from a recipe devised by Hazel Horrobin, who tests recipes for me and puts up two batches of marmalade a year. I have seen bitter oranges growing in Florida; they really ought to be more widely available.

I hate pale marmalade, and like thick strips of peel. The longer the first cooking of the oranges, the darker the marmalade. If you want the look of real 'Oxford' marmalade, add 30 g (1 oz, 1 big Tbsp) of black treacle (molasses).

Makes about 3 kg (6–7 lb)
2 kg (4 lb) Seville oranges
2 lemons
about 2 kg (4½ lb) sugar

In a pan with a lid, cover the fruit with water (you'll need about 2.5 litres/4 pints/10 cups). Bring to a simmer and cook with the lid on for at least 6–8 hours, more if you like the marmalade really dark. Take off the heat and leave overnight, still covered.

Take out the fruit, quarter it and take out the pips; tie the pips in a muslin bag to add pectin to the final preserve. The fruit should be soft now, but not squishy, so you can slice it exactly as thick as you want the final marmalade to be; but if the fruit has gone too soft, just chop it roughly.

Now put the cooking water into a preserving pan, heat gently, and stir in the sugar (which it is a good idea to warm gently in a low oven before using). Keep the temperature low until all the sugar has dissolved. Then bring to the boil, and boil hard for 5 mins with the muslin bag containing the pips, before adding the fruit. Keep at a gentle boil now until the setting point is reached – about 30 mins to an hour.

Skim the top, discard the bag of pips, let the marmalade cool a little, and pour into hot jam jars. Cover with a wax disc if you like, and a round of cellophane. Seal the jar or put a rubber band around the cellophane; and don't forget to label, including the date.

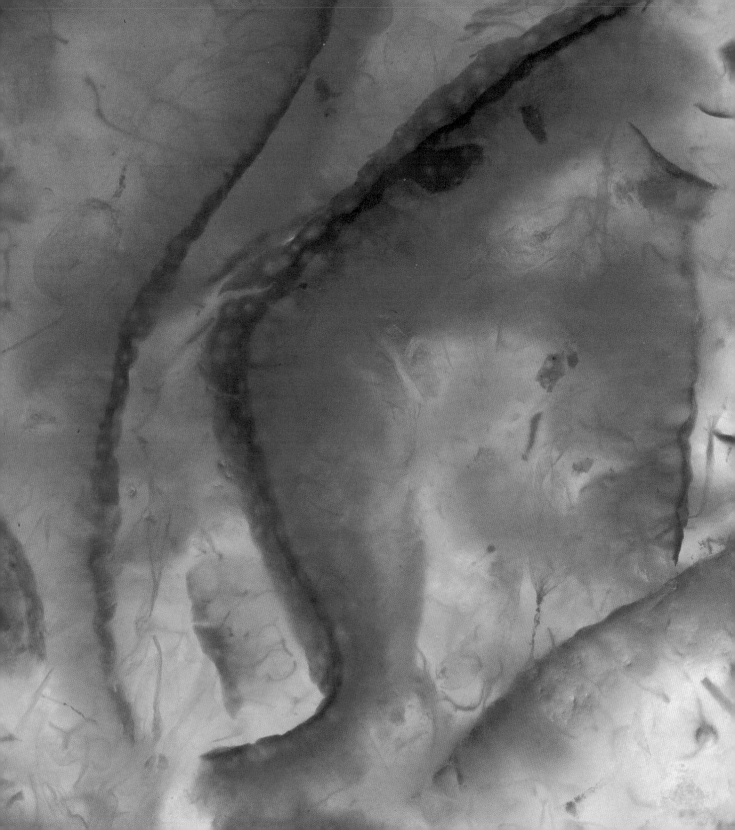

ADA GAIL'S AUTHENTIC JEWISH DILL-PICKLED CUCUMBER

This is it – the real thing. I have published this recipe before, in *The Official Foodie Handbook*, in *Out to Lunch*, in the Conran-Habitat *Cook's Calendar* and in the Time-Life *Good Cook* series. I have always got one detail or another wrong. Here is the correct recipe.

Makes 6 1-litre (2-pint) jars

18 sprigs of fresh dill
18 fat cloves of garlic, peeled
6 mild chillies, fresh or dried
36 black peppercorns
1 Tbsp pickling spice
1½ tsp alum (used to keep the pickle crisp; try to talk the chemist or pharmacist into selling you some)
3 kg (6 lb) pickling cucumbers about 8 cm (3 in) long, scrubbed and soaked overnight in water with a handful of salt
8.5 1 litres (14¼ pints, 9 quarts) water
350 g (12 oz, 1½ cups) coarse (Kosher) salt
250 ml (8 fl oz, 1 cup) cider or white wine vinegar
6 vine leaves, blanched if fresh (optional)

Into each of six sterilised 1-litre (2-pint) jars put 3 sprigs of dill, 3 cloves of garlic, 1 chilli, 6 peppercorns and a pinch each of pickling spice and alum. Pack the cucumbers in tightly.

Make a brine by boiling the water with the salt and vinegar, and pour the *hot* brine over the cucumbers, reserving any left over. Cover each jar with a vine leaf and seal. After 2 or 3 days you can expect to see some fermentation bubbles; in which case, top up with the boiling reserved brine and seal the jars again. When the brine clears, fermentation has stopped, and you can eat the pickles four or five days later. You probably won't need any urging, but it is best to eat it all up within a couple of months.

Green tomatoes, green beans, chillies and lots of other vegetables can be put up in the same way.

This recipe is illustrated on page 174.

MARROW CHUTNEY

I adore this recipe because it uses asafoetida, the smell of which you either like or loathe. The Romans were keen on it, and I am sure this Indian recipe would have been perfectly familiar to an ancient Roman. It's brilliant for using up overgrown marrows – the only use I have ever discovered for them, except for chopping them up as finely as possible and spreading the resulting paste in a thin layer over the compost heap. Once you've opened a pot of this chutney, keep it in the fridge.

1.5 kg (3 lb) marrow, peeled
2 Tbsp salt
6—12 dried chillies, with seeds for a hot chutney, without for a milder one
5 cm (2 in) ginger, grated
2 tsp amchoor (dried mango powder)
2 tsp ground turmeric
½ tsp powdered asafoetida
½ tsp ground fenugreek
175 g (6 oz, 1¼ cups) sultanas
175 ml (6 fl oz, ¾ cup) safflower or other neutral oil
2 tsp black mustard seed
more oil for topping up and sealing the jars

Slice the marrow into 7 cm (3 in) lengths, then in half, and cut out and discard the pithy centre. Dice the remaining strips into pieces of about 1.5 cm (½ in). In a glass or china or other non-reactive bowl, mix the marrow with the salt, then the finely chopped chillies, ginger, amchoor, turmeric, asafoetida and fenugreek, and let it marinate for half an hour before adding the sultanas.

Put the oil and mustard seed into a covered frying pan (large enough to hold the contents of the bowl) on high heat and treat like popcorn, removing the lid only when the popping has stopped. There will be a haze over the oil. Turn the marrow mixture into the pan and lower the heat. Cook for about 20 mins, until the marrow is tender and the sultanas have swollen. Most of the liquid should have evaporated and the oil separated.

Have plenty of hot jars ready to hold the chutney. Spoon out into the jars, and try to distribute the oil from the pan evenly among them, but don't fill right to the top. After the chutney has cooled, top up with oil to cover, if need be, and seal the jars. It's ready to eat as soon as it's made, but it does mellow with age.

Bibliography

These are the major sources consulted in the preparation of this book. The date given is that of the edition used. All books published in London, except where otherwise indicated.

ACTON, Eliza. *The Best of Eliza Acton*, 1988.
ALI-BAB, *Gastronomie Pratique*, Paris, 1928.
BARR, Ann and Levy, Paul. *The Official Foodie Handbook*, 1984.
BEARD, James. *Delights and Prejudices*, New York, 1990.
BEETON, Isabella. *Household Management*, 1861.
BERANBAUM, Rose Levy. *The Cake Bible*, 1992.
BISSELL, Frances. *The Real Meat Cookbook*, 1992.
BLACK, Maggie. *Food and Cooking in Mediaeval Britain*, 1985.
—. *Food and Cooking in 19th Century Britain*, 1985.
BLANC, Raymond. *Cooking for Friends*, 1991.
BREARS, Peter. *Traditional Food in Yorkshire*, Edinburgh, 1986.
BROOK, Stephen. *Liquid Gold: Dessert Wines of the World*, 1987.
BUDAY, George. *The History of the Christmas Card*, 1954.
CHRISTIAN, Glynn. *Delicatessen Food Handbook*, 1982.
CLARK, Eleanor. *The Oysters of Locmariaquer*, 1959.
COURTINE, Robert. *The Hundred Glories of French Cooking*, 1976.
—. *La Cuisine des Terroirs*, Lyon, 1989.
DAVID, Elizabeth. *Mediterranean Food*, 1950.
—. *French Country Cooking*, 1951.
—. *Italian Food*, 1954.
—. *French Provincial Cooking*, 1960.
—. *Spices, Salt and Aromatics in the English Kitchen*, 1970.
—. *English Bread and Yeast Cookery*, 1977.
DAVIDSON, Alan and Jane. *Dumas on Food*, 1978.
DAVIDSON, Alan. *Mediterranean Seafood*, 1972.
—. *North Atlantic Seafood*, 1979.
—. *On Fasting and Feasting*, 1988.
DIMBLEBY, Josceline. *The Josceline Dimbleby Christmas Book*, 1987.
ESCUDIER, Jean-Noel. *La Veritable Cuisine Provençale et Niçoise*, Paris, 1974.
FARMER, Fannie. *The Fannie Farmer Cookbook*, 1981.
FISHER, M. F. K. *The Art of Eating*, 1963.
—. (trans.) *Brillat-Savarin's The Physiology of Taste*, 1949.
FREEMAN, Sarah. *Mutton and Oysters: The Victorians and their Food*, 1989.
GAULT, Henri and Millau, Christian. *Guide Gourmand de la France*, Paris, 1970.
GRAY, Patience. *Honey from a Weed*, 1986.
GRIGSON, Jane. *Charcuterie and French Pork Cookery*, 1967.
—. *Fish Cookery*, 1973.
—. *English Cookery*, 1974.

—. *Vegetable Book*, 1978.

—. *Fruit Book*, 1982.

HARRISON, Michael. *The Story of Christmas*, n.d.

HARTLEY, Dorothy. *Food in England*, 1954.

HENISCH, Bridget Ann. *Cakes and Characters*, 1984.

HOM, Ken. *The Taste of China*, 1992.

KAFKA, Barbara. *Food for Friends*, New York, 1989.

—. *The Opinionated Palate*, New York, 1992.

KENNEDY, Diana. *The Cuisines of Mexico*, New York, 1972.

—. *The Art of Mexican Cooking*, New York, 1989.

LARKCOM, Joy. *The Salad Garden*, 1984

—. *Oriental Vegetables*, 1991.

LASSALLE, George. *The Adventurous Fish Cook*, 1972.

LEVY, Esther. *Jewish Cookery Book* (facsimile of 1871 edn), Garden Grove, CA, 1982.

LEVY, Faye. *International Jewish Cookbook*, 1992.

LOUSADA, Patricia. *Easy to Entertain*, 1986.

LUARD, Elisabeth. *European Festival Food*, 1990.

MACDONOGH, Giles. *A Palate in Revolution: Grimod de la Reynière and the Almanach des Gourmands*, 1987.

MCGEE, Harold. *On Food and Cooking*, 1984.

—. *The Curious Cook*, 1992.

MÉDECIN, Jacques. *Cuisine Niçoise*. 1983.

MENNELL, Stephen. *All Manners of Food*, 1985.

MONTAGNÉ, Prosper. *New Larousse Gastronomique*, 1977.

MONTEFIORE, Lady. *The Jewish Manual* (facsimile of 1846 edn), 1985.

OLNEY, Richard. *Simple French Food*, 1981.

—. *Preserving* (Time-Life Good Cook series), 1980.

ORTIZ, Elisabeth Lambert. *The Book of Latin American Cooking*, 1969.

PIMLOTT, J. A. R. *The Englishman's Christmas: A Social History*, 1978.

PININSKA, Mary. *The Polish Kitchen*, 1990.

RANCE, Patrick. *The Great British Cheese Book*, 1982.

—. *The French Cheese Book*, 1989.

REBOUL, J-B. *La Cuisinière Provençale*, 23rd edn, Marseille, n.d.

DE ROBECK, Nesta. *The Christmas Crib*, 1938.

RODEN, Claudia. *A New Book of Middle Eastern Food*, 1985.

—. *Middle Eastern Cooking*, 1986.

ROOT, Waverley. *The Food of France*, New York, 1977.

SCHARFENBERG, Horst. *The German Kitchen*, 1991.

SCHWARTZ, Oded. *In Search of Plenty: A History of Jewish Food*, 1992.

SIMON, André. *A Concise Encyclopedia of Gastronomy*, 1983.

SOKOLOV, Raymond. *The Jewish-American Kitchen*, New York, 1989.

—. *Why We Eat What We Eat*, New York, 1991.

SPURLING, Hilary. *Elinor Fettiplace's Receipt Book*, 1986.
STAVROULAKIS, Nicholas. *Cookbook of the Jews of Greece*, Philadelphia, 1990.
STEAD, Jennifer. *Food and Cooking in 18th Century Britain*, 1985.
STOBART, Tom. *The Cook's Encyclopaedia*, 1982.
TANNAHILL, Reay. *Food in History*, 1988.
VISSER, Margaret. *Much Depends on Dinner*, 1990.
—. *The Rituals of Dinner*, Toronto, 1991.
WHEATON, Barbara Ketcham. *Savouring the Past: The French Kitchen and Table from 1300–1789*, 1983.
WILSON, C. Anne. *Food and Drink in Britain*, 1973.

*Mail-order food and wine
for Christmas*

WINE

These wine merchants have especially good catalogues and several of them do
    special Christmas offers:

Adnams Wine Merchants, The Crown, High Street, Southwold, Suffolk IP18 6DP.
    Tel: 0502 724222; fax: 0502 724805.

Avery's of Bristol, 7 Park Street, Bristol, Avon BS1 5NG.
    Tel: 0272 214141; fax: 0272 221729.

Bibendum Wine Limited, 113 Regents Park Road, London NW1 8UR.
    Tel: 071 722 5577; fax: 071 722 7354.

Corney & Barrow Limited, 12 Helmet Row, London EC1V 3QJ.
    Tel: 071 251 4051; fax: 071 608 1373.

Farr Vintners Limited, 19 Sussex Street, London SW1V 4RR.
    Tel: 071 828 1960; fax: 071 828 3500.

The Fulham Road Wine Centre, 899–901 Fulham Road, London SW6 5HU.
    Tel: 071 736 7009.

Haynes, Hanson and Clarke, 17 Lettice Street, London SW6 4EH.
    Tel: 071 736 7878.

The Hungerford Wine Company, Unit 3, Station Yard, Hungerford,
    Berks RG17 0DY.
    Tel: 0488 83238; fax: 0488 84919.

Lay & Wheeler Limited, 6 Culver Street West, Colchester, Essex CO1 1JA.
    Tel: 0206 764446; fax: 0206 564488.

Morris & Verdin, 28 Churton Street, London SW1V 2LP.
    Tel: 071 630 8888; fax: 071 630 6227.

Le Nez Rouge, 12 Brewery Road, London N7 9NH.
    Tel: 071 609 4711; fax: 071 607 0018.

Raeburn Fine Wines, 23 Comely Bank Road, Edinburgh EH4 1DS.
    Tel and fax: 031 332 5166.

Reid Wines, The Mill, Marsh Lane, Hallatrow, Bristol, Avon BS18 5EB.
    Tel: 0761 52645; fax: 0761 53642.

Windrush Wines Limited, The Barracks, Cecily Hill, Cirencester, Glos GL7 2EF.
    Tel: 0285 650466; fax: 0285 654280.

The Wine Society, Gunnels Wood Road, Stevenage, Herts SG1 2BG.
    Tel: 0438 741177/740222; fax: 0438 741392.

Wine Cellars, 153/155 Wandsworth High Street, London SW18 4JB.
    Tel: 081 871 3979; fax: 081 874 8380.

Yapp Brothers PLC, The Old Brewery, Mere, Wilts BA12 6DY.
    Tel: 0747 860423; fax: 0747 860929.

OYSTERS

Loch Fyne Oysters Ltd, Clachan Farm, Ardkinglass, Cairndow,
    Argyll PA26 8BH.
    Tel: 04996 264/217; fax: 04996 234.

Cuan Sea Fisheries, Sketrick Island, Killinchy, Co Down BT23 6QH.
Tel: 0238 541461; fax: 0238 541787.
Seasalter Shellfish (Whitstable) Ltd, The Harbour, Whitstable, Kent CT5 1AB.
Tel: 0227 262003; fax: 0227 264829.
Sometimes have Whitstable natives number ones.

SMOKED SALMON

Scottish cure:

Loch Fyne, address above, also offers langoustine, smoked trout, kippers and other fish products. Their smoked salmon is my favourite of the Scottish cures.

Pinneys of Scotland Ltd, Brydekirk, Annan, Dumbriesshire DG12 5LP.
Tel: 0576 3777; fax: 0576 3466.
Mail-order smoked salmon and other smoked fish products to EC and Switzerland.

Cley Smoke House, Cley-next-the-Sea, Norfolk NR25 7RF.
Tel: 0263 740282. Wonderful kippers and bloaters as well.

London Cure:

Box's of Fulham, 110 Wandsworth Bridge Road, Fulham SW6 2TF.
Tel: 071 736 5766; fax: 071 736 4509.

TURKEY

J. N. Munson, Munson's Poultry, Emdon, Straight Road, Boxted, Colchester, Essex CO4 5QX.
Tel: 0206 272637; fax: 0206 272962.
Bronze, Black and White turkeys, sometimes geese and large chickens. The best I've found.

Anne Petch, Heal Farm, Kings Nympton, Umberleigh, Devon EX 37 9TB.
Tel: 076957 4341; fax: 076957 2839.
Hams, bacon, sausages, beef and rare breeds of lamb as well.

Bill and Charlotte Reynolds, Swaddles Green Farm, Hare Lane, Buckland St Mary, Chard, Somerset TA20 3JR.
Tel: 0460 234387; fax: 0460 234591. American Bronze turkeys.

Naturally Yours, Witcham Toll, Ely, Cambs CB6 2AB.
Tel: 0353 778723. 'Totally free-range' Norfolk Blacks.

GEESE

Judy Goodman, Goodman's Geese, Walsgrove Farm, Great Witley, Worcs WR6 6JJ.
Tel: 0299 896272.
Also J. N. Munson, and Naturally Yours, above.

HAM

Dukeshill Ham Co Ltd, Bridgnorth, Shropshire WV16 6AF.
Tel: 0746 35519; fax: 0746 35533. Real York hams and Wiltshire hams.
Also Anne Petch, above.

GAME

American list from *The Art of Eating* (Winter 1992), by Edward Behr
(subscription enquiries to this wonderful quarterly newsletter to: The Art
of Eating, PO Box 242, Peacham, Vermont 05862).

D'Artagnan (farmed birds, plus 'wild Scottish game' fresh in season), 399–419
St Paul Avenue, Jersey City, New Jersey 07306.
Tel: 800-327-8246.

Game Exchange (farmed plus Scottish game), PO Box 880204, San Francisco,
CA 94124. Tel: 800-426-3872.

Foggy Ridge Gamebird Farm (wild turkey, guinea fowl, quail and mallards),
PO Box 211, Warren, Maine 04864.
Tel: 207-273-2357.

Oakwood Game Farm (wild turkey, pheasant, partridge and mallards), Box
274, Princeton, Minnesota 55371.
Tel: 800-328-6647.

Wild Game, Inc. (birds plus Scottish game), 2315 West Huron, Chicago, Illinois
60612. Tel: 312-278-1661.

Wylie Hill Farm (pheasant, partridge and quail), PO Box 35, Craftsbury
Common, Vermont 05827.
Tel: 802-586-2887.

VENISON

Wild:

Highland Venison, Grantown-on-Spey, Morayshire PH2 63BR.
Tel: 0479 2255.
From a consortium of Scottish estates.
Also, Naturally Yours, above.

Farmed:

Fletchers of Auchtermuchty, Reediehill Deer Farm, Auchtermuchty, Fife KY14
7HS.
Tel: 0337 28369; fax: 0337 27001.

Moorland Larder, 113 East Street, South Molton, Devon EX36 3DB.
Tel: 0769 573554.

Round Green Farm Venison Company, Worsbrough, Barnsley, S. Yorks
S75 3DR.
Tel: 0226 205577; fax: 0226 281294.

Welsh Venison Centre, Middlewood Farm, Bwlch, Brecon, Powys LD3 7HQ.
Tel: 0874 730246; fax: 0874 730566.

CHEESE

Wells Stores, 29 Stert Street, Abingdon, Oxon OX14 3JF.
    Tel: 0235 535978.
Neal's Yard Dairy, 9 Neal's Yard, London WC2H 9DP.
    Tel: 071 379 7646; fax: 071 240 2442.
Jeroboams, 51 Elizabeth Street, London, SW1W 9PP.
    Tel: 071 495 3314; fax: 071 823 5623.
H. J. Errington & Co, Walston Braehead, Ogscastle, Carnwath ML11 8NE.
    Tel: 089 981 257.
    Whole cheeses, either Dunsyre or ewe's milk Lanark Blue. Humphrey
    Errington is probably Britain's most interesting cheesemaker.
Philippe Olivier, 43/45 rue Thiers, Boulogne-sur-Mer 62200 France.
    Tel: 21.31.94.74.
Mail order in France. UK mail order Rouxel Ltd, Unit 1, Chelsea Fields,
    Western Road, London SW19 2QA.
    Tel: 081 640 9928; fax: 081 640 9892.

CHRISTMAS PUDDINGS AND CAKES

Mosimanns, 11 Elvaston Place, London SW7 5QR.
    Tel: 071 823 9992; fax: 071 584 2467.
Meg Rivers Cakes, Main Street, Middle Tysoe, Warks CV35 0SE.
    Tel: 0295 888101; fax 0295 88799.

MISCELLANEOUS

Pickles and chutneys:
Wendy Brandon, Felin Wen, Boncath, Dyfed SA37 0JR.
    Tel: Tel: 0239 841568; fax: 0239 841746. Everything homemade, including
    mostarda di frutta.

Fruit:
Crapes Fruit Farm, Rectory Road, Aldham, Colchester, Essex CO6 3RR.
    Tel: 0206 212375. Rare and unusual apples by post.

Oil:
The Oil Merchant, 47 Ashchurch Grove, London W12 9BU.
    Tel: 081 740 1335; fax: 081 740 1319.
    Designer olive oils, and excellent balsamic vinegar.